Body Language

FOR

DUMMIES®

A Wiley Brand

3rd Edition

by Elizabeth Kuhnke

Body Language **For Dummies® 3rd Edition**

Published by: **John Wiley & Sons, Ltd,** The Atrium, Southern Gate, Chichester, www.wiley.com

This edition first published 2015

© 2015 John Wiley & Sons, Ltd, Chichester, West Sussex.

Registered office

John Wiley & Sons Ltd, The Atrium, Southern Gate, Chichester, West Sussex, PO19 8SQ, United Kingdom

For details of our global editorial offices, for customer services and for information about how to apply for permission to reuse the copyright material in this book please see our website at www.wiley.com.

For general information on our other products and services, please contact our Customer Care Department within the U.S. at 877-762-2974, outside the U.S. at (001) 317-572-3993, or fax 317-572-4002. For technical support, please visit www.wiley.com/techsupport.

A catalogue record for this book is available from the British Library.

ISBN 978-1-119-06739-9 (paperback); ISBN 978-1-119-07644-5 (ebk);

ISBN 978-1-119-07640-7 (ebk)

Printed in the United States Of America at Bind-Rite Robbinsville, NJ

10 9 8 7 6 5 4

Contents at a Glance

Table of Contents

Introduction

Body language speaks the truth. While the spoken word conveys facts and data – not all of which may be real – your body's movements, gestures and facial expressions never lie. No matter what words you choose – 'I love you', 'I'm disappointed', 'I'm happy', 'I'm sad' – if your body isn't reflecting what you're saying, your listeners will be confused and will believe what they see and sense rather than what you say.

All day, every day, your body relays messages about your attitude, intentions and general state of being. Although at times you're unable to control your body's movements, all is not lost however. With awareness and practice, you can determine what messages you relay through your gestures, postures and expressions.

Although body language began with our ancient ancestors (long before vocal sounds turned into sophisticated words and phrases), only in the last 80 years or so has body language been seriously studied. During that time, people have come to appreciate the value of body language as a tool for understanding and enhancing interpersonal communication. Politicians, actors, celebrities and other high-profile individuals recognise the important part that their bodies play in conveying their messages.

Each chapter of this book addresses a specific aspect of body language. In addition to focusing on individual body parts and their role in communicating your thoughts, feelings and intentions, you discover how to interpret other people's body language, giving you an insight into their mental state before they may be aware of it themselves. Approach body language in a respectful and responsible way and base your judgements on the clusters of movements you observe and the context in which you see them. Just as one word can't tell an entire story, nor can one gesture. By aligning your movements with your words, you experience the powerful impact of body language and the clear messages you can convey. By performing specific actions and gestures, you can create the corresponding mental states within yourself and others. By choosing your gestures and facial expressions, you can determine how others perceive you. Who knows? You may even become the person you want to be.

About This Book

For a subject that's relatively new to the study of evolution and social behaviour, you can find a sizeable amount of research on body language. As businesses expand across the globe and international travel is more accessible than ever before, people are recognising the impact of culture, gender and religious customs on body language and communication. While I've written the third edition of *Body Language For Dummies* from a mostly English-speaking Western perspective, Chapter 15 has been expanded to include body language in different cultures – what's acceptable and what could cause offence. Because of the vastness of the subject, I've been selective in what I've included and focus on how to use body language to enhance your personal and business relationships.

In this book I explain ways of recognising and identifying specific gestures, actions and expressions that both convey and negate the spoken message. By improving your reading of body language, understanding how your body conveys meaning and recognising how thoughts and emotions are reflected in your gestures and expressions, you have the upper hand in your interpersonal communications. Through body signals, you can direct the flow of conversation and facilitate meetings, discussions and everyday conversations with ease and effectiveness. I show you the impact of thoughts and feelings on gestures and expressions – yours *and* those of others.

The point of this book is for you to become conscious of the power of body language. To this end, I provide you with the means of identifying and interpreting non-verbal behaviour as well as offer you tips for sending signs and signals to facilitate clear and congruent communication.

Foolish Assumptions

I assume, perhaps wrongly, that you:

- Are interested in body language and know a little bit about the subject
- Want to improve your interpersonal communication
- Are willing to reflect and respond
- Expect the best of yourself and others

Icons Used in This Book

For sharpening your thinking and focusing your attention, let these icons be your guide:

 This icon highlights stories to entertain and inform you about people I know or people I've observed and the signals they've sent through their body language.

 Here's a chance for you to stand back and observe without being seen. By distancing yourself and taking a bird's eye view, you can see how others behave and then reflect on the outcome.

 This icon underscores a valuable point to keep in mind.

 These are practical and immediate remedies for becoming a skilled and confident body language practitioner.

 Here, you can have a go at putting theory into practice. Some of the practical exercises are designed to enhance your non-verbal communication while others aim to help you understand the meaning behind what others are saying.

 This icon highlights potentially awkward situations to avoid.

 This is information that you may find interesting.

Beyond the Book

Find out more about Body Language by checking out the bonus content available to you at www.dummies.com.

You can locate the book's e-cheat sheet at www.dummies.com/cheatsheet/bodylanguage, where you'll find handy hints and tips.

Be sure to visit the book's extras page at www.dummies.com/extras/bodylanguage for further information and articles.

Where to Go from Here

Although all the material in this book is designed to support you in being yourself at your best, not all the information may be pertinent to your specific needs or interests. Read what you want, when you want. You don't have to read the book in order, nor is there a sell by date for covering the material.

If you're interested in how body language conveys messages, begin with Part I. If you're seeking to improve your body language for a job interview or for playing politics in the professional world, have a look at Chapter 14. If you're curious about facial expressions, turn to Chapter 4. And if you want to know how to behave appropriately in cultures and countries different to your own, go to Chapter 15.

Now turn to a page, chapter or section that interests you and begin reading. Take away something useful and have fun in the process.

Part I
Getting Started with Body Language

In this part . . .

- Find out more about the origins of body language and how it's evolved.

- Discover how body language reveals people's attitudes, beliefs and emotions.

Figure 1-1:
His
gesture is
aggressive
while hers is
protective.

Creating an impression within moments

You can tell within the first seven seconds of meeting someone how she feels about herself by the expression on her face and the way she moves her body. Whether she knows it or not, she's transmitting messages through her gestures and actions.

You walk into a room of strangers and, from their stance, movements and expressions, you receive messages about their feelings, moods, thoughts and intentions. Look at the teenage girl standing in the corner. From her slouching shoulders, her lowered head and the way her hands fidget over her stomach, you can tell that this is not a happy camper.

Another young woman in this room of strangers is standing amongst a group of contemporaries. Her eyes twinkle, she throws back her head as she laughs, her hands and arms move with ease and openness and her weight is evenly distributed between her feet, which are placed beneath her, hip width apart. This woman is projecting an image of self-confidence and joie de vivre that draws people to her.

Early observations about body language

Before the twentieth century, only a few forays were made into identifying and analysing movement and gesture. The first known work exclusively addressing body language is John Bulwer's *Chirologia: or the Natural Language of the Hand*, published in 1644. By the nineteenth century, directors and teachers of drama and pantomime were instructing their actors and students how to convey emotion and attitude through movement and gesture.

In *The Expression of the Emotions in Man and Animals* (1872), Charles Darwin explores the connection between humans, apes and monkeys. These species use similar facial expressions, inherited from a common ancestor, to express specific emotions. Out of Darwin's work grew an interest in *ethology* – the study of animal behaviour.

In the late 1960s, Desmond Morris created a sensation when his interpretations of human behaviour, based on ethological research, were published in *The Naked Ape* and *Manwatching*. Further publications and media presentations continue to reveal how much our non-verbal behaviour is based on our animal nature.

Like it or not, how you position your head, shoulders, torso, arms, hands, legs and feet, and how your eyes, mouth, fingers and toes move, tell an observer more about your state of being than any words you can say.

Transmitting messages unconsciously

In addition to your ability to consciously choose precise gestures and actions to convey a particular message, your body sends out signals without your awareness. Dilated or contracted pupils and the unconscious movements of your hands and feet indicate an inner emotion that you may wish to conceal. For example, if you notice that the pupils of someone's eyes are dilated, and you know that she's not under the influence of drugs, you'd be correct in assuming that whatever she's looking at is giving her pleasure. If the pupils are contracted, the opposite is true.

While body language speaks volumes, be careful when ascribing feelings and attitudes based solely on non-verbal behaviour. Individual signals can be easily overlooked or misidentified if they're taken out of their social context. Look for clusters of gestures and expressions that involve several parts of the body. Also observe breathing patterns to gauge someone's internal state. For more about how your breathing patterns influence the way you behave, have a look at *Communication Skills For Dummies* by Elizabeth Kuhnke (Wiley). At times, you may want to conceal your thoughts and feelings, so you behave in a way that you believe hides your true emotions. And then, wouldn't you know it, out pops a giveaway gesture, barely perceptible to the untrained eye, sending a signal that all's not what it appears. Don't kid yourself that no one notices. Just because these micro-gestures and -expressions are fleeting doesn't mean that they don't send powerful messages.

In the 1970s, Paul Ekman and Wallace V. Friesen developed the Facial Action Coding System (FACS) to measure, describe and interpret facial behaviours. This instrument is designed to gauge even the slightest facial muscle contractions and determine what category or categories each facial action fits into. It detects what the naked eye can't and is used by the police, film animators and researchers of human behaviour.

According to research conducted by Professor Mehrabian, when people are discussing feelings and emotions in a face-to-face setting and an incongruity exists between the words themselves and the way you deliver them, 7 per cent of the message received is conveyed through your words, 38 per cent is revealed through your vocal quality and a whopping 55 per cent of your message is expressed through your gestures, expression and posture. Mehrabian's premise is that your non-verbal behaviours are directly tied to your feelings, whether you're conscious of the connection or not. Although sceptics contest Mehrabian's figures, the point remains that body language and vocal quality significantly contribute to the meaning of the message.

Gunther is the CFO of a global corporation and is a charming, successful and popular man. In addition, he is used to getting what he wants, when he wants it. You know the time has come to step lively when Gunther points his index finger in your direction, raises his chin, lifts his eyebrows and barks out a rapid-fire command, even if he has a smile on his face. For more about how smiling informs communication, flip to Chapter 6.

Substituting gestures for the spoken word

Sometimes a gesture is more effective in conveying a message than any words you can say. Signals expressing love and support, pleasure and pain, fear, loathing and disappointment are clear to decipher and require few, if any, words for clarification. Approval, complicity or insults are commonly communicated without a sound passing between lips. When you frown, smile or sneer you don't need words to clarify your meaning.

When words aren't enough or the word mustn't be spoken out loud, you can gesture to convey your meaning. For example:

✔ Putting your index finger in front of your mouth while at the same time pursing your lips is a common signal for silence.

✔ Putting your hand up sharply with your fingers held tightly together and your palm facing forward means 'Stop!'

✔ Winking at another person hints at a little secret between the two of you.

✔ Putting up your middle finger is an obscene gesture conveying contempt.

Figures 1-2 and 1-3 illustrate these behaviours.

Figure 1-2: She's sending a clear message without saying a word.

Figure 1-3: Wide eyes, open mouths and hands to head and face gestures tell you that these people have witnessed something shocking.

ANECDOTE

Nick and Holly were involved in a tough business negotiation. At one point during the meeting, Nick started to give away too much information. Holly calmly placed her index finger over her lips while resting her chin on her thumb. This was a sign to Nick for him to listen more and talk less.

Gesturing to illustrate what you're saying

When you describe an object, you frequently use gestures to illustrate what the object is like. Your listener finds it easier to understand what you're saying when your body creates a picture of the object rather than relying on words alone. If you're describing a round object, for example a ball, you may hold your hands in front of yourself with your fingers arched upward and your thumbs pointing down. When describing a square building, you may draw vertical and horizontal lines with a flat hand, cutting through the space like a knife. If you're telling someone about a turbulent ride on a boat or plane, your arms and hands may beat up and down in rhythmic fashion. You may hold your arms out wide when describing a large object and hold your fingers close together when you're illustrating a small point (see Figure 1-4). The point is that gesturing is a practical way to convey visual information.

Figure 1-4:
Her tight, contained gesture is describing something small.

Because some people are more comfortable processing information through the visual channel, illustrate your messages through gestures. This helps create a clear picture and adds energy to your voice. If you want to help a blind person experience what you're describing, hold her hands in the appropriate position.

Lotsie is a dedicated traveller and frequently speaks to students about her adventures. As she describes her climb up Mount Kilimanjaro she acts out those moments when the air is so thin that she's hardly able to breathe and when she struggles to put one foot in front of the other. She mimes leaning on her walking stick, bending over with the weight of her equipment, gasping for air and pausing between shuffled steps as she puts one foot in front of the other. Her listeners share her pain and determination through her gestures, posture and facial expressions.

Physically supporting the spoken word

Appropriate gestures add emphasis to your voice, clarify your meaning and give impact to your message. Whether you're sending out signals of interest or signs of disgust, when your body movements reflect your emotions you help your listener understand how you're feeling.

In addition to reinforcing your message, specific hand signals reflect your desire to communicate clearly. Watch well-schooled politicians standing at the podium. See how their hands move in a precise, controlled manner (see Figure 1-5) – no wasted gestures, just those specific ones that tell the tale they want you to believe.

When you're making a formal presentation, use illustrative gestures to help your audience remember the points you're making.

During the introduction to your presentation, as you establish the points to be covered, list them separately on your fingers. You may hold your fingers up in front of you, or touch them individually on one hand with a finger from your other hand as you say the point. When talking about point one in your presentation, point to the first finger, or gesture to it; when you reach point two, point or gesture to your second finger, and so on. This technique helps both you and your listener focus on the subject and stay on track.

Note: Many British and American people begin counting with their index finger. Many Europeans begin counting with their thumb. See Chapter 15 for more on cultural differences in body language.

Figure 1-5:
This precise chopping gesture demon-strates firmness and conviction.

Experienced lawyers, celebrities and anyone else who takes their public persona seriously strive to emphasise their messages through considered movements, gestures and facial expressions. By carefully timing, focusing and controlling their actions, they court the people they want by using open, welcoming gestures and dismiss others with a flick of the wrist.

When you're giving bad news and want to soften the blow, adapt your body language to reflect empathy. Move close to the person you're comforting and tilt your body towards hers (see Figure 1-6). You may even touch her on the hand or arm or place your arm around her shoulder if she doesn't object.

Revealing feelings, attitudes and beliefs

You don't have to tell people how you're feeling for them to know. Look at someone deep in thought. As she leans forward, looks downward, wrinkling her forehead in contemplation and rests her chin on her hand, she's replicating Rodin's sculpture, *The Thinker*. Equally so, a child throwing a tantrum with stomping feet, clenched fists and a screwed up face is letting you know that she's not happy. The body says it all.

Figure 1-6:
The woman on the right is expressing her care and concern for the other woman who appears depressed.

Think of your body as if it were a movie screen. The information you project derives from your inner life of thoughts, feelings and intentions. Your physical body is the vehicle onto which the information is displayed. Whether you're anxious, excited, happy or sad, your movements and expressions tell your tale. Here are some examples:

✔ People who feel threatened or unsure of themselves touch their bodies as a means of self-comfort or self-restraint. Gestures such as rubbing their foreheads, crossing their arms and holding or rubbing their fingers in front of their mouths provide comfort and protection (see Figure 1-7).

✔ People who perform specific gestures reserved for religious rituals reveal their beliefs and values. Upon entering a Catholic church, the congregation dip their fingers into holy water and cross themselves. Before entering the home of many Jewish people, you may touch the mezuzah by the front door. Muslims bow in prayer facing east. By performing these gestures, people are demonstrating their respect for the culture, its traditions and values. See Chapter 15 for more about cultural differences and body language.

Figure 1-7:
Both men
are holding
back and
seeking
comfort.

✔ People in a state of elation often breathe in deeply and gesture outwards with expanded arms. Pictures of winning sportspeople frequently show them in the open position with their arms extended, their heads thrown back and their mouths and eyes opened in ecstasy.

✔ Footballers who miss the penalty kick and city traders who get their numbers wrong often walk dejectedly, with their heads down and their hands clasped behind their necks. This hand position is a comforting gesture and the head facing downwards shows the individual's despair.

✔ People who are despondent, or feeling down and depressed, reveal their feelings by the slouch in their step, their drooping heads, limp lips and downward-cast eyes. Positive people, on the other hand, reveal their feelings with an upright stance, a bounce in their step, lifted lips and eyes that twinkle with liveliness and engagement.

✔ Not every bent head signals depression. Sometimes it just means that you're reflecting, thinking or absorbing information. If you're thinking hard for example, your head most likely rests in your hand or on your fingertips unless you're pacing the room as you consider your options, in which case you still might rest your chin on your thumb as you stroke your cheeks and lips with your index finger. You can find out more about body language and mental states in *Persuasion & Influence For Dummies* by Elizabeth Kuhnke and *Neuro-Linguistic Programming For Dummies* by Romilla Ready and Kate Burton (both Wiley).

Kate's mother is 94 and lives in a nursing home. Often, when Kate visits her, the elderly woman doesn't recognise her. While Kate is used to this situation, she still feels sad as she considers the passage of time and family relationships. When she speaks of her mother her voice is low, her eyes are downcast and her shoulders slightly slumped. Kate's own daughter, Rosie, recently had a baby girl, Kate's first grandchild. As Kate speaks of little Sienna, her eyes sparkle, her voice lifts and her chest expands with happiness. Kate's different postures and facial expressions project the differences in her feelings.

Holding your hands over or near your heart, as shown in Figure 1-8, is an expression of how much something means to you. You often see this gesture when people give and receive compliments.

Figure 1-8:
The hands over the heart, the tilted head and the open smile indicate happiness and appreciation.

Noticing your own body language

My husband suggested that people may only demonstrate body language when someone else is around to see and respond to it. I found that an interesting thought and retired to my office to consider the implications on my own postures and gestures. As I sat at my desk reflecting on what he said, I noticed I was leaning back in my chair with my head tilted upwards, one arm folded over my body supporting the elbow of my other arm. My chin was resting lightly on my thumb as my index finger gently stroked my cheek. I couldn't help but think of the question: 'Do falling trees in the forest make a noise if no one's around to hear it?'

Examining Key Types of Gesture

Humans are blessed with the ability to create a wide variety of gestures and expressions from the top of the head to the tips of the toes. Gestures can show intention, such as leaning forward just before rising out of a chair, and no intention, such as crossing arms and legs. Certain gestures, frequently referred to as signature gestures, are acts you perform and by which you are identified. Others are displacement gestures: you perform them for no reason other than to shift some energy. Local customs call for specific gestures and other gestures are universal, performed and interpreted the same way across the globe.

Unintentional gestures

Unintentional gestures are types of body language that inhibit your ability to act. They hold you back from speaking and make it hard for your body to budge. As opposed to intentional gestures – those movements you specifically choose to support your spoken message – unintentional gestures usually surface without conscious thought.

Examples of unintentional gestures are:

- Folded arms
- Lips pressed together
- A hand or finger in front of the mouth
- Crossed legs

When your arms are folded you can't strike out. When your lips are sealed your thoughts remain silent. When your legs are crossed you can't run away. These gestures prevent you from moving and speaking, which may not be such a bad thing. Standing or sitting with your legs crossed is no position to take if you want to get somewhere quickly. The scissor stance is a prime example of a gesture that keeps you in your place. One leg is crossed over the other, rendering you immobile (see Figure 1-9). When someone adopts this position, you know she's staying put.

Because the scissor stance contains no sign of impatience, the gesture can come across as submissive. You take up less space as you make yourself smaller. Men seldom adopt this stance while women frequently do. Physiological reasons make the pose more or less comfortable for the two genders. People who move freely, not locking themselves into awkward physical positions, are considered to be more dominant than those who are constrained and hesitant in their movements.

Figure 1-9:
Crossed arms and legs, fingers cupping the mouth and chin, and a side-ways look tell you she's holding something back.

Signature gestures

A signature gesture is one that you become known by, a common gesture that you perform in a particular way. Some examples are:

- ✔ Twirling your hair around your finger
- ✔ Pointing your finger
- ✔ Sticking your tongue out
- ✔ Patting your eyebrows
- ✔ Stroking your throat
- ✔ Winking

You provide clues about your personality through your signature gestures. They set you apart from others and draw their attention to you.

Red carpet sweetheart Shailene Woodley understands the value of having a gesture to add to her brand. One of the originators of the sassy hand on the hip photo pose, she has replaced that ubiquitous gesture with a double-handed Hang Ten pose, also described as Cowabunga Hands by *Cosmopolitan* magazine. Extend your thumbs and little fingers on each hand while folding your middle fingers into your palms, and bingo – you look like a rock star. You could also adopt Miley Cyrus's go-to signature pose by quirking, commonly known as sticking out your tongue. Watch Andy Murray after a big win on the court. The British number one tennis player points both index fingers skyward and makes a little head nod as if he were communicating with someone above. Sticking with the tennis champions, Rafael Nadal is recognised by his signature gesture of tugging at the back of his shorts just before serving. When the Seattle Mariners' closing pitcher Fernando Rodney saves a game, he points to the sky as if shooting an arrow in a movement similar to Usain Bolt's 'To Di World' gesture (see the nearby sidebar for details).

The late Diana, Princess of Wales's most vividly remembered signature gesture was her lowered head and eyes looking upward from beneath her lashes and brows. This look was so closely identified with the princess that it's become known as the Shy Di look.

Frequently referred to as the Power Pose, in which you put your hands in front of your stomach, thumbs pointing upwards and fingertips touching, with your thumbs and index fingers forming a rough diamond shape, this action is one of German Chancellor Angela Merkel's most recognised poses. Known in Germany as the Merkel-Raute (The Triangle of Power), this posture is synonymous with Merkel's reputation for strong leadership and a safe pair of hands. The gesture has been used by Merkel's party, the Christian Democratic Union (CDU), for publicity purposes and the emoticon <> referencing the gesture is used in its internet communications.

Celebrating victory with a lightning bolt

After Jamaican sprinter Usain Bolt picked up gold at the Beijing Olympics in 2008 he adopted a pose that's become synonymous with the star athlete. The gesture, which Bolt calls 'To Di World', is now referred to colloquially as 'bolting'. To adopt this pose, you spread your feet, lean backwards, cock your right arm while you extend your left one forward and point both index fingers towards the sky. Although then-International Olympic Committee boss Jacques Rogge branded it 'disrespectful' and 'showboating', Bolt continues to celebrate his victories with this gesture. During his visit to Jamaica in March 2012, Prince Harry received world media attention when he and Bolt adopted the pose together on a Jamaican running track. Bolt has incorporated the pose into his Puma sponsorship campaign as well as in a commercial promoting tourism in his homeland.

Toby is a quiet, task-orientated, focused man. His boss, Annie, is highly energetic with a mind that skips and leaps from one project to the next. Frequently, Annie asks Toby to do one task, only to interrupt his concentration by asking him to do something else, often unrelated. When Toby pats his eyebrows with the tips of his fingers, Annie recognises his signature gesture of impatience and frustration and quickly backs off, letting him get on with what he has to do.

If you want to be easily identified and remembered, you can create your own signature gesture. Consider Victoria Beckham's sexily defiant pout and Mo Farah's 'Mobot'.

Fake gestures

Fake gestures are designed to camouflage, conceal and fool. They pretend to be something when they're actually something else. You're able to tell a fake gesture from a real one because some of the genuine gesture's parts are missing.

Some gestures that are commonly faked are:

- ✔ Smiling
- ✔ Frowning
- ✔ Sighing
- ✔ Crying
- ✔ Holding your body as if in pain

Anna is a highly motivated, recently qualified lawyer in a large London firm. She knows that, in part, her success depends on her ability to get on well with clients and colleagues. One day, her supervising partner invited her to attend a client meeting and to put together the remaining briefs that a previous trainee had begun and hadn't had time to finish. Anna, already overloaded with work, stayed at the office until well past midnight. In spite of little sleep and over an hour's commute that morning, she arrived, shortly before the meeting's 8 a.m. start looking smart and ready to go. At one point during the session, the client remarked that some information seemed to be missing. The partner shot Anna a glance of annoyance before covering up his feelings with the hearty remark, 'Well, she's new on the job. We'll let her get away with it just this once.' To cover her fury and shame, Anna put on what she calls her 'smiley face', a big toothy grin and offered to find the missing materials. Anna's teeth were clenched, and her eyes didn't crinkle, which they would have were her smile sincere. She was tired, hurt and humiliated and anyone paying attention would have seen that her grin was fake.

To avoid being fooled by a fake gesture, observe all the signals.

Micro-gestures

Teeny weeny, so small that they sometimes take highly specialised equipment to see them, micro-gestures flicker and flash across your face faster than a speeding bullet. Unfortunately, you're at the mercy of your micro-expressions as you don't choose them and they tell an observer a lot about your internal state at that moment.

Although you may choose to smile, pout or frown, you may not want a micro-gesture of fear, loathing, love or disgust to flicker across your face. The good news is, if you're a careful observer you can figure out how someone's feeling from their micro-expressions. The bad news is, an adept observer can spot your emotions through the same channel.

A list of the more common micro-gestures includes:

- ✔ Movement around the mouth
- ✔ Tension at the eyes
- ✔ Flaring of the nostrils

Erik, one of my clients, is the newly appointed CEO of a global corporation. In his position, he's used to being the centre of attention. Erik recently entered a room where I was speaking with one of his colleagues whom I'd not met before. Erik winked and smiled as he asked if we were talking about him.

Although he robustly said, 'Good. I'm glad' when I told him that we weren't, I noticed a momentary flicker of surprise cross his face. (Turn to Chapter 5 for more about spotting when someone's surprised.)

Displacement gestures

When you experience conflicting emotions, you may engage in self-directed gestures that release nervous energy and provide a temporary feeling of comfort. Drumming fingers, flicking feet, fetching a glass of water when you're not even thirsty – these are the types of behaviour of someone who's looking to refocus or vent some pent up energy. Called displacement activities, they're a conduit for excess energy that's looking for somewhere to go.

Some examples of displacement gestures are:

✔ Fiddling with objects

✔ Tugging at your earlobe

✔ Straightening your clothes

✔ Stroking your chin

✔ Running your fingers through your hair

✔ Eating

✔ Smoking

Some smokers light up a cigarette, take a puff or two and then put it out or leave it in the ashtray barely smoked. These people may not actually want the cigarette, but need a gesture to take their mind off something else.

I knew the time had come to stop smoking when I had three cigarettes on the go in a four-room apartment. I was working in New York, living on my own, making barely enough to pay my monthly bills and wondering what life challenges were coming next. I was frustrated and feeling anxious. One morning, while I was in the kitchen making coffee, I lit up a cigarette. When the phone rang, I answered it in the living room, leaving the cigarette burning in the kitchen. While speaking on the phone to my soon-to-be ex-husband, I lit another cigarette, which, after a drag or two, I stubbed out in the ashtray on my desk. I went to the bathroom to get ready for work. Here, too, I lit a cigarette, which I occasionally puffed on as I applied my make-up. In the course of less than ten minutes I had lit three cigarettes, none of which I was interested in smoking and all of which were props for displacing nervous anxiety. Rather than verbalising my feelings, I let my gestures do the talking.

Words convey information. Gestures reveal emotions. If someone's feeling anxious, she may fiddle with her keys, twist the ring on her finger or pull at her clothes to manage her discomfort.

If you see someone being scrutinised, look to see what her hands are doing. If she's gently rubbing her stomach, stroking her sternum or running her fingers up and down her throat, you may assume that she's feeling the pressure and is doing her best to calm and comfort herself without calling attention to it.

Universal gestures

Universal gestures, such as blushing, smiling and the wide-eyed expression of fear, mean the same thing around the world. These gestures stem from human biological make-up, which is why you can easily recognise the signs. See Chapter 15 for more about gestures in different cultures.

Smiling

From the sands of the Middle East to the shores of Malibu, humans are born with the ability to smile. From the earliest days in a baby's life, her facial muscles can form the upward turn of the lips and the crinkling around the outer edges of the eyes to create a recognisable grin.

Sure, each person may have her own unique way of smiling. Julia Roberts is easily recognisable by her toothy wide smile. Keira Knightley prefers the slightly pouty smile. Jennifer Lawrence's smile is so engaging that some of her fans call it addictive. The point remains that anyone with working facial muscles who's conveying a genuine smile lifts her lips in pleasure while the outer muscles around her eyes crinkle.

In Western cultures people smile as a sign of recognition and acknowledgement, whether they know you or not. In China, don't feel left out if no one smiles at you as you walk through their towns. The Japanese smile when they're confused, angry or embarrassed. In the former USSR you're perceived as suspicious if you smile at strangers in public. See Chapter 15 for more about smiling in different cultures.

Blushing

Blushing, caused by blood flowing to your chest and face, is a universal response when feeling passionate or embarrassed. No matter where your passport takes you, when you see someone blush you know she's consumed with embarrassment.

To control the blushing take several slow, deep breaths from your diaphragm to steady your nerves and control the blood flow. For more about how breathing can help control nervous energy, see *Persuasion & Influence For Dummies* by Elizabeth Kuhnke and *Voice and Speaking Skills For Dummies* by Judy Apps (both Wiley).

Tom and Louise have been dating exclusively for nine months. While they're enjoying one another's company and may some day make a serious commitment, they're in no hurry to formalise their relationship. When Louise's father asked Tom what his intentions were, both Tom and Louise blushed, embarrassed at having been put on the spot.

Crying

Crying is a universal sign of sadness. One of a healthy baby's first actions is to let out a walloping great cry when she first enters this world, having been torn from the comfort and safety of her mother's womb. No one had to teach her how to cry; she was born with the innate ability to express her unhappiness.

If you feel tears well up in your eyes and you want to stop them from flowing down your face, fix your gaze at the point where the ceiling and wall meet. Performing this action focuses your attention onto a meaningless and unrelated subject and frees your mind of upsetting thoughts. Another way to prevent your tears from flowing is to press your tongue firmly against the roof of your mouth as you remind yourself that in a few moments what's troubling you will be over. If, however, you feel the salt of your tears about to splash down your face, you could acknowledge what's happening and move on. Sometimes accepting what's about to occur is enough to make it stop.

Shrugging

Shrugging is a gesture that people use when they need to protect or distance themselves from something they'd rather avoid. In the full shrug your head dips into your rising shoulders, the sides of your mouth turn down and your palms turn upwards as you raise your eyebrows.

The shrug can indicate:

- Indifference
- Disdain
- Lack of knowledge
- Embarrassment

To know which attitude is being expressed, you have to identify what the other body parts are doing at the same time.

Television versus radio

In the early 1960s, little was known about body language. Yet John F. Kennedy intuitively knew how to use it. Prior to their first televised debate in 1960, JKF and Richard Nixon posed for a media photo call. Kennedy placed himself to the right of Nixon and shook Nixon's hand. The resulting photograph showed Kennedy applying the upper-hand position, causing Nixon to appear diminished in stature. This was one of Kennedy's favourite gestures. The Nixon–Kennedy election debate that followed this photo call was a further testimonial to the power of body language. Most of the Americans who only heard the debate on the radio believed that Nixon out-performed Kennedy. However, the majority of those who saw the debate on television believed Kennedy was the victor. The media savvy Kennedy knew how to use his body to manipulate public perception and did it with grace, charm and ease.

Anne, a French woman, heads up her organisation's public relations department. Chad, one of her internal clients, makes Anne's life difficult as he frequently fails to prepare for the presentations Anne writes for him, is late in responding to her requests for information, and often argues with her directives. When I asked Anne how she finds working with Chad, she closed her eyes, pursed her lips, raised her shoulders holding her palms upwards and uttered the dismissive 'puh' sound as a quick blast of air escaped from her mouth. 'I don't think much of him' was her message.

Getting the Most Out of Body Language

People in powerful positions know how to use their bodies to greatest effect. They stand tall, chests open, shoulders back and down, and, when they move, they do so with purpose. They choose their gestures with care to reflect their sense of who they are and how they want to be perceived.

Powerful people know where to position themselves in relation to others. They know that if they stand too close they're perceived as overwhelming or threatening, while if they stand too far away they come across as distant. They know that the gestures they use and how they use them have a powerful impact.

A major part of your message is conveyed through your posture, movements and facial expressions. Being aware of the impact of your body language enables you to act confidently, knowing that your message is received in the way you intend.

Becoming spatially aware

Understanding how to position yourself in relation to other people is a skill that some people just don't seem to have. Someone is either up so close and personal that you can smell her coffee breath or she stands just slightly too far away, making her appear uninterested and disengaged. Others know just how close to come. They understand and respect the different parameters people place around themselves, and being with them is comfortable.

Think of yourself as having a personal, individual space bubble that you stand, sit and move in. This invisible space expands and contracts depending on circumstances. For example, when you're with people you like, you tend to close the gap between yourselves. When you're with people you don't know well or whose company you don't enjoy, you may find that you're more comfortable when you expand the space. People who grew up in the country and now live in crowded cities frequently complain about lack of space while people who were raised in metropolitan areas adapt to confined conditions more readily.

The study of *proxemics* – how people use and relate to the space around them for purposes of communication – was pioneered by Edward T. Hall, an American anthropologist, in the 1960s. His findings reveal the different amounts of personal space that people feel they need depending on their social situation. Robert Sommer, an American psychologist, coined the term 'personal space' in 1969. He defined it as the 'comfortable separation zone' people like to have around them.

Chapter 12 takes a look at how circumstances determine at what distance you're most comfortable, and how best to position yourself in relation to another person, whether standing, sitting or lying down.

Anticipating movements

If you're able to anticipate another person's movements you can predict what they're going to do next, giving you the upper hand by eliminating the element of surprise.

The American anthropologist, Ray Birdwhistell, pioneered *kinesics* – the study of body movement and verbal communication. Replaying in slow motion films of people in conversation, Birdwhistell was able to analyse people's actions, gestures and facial expressions.

Consider these examples:

- ✔ Spotting the subtle gestures a person makes in preparation for rising from a seated position let's you know that it's time to move on.

- ✔ Recognising when a person is about to strike out in anger gives you enough time to protect yourself.

- ✔ Seeing that someone wants to speak enables you to give them the chance to be heard.

- ✔ Noticing that your partner is leaning towards you with pursed lips offers you the chance to pucker up or pull away, depending on your mood.

Anticipating a movement can save your life, keep you from harm and even bring you great happiness. By predicting gestures, you gain the upper hand in figuring out your response before the other person has completed her action.

Creating rapport through reflecting gestures

In order to establish rapport – a state of understanding feelings and communicating well – you accept and connect with other people, treating one another with respect. Rapport assures that your communications are effective and lead to results that satisfy both parties' needs.

Training the brain

If you ever wonder what makes footballer Cristiano Ronaldo so good at intercepting the ball, consider his ability to read body language. Research conducted by Dr Daniel Bishop at Brunel University shows that highly skilled footballers activate more areas of their brain when seeing the opponent coming their way than do less-experienced players. Brain scans show that they have developed a checking system that inhibits their urge to react instinctively, making them less likely to be misled by deceptive movements. The mirror neuron system (MNS) of an experienced player is more developed than that of a rookie. The MNS helps predict opponents' actions, ensuring that they won't be caught off guard or out of position. Bishop's premise is that players can be trained to anticipate their opponents' moves and by focusing on a consistent centre point, such as the chest, a player can take away the opponents' element of surprise.

You can create rapport in many ways, including touch, word choice and eye contact. You can also create rapport by reflecting another person's movements. By mirroring and matching the other person's gestures and behaviours, you're demonstrating that you know what it feels, sounds and looks like to be in her shoes. If connecting with others and behaving respectfully is important to you, mirroring and matching their behaviour helps you achieve that goal. For more information about the benefit of mirroring and matching others' actions, check out Chapter 14.

A fine line exists between reflecting another person's gestures and mimicking her. People who are being mimicked quickly figure out what you're doing, recognise your insincerity and question your motives.

Becoming who you want to be

How you present yourself, how you move and gesture, how you stand, sit and walk all play their part in creating the image you present and determining people's perceptions of you. By developing an arsenal of postures, positions, gestures and expressions, you can project a plethora of attitudes. Positive body language – through which you establish eye contact and move with purpose – comes across as strong, engaged and vibrant. Negative body language – whereby you avoid looking at another person and fold into yourself – communicates weakness, dullness and a disconnect between yourself and others. How you move your head, face, torso and limbs determines how you're perceived and the results you achieve.

Actors know how to create a character from both within – the character's history, present life, beliefs, attitudes, thoughts and feelings – and without – her physical attributes, including how she looks and behaves. They draw upon the technique of acting 'as if', that is, behaving as if they were the character. Working from the outside in, actors consider how their character sounds, moves and gestures. They ask themselves:

- ✔ How would the character walk, sit and stand? Would she move like a gazelle, lumber along like a sleepy bear or stagger in a zigzag pattern like someone who's had one drink too many? Is her posture upright and erect or slouched and limp?

- ✔ What gestures would convey a particular mood or emotion? Slow, deliberate and carefully timed gestures create a different impression from those that are quick, spontaneous and unfocused.

By adopting the appropriate behaviours, the actor creates an attitude, emotion or feeling that the audience recognises and understands. The same is true for the layperson. By acting in a particular manner you can create an image and become that character. As Cary Grant said, 'I pretended to be someone I wanted to be until finally I became that person.'

The way you act makes an impression. How you're perceived – dumb or sultry, champion of the people or chairman of the board – is up to you. The key is to adopt the appropriate behaviours. To do that, keep these points in mind:

- ✔ **Make sure that your gestures reinforce the impression you want to make:** For example, the higher up the command chain, the more contained the gesture (which is why you never see the chief executive running down the hall).

- ✔ **You can modify your gestures to suit the situation:** When you're hanging out with friends your body language is loose and relaxed. When meeting a client or your partner's parents for the first time, your body language is more contained and formal. Follow the lead of the other person and reflect what you're observing to create rapport.

Pick an attitude that you want to project. Determine the appropriate gestures and expressions. If you struggle to come up with ideas of your own, model the gestures of someone you think successfully conveys the image you want to portray.

When I experienced my first tax audit, I felt quite nervous. Tom, my financial director, and Ron, my accountant, are in charge of the business's finances and when they say how much I owe and where I'm to sign, I do as I'm told. Tom arrived at the office wearing a suit and tie for the meeting with the tax inspector. Our office is normally quite informal and Tom's change of clothes and serious demeanour told me that we were to leave out the jokes. I dressed in a suit like Tom and also adjusted my behaviour to mirror his, which was thoughtful, serious and open. We wanted to demonstrate that, in addition to the business having a strong creative base, its financial backbone is firmly in place.

Reading the signs and responding appropriately

Recognising, interpreting and responding to other people's body language is a stepping stone to effective communication. By observing how people move and gesture, you get a glimpse into their thoughts, emotions, and intentions. You can tell, for example, how someone is feeling by the way she stands. You can see what kind of mood a person is in by the speed of her gestures. You can spot someone's attitude by the tilt of her head. By having an insight into someone's thoughts and emotions, you're forewarned and forearmed for whatever may happen next.

Say that you're with a friend. You notice her sitting with her head hanging down, her eyes looking moist and her arms wrapped around her body. Her body language is indicating that she's depressed and might benefit from a little tender loving care. You gently put your hand on her arm and she begins to perk up because you responded to her signals.

Perhaps you're at a party and notice that some of the guests who have had more than their fair share of drink are beginning to go from jovial to rowdy. The lads pushing and shoving one another signals that this could be the time for you to leave. By reading body language effectively, you can tell when to stay and when to go.

Holly unexpectedly popped round to have a chat with her colleague, Tony. Tony was rushing to complete a project and had little time to stop for a gossip. As they're friends, Tony looked up at Holly and smiled and nodded when he saw her. He also stayed seated at his desk and didn't maintain eye contact. He kept his fingers on his keyboard, looked back at his computer screen and resumed typing. Holly sensed from Tony's body language that now was not a convenient time for them to speak, and she quickly left.

Appreciating Cultural Differences

How much more exciting, interesting and stimulating it is to live in a world with difference and diversity, rather than one in which everything's the same. Even though you appreciate the differences between cultures and nationalities, you may sometimes find yourself confused, scared or even repelled by displays of body language that are very different from what you're used to.

Because people in one culture act differently to people in another doesn't suggest that one is right and the other wrong. When it comes to cultural differences, the operative verbs are 'to respect' and 'to value'. Valuing behaviours that vary so much from those that you grew up with, and were taught to believe in, can be hard. To create respectful, positive relationships between different cultures and nationalities, you need to expand the way you think and work. If you remember nothing else from this paragraph, remember that in multicultural encounters, respect for others' ways of being is paramount. That doesn't mean having to agree with all the behaviours you see in your travels. Instead, accept that differences do exist, and then decide how best to respond.

Chapter 15 looks at different cultures and how behaviour and body language impact upon communication between nations.

People of different nationalities and cultures use their bodies differently. An acceptable gesture in one country may land you in jail in another. Before visiting or moving to another country, do your homework and find out what's suitable and what's not.

Chapter 2

Looking Closer at Non-Verbal Gestures

In This Chapter
▶ Looking into the origins of body language
▶ Conveying information through body language
▶ Considering what you can discover from others' gestures

*W*hether you like to think of yourself as an animal or not, the truth is, you are. And like all animals, the way you gesture, move and position your body tells an observer a lot more about you than the words you say.

Throughout the animal kingdom, body language is a constant and reliable form of communication. Whether on two, four or more legs, homo sapiens and every other animal are constantly sizing one another up as they prepare for a friendly, or unfriendly, encounter. Because of the structure and programming of the human body, you can send a plethora of silent messages, whereas other animals are more limited in the number of signals they can convey.

In this chapter, I revisit our ancient ancestors to see where body language began and how it evolved. You discover that the way you use your body conveys how you're feeling, what you're thinking and your general state of being. You find out how body language reveals the feelings and attitudes you may prefer to leave unsaid, as well as how your movements support your spoken message.

Observing the History of Body Language

For over 100 years, psychologists, anthropologists and even zoologists have been studying non-verbal behaviour throughout the animal kingdom to understand its implications, applications and ramifications in the field of human communication. These experts recognise that applying knowledge of non-verbal behaviour in practical settings allows people to communicate more successfully than if they rely purely on the spoken word.

According to research into primate behaviour, you can be safe in betting that non-verbal behaviour, including gestures and facial expressions, is a reliable source for conveying messages and supporting the spoken word.

Aping our ancestors

Charles Darwin concluded that humans' ability to express thoughts, feelings and intentions through posture and gesture stems from prehistoric apes that most resemble today's chimpanzees. Like humans, chimpanzees are social animals that live in groups. As with humans, chimpanzees' needs are based around successful communication and co-operation in order to survive. As chimpanzees have yet to develop the ability to speak, they primarily rely on non-vocal means such as stance, facial expressions and touching gestures to show who's in charge, demonstrate affection and alert others to danger.

Darwin published his findings in *The Expression of the Emotions in Man and Animals* in 1872. Regarded as the most influential pre-twentieth century work on the subject of body language, this academic study continues to serve as the foundation for modern investigations into facial expressions and non-verbal behaviour. Over 140 years after its original publication, Darwin's findings about posture, gesture and expression are consistently validated by experts in the field.

Gestures first, speech second

Extensive research into the foundations of communication suggests that spoken language evolved from gesture. In evolutionary terms, speech is a relatively new means of communication, having only been a part of man's communication process for somewhere between 500,000 and 2 million years.

According to Frans de Waal of the Yerkes National Primate Research Center in Atlanta, Georgia, gestures appeared first in human development, followed by speech. An example of this progress can be seen in the behaviour of infants. Babies quickly discover which gestures to use, and how to use them to get what they want. Shaking heads, grasping fingers and kicking heels send explicit messages to watchful observers.

Studying the behaviour patterns of apes and monkeys, de Waal concludes that gestures used as specific signals are a more recent addition to the communication chain, coming after vocalisations and facial expressions. Apes, who are genetically close to humans, use specific gestures for sending precise messages, while monkeys, who are further removed from humans, don't.

Although humans' ability to communicate effectively has evolved with the development of speech, body language continues to be the most reliable source for conveying thoughts, feelings and intentions.

Understanding the Nuts and Bolts of Body Language

The primary purpose of the spoken word is to convey information, facts and data, whereas body language is designed to relay unspoken thoughts, emotions and intentions. You may argue that words also relay thoughts, emotions and intentions, and you'd be right. Sometimes. Think back to those occasions when you said words like, 'I'm fine; there's no problem; I think you're great; I couldn't be happier' when you really meant, 'I'm annoyed; there's a huge problem; I think you're hideous; I couldn't be more miserable'. If the person you were speaking to was a careful observer, he would have noticed that, while your words were sending out one message, the way you delivered them sent out a conflicting one. The result? Confusing communication.

When observing body language, always take into account the context in which the gesture is being performed. In addition, consider other movements and facial expressions the individual is making before drawing a conclusion.

Kinesics: The categories of gesture

The American anthropologist Ray Birdwhistell was a pioneer in the study of non-verbal behaviour. He labelled this form of communication 'kinesics' as it relates to movement of individual body parts, or the body as a whole. Building on Birdwhistell's work, Professor Paul Ekman and his colleague Wallace V. Friesen classified kinesics into five categories: emblems, illustrators, affective displays, regulators and adaptors.

Kinesics conveys specific meanings that are open to cultural interpretation. The movements can be misinterpreted when communicating across cultures as most of them are carried out with little if any consciousness. In today's global environment, awareness of the meanings of different kinesic movements is vital to avoid sending the wrong message. (To find out more about kinesics across different cultures, see Chapter 15.)

Context clues: Studying gestures in chimps and bonobos

Studying humans' closest primate relatives — chimpanzees and the black-faced bonobo — research conducted by Amy Pollick and Frans de Waal concluded that the meaning of a gesture depends on the context in which the gesture is made, as well as on other gestures that are occurring at the same time. Observing a captive test group of chimps and bonobos, the researchers identified 31 gestures – defined as any movement of the forearm, hand, wrist or fingers used solely for the purpose of communication. In addition, they identified 18 facial or vocal signals and recorded them in the context in which they were made. The facial and vocal signals had practically the same meaning in the two species. The gestures had different meanings.

The common signal for fear in chimps is a 'bared-tooth scream'. The 'up and out' gesture of reaching with the palm facing upward has different meanings. Depending on the context, it can be interpreted as begging for food or money as street beggars do, or begging for a friend's support. The open-handed gesture can frequently be seen after a fight where reconciliation is sought. This versatility demonstrates the necessity for context to be taken into consideration before interpreting the meaning of a gesture.

Emblems

Emblems are non-verbal signals with a verbal equivalent, and are easily identified because they're frequently used in specific contexts. Because emblems are quick to use and unambiguous in their meaning, the person receiving the gesture immediately understands the message – as long as he comes from the same culture as you. Keep in mind that easily understood emblems in one culture may be puzzling in another.

Examples of emblems include:

- **The V sign:** During the Second World War Winston Churchill made the victory sign popular. The palm of the hand faces forwards with the middle and forefingers held erect. Over 70 years later this gesture continues to represent peace. Turn the palm of your hand towards you and flick your fingers once quickly and the gesture becomes quite rude.

- **The raised arm and tightly closed fist:** Generally this gesture is used as an expression of resistance, pride, militancy, solidarity and defiance, which makes it such a powerful symbol. In 1990, Nelson Mandela walked free of prison holding this position. Among black rights activists in the United States, the raised fist is known as the black power salute. Athletes also use a closed fist pumping gesture to spur themselves on.

> ✔ **The finger:** Americans hold the middle finger of the hand in an upright position, with the back of the hand facing out. In Britain, people tend to hold up their index and middle fingers with the back of their hand facing out. Both gestures mean the same thing and the meaning's quite rude.
>
> ✔ **The cuckold:** Your index and little fingers are extended pointing forward with your palm facing down, making 'horns'. Your thumb crosses over your two middle fingers. Use this gesture in Italy and you're telling someone that his partner has been unfaithful. In Texas, this gesture is the sign for fans of the University of Texas Longhorns football team and has nothing to do with infidelity.
>
> ✔ **The OK sign:** A circle made with the thumb and forefinger means 'okay' in many parts of the world, but in other places it can be interpreted as 'zero', 'nothing' or as an obscene gesture representing a body orifice.

Because of different interpretations of the same gesture between cultures, the correct reading is dependent on the context in which the signal occurs.

Illustrators

Illustrators create a visual image that describes, accentuates or reinforces what the speaker is saying. They are used to help define physical, concrete items as well as indicate levels of enthusiasm. Examples are pointing when giving directions, showing the size or shape of an object, raising your hands in the air as a sign of joy, and standing tall to demonstrate pride or confidence. Illustrators tend to be subconscious movements, occurring more regularly than emblematic kinesic movements. How you synchronise illustrators in relation to how you're speaking shows whether they're an unconscious movement or if you're using them deliberately for effect. When the gesture is unconscious the preparation for the gesture begins before you speak. When someone uses illustrators consciously you may notice a slight pause between the words and the gesture. How and how many illustrators are used differs from culture to culture. In general, Latinos rely on illustrators more than their Anglo-Saxon counterparts, who incorporate them into their way of communicating more than most Asian cultures. In some Asian cultures, extensive use of illustrators is often interpreted as a lack of intelligence. In Latin cultures, the absence of illustrators indicates a lack of interest.

Affective displays

Affective displays are movements, including your gait and facial expressions, which contain emotional meaning. For example, bouncing on the balls of your feet can indicate excitement or impatience, a genuine broad grin signals pleasure and covering your eyes, ears or mouth indicates that you don't want to see, hear or verbally respond to what's happening. Holding on to your own hands or wrapping your arms around your body can indicate worry or concern as you literally hold yourself together. Self-preening is an affective display that can indicate a desire to be liked or noticed. Because affective displays are spontaneous, they may send out signals you'd rather not reveal because of social norms or what you want to achieve in your communication. Less conscious than illustrators and occurring less frequently, affective displays convey universal emotions – such as love, frustration or anger – and can be understood fairly easily, though the degree and frequency with which they occur is determined by cultural mores.

A lack of affective displays doesn't indicate a lack of emotion. Cultural considerations determine what is acceptable behaviour. A person from Japan expressing anger shows significantly fewer affective displays than his Italian counterpart. This doesn't suggest, however, that the Japanese person is feeling any less annoyed. The Japanese are taught to contain their emotions whereas Italians are encouraged to express them fully.

Regulators

Regulators are body movements that control, adjust and sustain the flow of a conversation. They're associated with turn-taking in a conversation and they influence the ebb and flow of the discussion. For example, starting to move away from someone indicates that you want the communication to end; raising a finger or lifting your head indicates that you want to speak, and showing your palm signals that you want the other person to stop (see Figure 2-1). Further examples of regulators include head nodding and eye movements.

Because of cultural differences in the use of regulators, the way in which people respond to the flow of information can be confusing. A misinterpreted regulatory signal in international politics and business can lead to serious consequences. See Chapter 15 for tips about how to behave in different cultures.

Figure 2-1: By turning her head away and putting her hand in the 'stop' position, the woman on the left is demonstrating her unwillingness to engage.

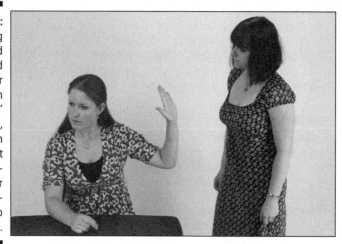

Adaptors

Adaptors include changes in posture and other movements, made with little awareness. These body adjustments are to perform a specific function, or to make the person more comfortable. Because they occur with such a low level of awareness, they're considered the keys to understanding what someone's really feeling. Adaptors principally comprise body-focused movements, such as rubbing, touching, scratching and twitching.

Adaptors are triggered by situational circumstances and tend to increase as anxiety levels rise. They are not intended to progress or support the conversation.

The significance given to adaptors may be overstated as well as oversimplified. Many adaptor movements, such as shifting position while seated, may be simply a way of resolving a specific physical situation, such as being uncomfortable, rather than revealing deep-felt emotions and attitudes. Always look for a cluster of gestures and take into account context when reading body language.

Inborn responses

A newborn baby latches onto its mother's breast and begins to suckle. A child born blind and deaf smiles, frowns and cries. These reactions aren't taught; rather, they're inborn responses to specific stimuli and require no practise or knowledge. They're performed unconsciously, unprompted and without self-analysis.

Some movements are so familiar that you take them completely for granted. If asked how to do them, you wouldn't have a clue. Take, for example, interlocking fingers. Every person has a dominant thumb, which consistently rests on top of the other when you interlock your fingers. If you were asked which of your thumbs rests on top you probably wouldn't know and would need to look to find out. This doesn't mean that you can't reverse the position and put the other thumb on top. Do it and see what happens. Feels strange, awkward and not quite right, doesn't it?

The study of animal behaviour, especially as it occurs in a natural environment, was pioneered by Irenaus Eibl-Eibesfeldt, an Austrian scientist and head of the Max Planck Institute for Behavioural Physiology in Germany. His interest in humans as 'signal carriers' significantly contributed to the field of human ethology, including the study of inborn actions.

An inborn action works like this: think of your brain as being programmed like a computer. It's encoded to connect precise reactions with particular stimuli involving inputs and outputs. The stimuli, or input, triggers a reaction, or output. The process is straightforward and simple, requiring no prior experience or learned behaviour.

An example of inborn behaviour is the rapid raising and lowering of the eyebrows as a sign of greeting, a gesture that can be seen around the world. Stamping feet in anger and baring teeth when enraged are also inborn behaviours. It seems that no matter how far humans evolve from their prehistoric relatives, some things never change.

Learned gestures

The English zoologist, human behavioural scientist and author, Desmond Morris, concludes that human beings have an abundant variety of actions that, in addition to being genetically inherited, are learned behaviours. Some of these behaviours are discovered, others are absorbed, some are taught and still others are acquired in a combination of ways.

Discovering actions for yourself

Most people around the world are born with similar hands, arms and legs, and move and gesture with them in pretty much the same way. An African warrior, a London banker and a Minnesota farmer with their similar arms, all discover, at some point in their lives, how to fold them across their chests. No one taught them how to take that pose. During the growing up process, as they became familiar with their bodies, they unconsciously discovered they were able to do this. Most of the time, you don't even know how you perform the gesture. When you cross your arms over your chest, which one's on top? See what I mean?

Absorbed actions

Observe a group of teenage girls, watch the boys in the boardroom or celebrities on the red carpet and you notice that within each grouping a similar pattern of behaviour exists. Humans are imitative characters, easily influenced by the actions of others, especially if the others are considered to be of a higher status. The higher the status, the more they're copied. Unaware of what they're doing, people within the individual groups replicate the actions, gestures, postures and expressions of the group's alpha person.

You absorb most from those you admire.

Trained actions

Some actions have to be learned. For example, say you want to wink. You give it a go and it doesn't quite work. You give it another go. This time you're a little better, still with plenty of room for improvement. Desperate to be an adept winker, you deliberately and doggedly practise until you manage to close one eye while the other remains open. You learn how to wink.

Most of you aren't going to join the circus, where somersaulting and walking on your hands is required, but at some time in your lives you shake hands with other people. Having an adept teacher helps. Watch a parent showing his child how to shake hands properly and you see a trained action being taught. See Chapter 9 for more about different kinds of handshake.

Refined actions

Consider the way you cross your legs. As a child, you discover that sitting with your legs crossed can be a natural and comfortable position. You cross your legs, giving the action no further thought. Then society intervenes. As you mature, you emulate the way other members of your gender, nationality, age group and social class cross their legs and before you know what's hap-pened, you've refined the way you sit. (See Figure 2-2.)

Awareness of cultural differences can influence your actions. With the exam-ple of crossing your legs in mind, be aware, for example, that showing the soles of your feet is viewed as rude and insulting in many Asian countries, where the soles of your feet, sandals or shoes are considered unclean. If in doubt, point the soles of your feet toward the floor. (For more about cultural differences and body language, see Chapter 15.)

If you're feeling uncomfortable when mixing with a group of people you don't know well, and you can't figure out why, consider the implications of cultural differences. You may notice, for example, that the others are moving, acting and gesticulating in a manner different to you. Even though the differences may be subtle, they're detectable. (See Chapter 15 for more about culture, customs and body language.)

Figure 2-2:
Different attitudes are conveyed through the way you cross your legs.

Offering a Final Word on Non-Verbal Gestures

Charlie Chaplin and Gloria Swanson were great actors of the silent screen. They were expert in manipulating their bodies, moving and gesturing to convey messages to their audiences. With the advent of the talkies, the only actors who survived were those who were able to communicate successfully by combining their vocal and physical skills. Many a pretty face fell onto the cutting room floor for want of a decent voice.

Dancers, mime artists and people who can't speak face the challenge of conveying emotion relying solely on the use of their bodies. Posture, position, movement and expression reveal their attitudes, thoughts and intentions.

Researchers have observed and documented almost 1 million different types of signals and gestures.

You don't have to be a professional performer for your body to expose, both consciously and subconsciously, your emotions, thoughts, and intentions. Nor do you have to be a mind-reader to understand the people you interact with. You simply need to be aware of and understand how body language influences communication. Some movements and expressions are subtle, some are obvious. Some are designed to reveal; others seek to hide. All body movements and facial expressions tell a story. You just need to know what to look for to understand the tale.

Throughout this book I explore and interpret the various signs and signals, gestures and movements, plus postures and facial expressions the body makes and offer suggestions of how you can use your body to enhance the way you communicate. Let's get started.

Part II
Starting at the Top

 For some online extras about Body Language, head online and visit www.dummies.com/extras/bodylanguage

In this part . . .

- ✔ Explore how to recognize and interpret messages conveyed through body language.

- ✔ Discover how the tilt of your head can convey sympathy.

- ✔ See how the size of your pupils can reveal your emotions.

- ✔ Learn how you reveal more than words can say with the twitch of your lips.

Chapter 3

Heading to the Heart of the Matter

• •

In This Chapter

▶ Using your head to display power

▶ Nodding your head in agreement

▶ Tilting your head to indicate interest

▶ Discerning the meaning of other head movements

• •

*W*hether you hold it high, cant it in contrition or drop it in despair, the way you position your head reveals what you think of the person, place or thing you're encountering. How you place and pose your head indicates whether you're feeling aggressive, flirtatious or are bored to distraction.

Head movements have many purposes. They reveal attitudes, replace the spoken word and support or challenge what's said. You can steer someone to look or move in a specific direction by using your head to guide her, or you can point with your head when finger pointing would be rude or inappropriate.

Head nods and chin thrusts emphasise words and phrases. In a meeting, the chairperson nods her head to indicate who may speak next. At the dinner table parents bob their heads while looking at their children, indicating it's time to tuck into dinner. The bouncer at the nightclub bows his head towards you and you're in the door.

In this chapter you discover how a slight shift in action or angle can make the difference between being perceived as interested or dismissive, thoughtful or arrogant, playful or angry.

Demonstrating Power and Authority

Power is, indeed, a heady thing, and people with power, whether they're aware of it or not, position their heads in ways that reinforce their supremacy. Particular positions of the head correspond to the kind of power you hold. Lift your head and tilt it backward, and you convey a sense of superiority; raise your head and thrust your chin forward, and you send out a sign saying, 'Don't mess with me!' The following sections explain the meanings behind head signals.

The way you hold your head creates both positive and negative feelings in other people. Make sure that your head position elicits the response you want.

Signalling superiority

So, you've recently been appointed president of your company, running club or choral society. Upon hearing the news you lift your head and square your shoulders. Already, your body language reflects your position of privilege and authority.

Although you may believe that all people are created equal, when you're in charge your body sends out signals indicating that you're the alpha dog. Sure, you may choose to drop your head in a moment of thought or as a sign of respect, or even to demonstrate humbleness, but when you want people to pay attention and focus on you, your head rises.

If you find yourself feeling blue, down in the dumps or just not quite on top of your game, raise your head and hold it in an upright position for 60 seconds. Notice your mood shifting from low to high. If you're feeling really down, it may take a few extra moments to feel the change. Don't lower your head until you notice the sense of strength and power.

Demonstrating arrogance

If you're not sure whether someone's demonstrating assertiveness or arrogance, look at the tilt of the head and the position of the chin. If the head is lifted from the crown and the chin is parallel to the floor, you're looking at an assertive position. If the head is tilted back and the chin is thrusting forward, you've spotted a case of arrogance.

Occasionally, what appears to be arrogance isn't that at all; it's camouflaged insecurity. If someone tilts her head away from you, so that she looks downwards over her shoulder, she's put a barrier between the two of you. Although the raised head, forward-thrusting chin and downward gaze imply arrogance, the underlying message is defensiveness. Look into her eyes and at her mouth for further signs. (Check out Chapter 5 for more about the many messages the eyes send and Chapter 6 for the meaning of lip movements.)

Al is a solicitor at a top law firm. His first attempt at becoming a partner was unsuccessful. The human resources team and existing partners told him that he came across as arrogant and aggressive. Although I thought these were natural traits in a lawyer, the partners thought that his body language put people off. At first glance, Al's behaviour can be perceived as haughty. He often lifts his head, juts out his chin, slightly turns away from you when he speaks, frequently crosses his arms over his chest, and when challenged adds what sounds like a sarcastic laugh to the ends of his sentences. These behaviours create an impression of egotism, belligerency and aggressive superiority that make others feel uncomfortable and threatened. What those of us who know him well recognise, however, is that these actions are covering up his sense of insecurity. His lack of body awareness combined with his self-doubt is sending out negative messages. (If you want to read more about how body language impacts on perceptions, have a look at *Persuasion and Influence For Dummies* by Elizabeth Kuhnke (Wiley).)

Displaying aggression

If someone approaches you in an aggressive state you may notice, if you have the time and the courage, that the head is thrust forward from the shoulders as if it were a weapon. In extreme cases, someone who's really angry may use the head as a missile, projecting it forward in a head butt to hit the other person. Ouch.

George was leisurely driving along a narrow country lane when a speeding sports car came careering around a corner and almost rear-ended him. Experiencing a combination of fear, anger and moral outrage, George stopped his car, forcing the other driver to brake hard to avoid running into him. The driver leapt out of his car and approached George, who wisely stayed in his vehicle. In a flash, George noticed that the other man's face was red with anger, his fists were clenched in front of him and his head was jutting forward from his shoulders, neck sinews extended, jaw tight, lips snarled and teeth clenched. Wisely, George recognised the signs of extreme aggression, kept his windows up, locked the doors and called the police.

Showing disapproval

Remember when you were called into the head teacher's office and you knew it wasn't because you'd won the citizenship prize? Or, perhaps more recently, when your boss summoned you to inquire why you hadn't met your monthly target? Or that time your tennis partner threw you a look after you hit the ball into the net to lose the final point in the tournament? We've all been on the receiving end of the disapproving look. My children assure me that I've been known to give them the look, too.

As with all gestures, the disapproving look involves several actions. You tip the top of your head forward and your chin dips down. Your brow furrows and your lips purse.

You can show disapproval by holding your head upright over a straight body, folding your arms over your chest, closing your lips and staring with icy precision at the object of your displeasure (see Figure 3-1).

If you want to practise showing disappointment or disapproval, stand or sit in an upright position. Hold your head still, feeling the crown rise as the back of your neck lengthens and your chin remains horizontal. Place an imaginary person in front of you and look her squarely in the eye as if to say, 'There's no room for argument or excuses here.' You can also show disappointment by lowering your head, staring at the floor, pursing your lips and picking at your clothes with your thumb and index finger as if removing an invisible bit of fluff.

To read body language accurately, you must observe all the gestures a person is making. The full message lies in the combination of actions, not in a single movement.

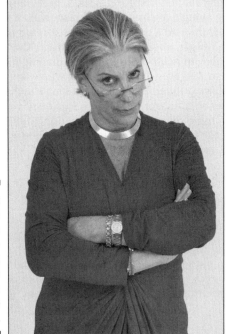

Figure 3-1:
A furrowed brow and a forward-tilting forehead imply a negative attitude.

Conveying rejection

The head shake is the commonest way to express a negative reaction. Babies rejecting the breast, bottle or a spoonful of food turn their heads rapidly from side to side. Anthropologists believe that, for adults, the action of turning the head horizontally from left to right with equal emphasis on each side to express rejection stems from our earliest days.

The head shake has two speeds of delivery:

- ✔ **Fast:** If the listener shakes her head rapidly and her lips are parted, she's indicating that she disagrees and wants to take over the speaker's role. If, however, she nods up and down at a slower pace, she's indicating that she concurs with what she's hearing.

- ✔ **Slow:** A slow back and forth sideways turning indicates the listener's incredulity at what she's just heard.

John and Caroline were discussing a possible candidate to join their team. John was in favour of the applicant while Caroline was doubtful. During their debate Caroline nodded quickly in disagreement, inhaling with her lips slightly parted, indicating that she'd heard John's point and wanted to interject. John raised his hand to silence her, at which point Caroline slowly exhaled and shook her head from side to side, indicating that she couldn't believe what she was hearing. (For more about the power of hand signals, see Chapter 9.)

Catapulting to intimidate

At work you often see people sitting at their desks, hands clasped behind their heads, elbows pulled back, with their chests puffed out. This position, known as the 'catapult', increases your size as your body expands. While you may sit in this position to stretch and relax, others may adopt the pose as a means of controlling feelings of aggression.

The catapult can make you appear self-satisfied, smug and even threatening, depending on your facial expression. (Turn to Chapter 4 for more about how facial expressions convey messages.) If you decide the catapult is the pose for you, make sure that you use plenty of antiperspirant (see Figure 3-2). Underarm stains and the smell of sweat demonstrate anxiety. Not pretty.

Choose your gestures carefully. If your boss calls you into her office to have a word with you, leave your catapult outside unless you're prepared for a counter-attack.

Figure 3-2:
Avoid the
catapult
position if
you're prone
to underarm
sweating.

Tossing your head in defiance

A woman frequently tosses her head to show disdain or haughtiness. She flicks her head backwards and gives it a small shake indicating that she has no interest in or intention of engaging with someone else. A person intent on delivering a double-punch gibe holds her head high and throws it back as she lays on the verbal charge.

If you want to see a clear example of the haughty head flick, tune into *Downtown Abbey*. Maggie Smith's portrayal of Lady Grantham is dotted with disdainful shakes of the head.

Beckoning with your head

When you want to attract someone's attention, be it a potential lover or a helping hand, and a shout or even a wave would be an unsuitable choice, the head beckon is an effective gesture. This movement is a diagonal backwards throw and may be repeated several times depending on how urgent your request is.

Alex is Debra's ballroom dancing teacher. During one performance of the bachata, he sensed her uncertainty about which hip she was to flick. Rather than shouting out 'left!', he quickly flicked his head in that direction, saving Debra the disappointment of losing points in the competition.

Touching someone on the head

The head is a special part of a person's body. Strong, sensitive and in some cultures seen as spiritual, it holds and protects the brain, the body's command centre. In addition, your sensory organs – mouth, eyes, ears and nose – are held in the head. Your head holds your thoughts and intentions, and reveals your emotions through your facial expressions.

The hand is the part of the body that can caress and console. It can also be an instrument of harm and offense. Touching another person on her head is an intimate gesture, implying fondness and care. The gesture is parental and is also tinged with a touch of superiority. While you may touch your friend's child on the head, you'd get tongues wagging if you did the same to your boss.

The person in the position of authority, be she taller, older or wiser than you, has implicit permission to place her hand on your head – not that she necessarily should or will.

If someone touches you in a way that makes you feel uncomfortable, tell her to stop. No one has the right to touch you without your permission.

As a result of child protection regulations, teachers, care givers and other people in authority no longer have permission to touch their charges on the head or anywhere else on the body and can be punished if they do so.

Showing Agreement and Encouragement: The Nod

The nod is an easily recognised and frequently used head movement in most cultures. As with many gestures, the head nod doesn't have just one meaning. In addition to signalling affirmation, agreement, acknowledgement and approval, this up-and-down movement is a gesture of recognition, comprehension, encouragement and understanding. To confuse the issue, in some cultures the head nod means 'no'. (See Chapter 15 for further insights into the impact of culture on body language.)

Sometimes people nod their heads as if agreeing when they have just the opposite thought in mind. To avoid being duped, look at every aspect of a person's body language.

If you want to establish a positive environment but you're not feeling quite so perky, nod your head intentionally and, before you know it, you'll be feeling quite jolly. By consciously nodding your head you can create positive feelings. Your movements influence your emotions. Head nodding is catching. If you nod your head at someone, she usually nods in return. This is true even if the other person doesn't agree with what you're saying. And as for creating rapport, gaining agreement and getting support, the head nod is a great place to start.

Encouraging the speaker to continue

When you're listening to another person and you want to keep the conversation going, nod your head. By nodding in a measured manner, you indicate that you're paying attention and want the speaker to continue. This slow, rhythmic nodding encourages the person speaking to say more and talk longer. Likewise, if you fail to nod your head while listening, the speaker thinks you aren't interested or paying attention. She finds it difficult to continue and quickly ends the conversation.

Start a conversation with someone you know well. As she speaks, nod your head in encouragement. See what effect your head movements have. Then stop nodding altogether and observe her reaction.

Research shows that listeners who nod their heads frequently during an interaction can prompt the speaker to generate three to four times more information than when no head movement occurs. Experienced interviewers employ the head-nodding technique to obtain additional information and generate further discussion.

Showing understanding

Although the slow head nod encourages the speaker to continue, shifting gears and speeding up your nodding indicates that you understand what she's saying. The fast head nod demonstrates a sense of urgency and shows that you support what the speaker is saying. The gesture can also mean that you want to interject and take over the speaker's role. As with all body language, you have to look at the cluster of gestures to determine what messages are being sent.

You can tell the difference between someone who's interested and encouraging as opposed to someone who wants to take over the conversation by observing where she's looking. If the listener is looking at the speaker, she's demonstrating support. If she's looking away from the speaker and her lips are parted, she's indicating that she wants to take over the conversation (unless she's distracted, of course).

When you're speaking and you want to confirm your listener's level of support, sneak a peep at her eyes. If they're enlarged and focused on you, she's paying attention. If her eyes are dull and lifeless, she's probably bored or uninterested.

The strength of the nod – the degree of the up-and-down action – indicates the listener's attitude. When you agree with what you hear, you nod your head firmly in confirmation. If you nod your head slowly, you're still considering your options.

When making a formal presentation, the head nod is a practical gesture for emphasising words and phrases. Use it sparingly. Too much repetition reduces the impact of any technique.

Affirming with a micro-nod

Often people end their statements with a barely perceptible dip of the head. In a quick motion, the head pulls downward followed by a softer return to the upright position. The action affirms and emphasises the speaker's commitment to what she's just said and can be perceived as a slight attack. Former United States president, George W. Bush, frequently uses this gesture when uttering his trademark phrase, 'make no mistake about it'.

Displaying Attention and Interest

Tilting or cocking your head indicates that you're interested in what you're observing. Although men tilt their heads by raising the chin and pulling the forehead back, women prefer the head cock in which the chin is slightly lowered and the head is held at an angle towards the subject of interest. This section covers all manner of head tilts and cants.

Whether you call the action tilting or canting, when people and animals hear or see something that grabs their attention, they incline their heads towards the point of interest. The head tilt – or cant – is an instinctive gesture that people and animals adopt when listening attentively.

When you tilt your head in an upward movement you make yourself taller, sending out a sign of power. A sideways tilt of the head shows appeasement as well as flirtation. The sideways head tilt is particularly seductive because it exposes a woman's neck, making her look vulnerable and submissive.

Because the head tilt conveys submission, be sure to keep your head upright when making a serious point.

Tam is head of PR for an international telecoms company. Although she is excellent at her job, she initially struggled to get the men in the organisation to take her seriously. Several senior male members of the executive committee described her behaviour as flirtatious and provocative, which apparently made them uncomfortable. When presenting at meetings, she tended to cant her head while smiling seductively and looking out from under her eyebrows. These behaviours were undermining her stature, power and authority. Tam was shocked when she saw herself on a video recording. After exploring the negative impact of her body language, and finding more appropriate gestures for getting what she wants at work, Tam now presents with authority, holding her head high, and saves the cant for the weekends.

If you want to gain someone's compassion, tilt your head to one side, smile warmly and gaze at the person with expectation. This gesture is similar to that a child uses when seeking approval, comfort, rest or tender bodily contact. Although you may not go so far as pressing your body against your companion's, the head tilt alone is enough to stir up protective emotions.

If you want to show that what you're saying isn't meant to be taken too seriously, give a short, sharp downward tilt of your head, and add a wink of the eye. People recognise this gesture as a friendly acknowledgement, both humorous and conspiratorial.

Cocking the head

Cocking your head involves a dip of the forehead and a twist of the chin as you incline your head towards another person. This gesture is frequently used as a non-contact greeting and relates back to the days when men doffed or touched their hats in recognition, or tugged their forelocks in acknowledgement, of another person. Dipping your head is a submissive gesture and demonstrates a subservient position. The head cock is a teasing, cajoling action intended to break down a person's resistance. Women appear appealing and provocative when they employ this gesture, eliciting nurturing and protective feelings from the person they're seeking to entice. Men who cock their heads are seeking sympathy or reassurance, or are simply showing that they're not the rough, tough, ruthless character people think they are.

Who cants the most?

An Italian research project investigating head positions in paintings from the thirteenth to the nineteenth centuries revealed that commissioned portraits of powerful men seldom depict them with their heads canted. Religious and pious figures are frequently portrayed in this attitude, however. The study also found that female figures are depicted with their heads canted more frequently than male figures.

Recall Clark Gable as Rhett Butler in *Gone with the Wind*. With great charm, he cocked his head to those with whom he courted favour, whether it was Mammy, the ladies of southern society or one of his jailors. The overriding effect of the head cock on the recipient is a rush of protective and compassionate feelings. Unless, that is, you know that you're being manipulated, in which case you may just feel annoyed.

When you're listening, you unconsciously copy the other person's head movements, establishing rapport through shared behaviour.

Sitting tête à tête

People who put their heads closely together are showing that a tie exists between them and no room is available for anyone else. The physical closeness reflects their bond. The action is one of exclusion and prevents others from overhearing what they're saying.

The next time you're sitting with your friends having a good gossip or sharing a risqué joke, observe how your heads come close together. When the punch line is delivered, or the dénouement of the story is revealed, note how the position of your heads changes, either coming in even closer with the thrill of conspiracy or pulling back with relief.

Indicating Submissiveness or Worry

Charles Darwin concluded that people lower their heads when they're feeling submissive. The act makes a person look smaller and less threatening. If our intention, conscious or not, is to appear compliant, dipping, tilting, canting and cocking the head all do the job. Research also shows that self-touching gestures, such as holding your head at the back of your neck and placing your hands on top of your head like a helmet, provide comfort, reassurance and protection, and help to alleviate your stress.

Dipping and ducking

If you've ever walked between two people who are deep in conversation, you may have ducked your head to avoid invading their space. In addition to making yourself smaller, this deferential gesture serves as an apology for any inconvenience you may have caused by penetrating their territory. (See Chapter 12 for the rules surrounding personal space.)

Some people make a slight involuntary dip of their heads when they acknowledge someone they think is superior to them.

If you want to impress your partner's parents, dip your head when you meet them. They'll be impressed by your deferential behaviour.

Cradling for comfort

The childhood memory of being held and comforted during times of distress lingers and lives on in your adult life. Your neck is one of your body's most exposed, and therefore vulnerable, areas. Clasping your hands behind your neck is a subconscious way to protect, calm and comfort yourself (see Figure 3-3).

Figure 3-3:
The head
cradle
provides
comfort and
security.

The sensation of having the back of the neck supported creates a sense of security. In times of insecurity, people can often be observed with their hands holding the back of their necks. Subconsciously, they're protecting themselves from real or imagined threats. This gesture provides comfort and reassurance.

Clasp your hands behind your neck and give a little squeeze to relieve tension and tired muscles and provide yourself with a sense of reassurance.

Sean attended an all-day board meeting during which several contentious issues were raised. At one point meeting he sat back in his seat, put his hands behind his head and began to rub his neck. He then changed positions, moving forward in his chair and resting his elbows on the table, and continued massaging his neck. After a few moments, he clasped his hands on the table, took a deep breath and addressed the group with new-found focus and purpose. He had become re-energised by the few moments of self-comfort.

Clasping the head

When the stakes are high, be they on the sporting field or trading floor, at campaign headquarters or the site of a disaster, and tension is in the air, people frequently hold onto their heads as if they're creating a crash helmet. The head clasp is a protective gesture in which the hands rise up and cover the top of the head. Head clasping is a natural response to calamity and acts as a protective device.

Jeni and her son Ben were cuddled on the couch watching a football match. When their team's goalkeeper failed to deflect the winning goal, both Jeni and Ben grabbed their heads in disbelief, mirroring the action of the disappointed and furious team manager.

Showing Boredom

A bored person props her head in her hand. Her eyes droop at half-mast and before you know it she's nodding off (see Figure 3-4). Resting your head in your hand is reminiscent of your childhood, when someone would support your head when you were tired. You rest your head in the palm of your hand because your head feels too heavy to stay upright on its own. Your palm cushions your jaw, your fingers cradle your cheek and your chin drops in a nod.

Figure 3-4:
A drooped head, glazed eyes and slack facial muscles indicate boredom.

Boredom and burnout

According to Ramon Greenwood, senior career counsellor at Common Sense At Work (www.commonsenseatwork.com), critical boredom, in which you're tired of your day-in-day-out job, is more dangerous than being bored with a specific part of your work. His research shows that being bored with at least one-half of a person's tasks for any particular job is usual. Being bored by the job itself can lead to burnout. Signs of burnout include fatigue, low morale, fear, despair, absenteeism, hostility (at home as well as at work), increased health problems, and substance abuse – which are all threatening to your health and your career. Boredom and burnout often result over time from bringing more ability to a task than is required. Stated differently, when the job doesn't fully engage you, you may find yourself feeling restless and out of sorts. According to the American Psychological Association, signs of boredom are similar to signs of depression. Common symptoms include changes in sleeping and eating patterns as well as loss of pleasure and purpose. The two groups of people most likely to commit suicide are teenagers and the elderly. Both groups described themselves as bored. This information gives added meaning to the expression 'bored to death'.

Before determining if you're boring someone, look into her eyes. If they're bright and alight, you've got her interest, even if she's resting her head in her hand. If her eyes are dull and unblinking, she's tuned you out.

Indicating You're Deep in Thought

Some of the most misinterpreted gestures are those that demonstrate pensiveness or deep thinking. Auguste Rodin's sculpture, *The Thinker*, is the prototype for the thinking position. The subject has his head resting on his hand and is in a forward-leaning position.

When you're deep in thought, you likely place your hand on your cheek as you reflect, contemplate or consider your options. It doesn't matter if you're leaning back in your chair or are perched on the edge of your seat; your hand usually ends up supporting your head while you ponder the possibilities. If your eyes are active and regularly blink, they show that you're considering your options.

You can tell when people are deep in thought or bored to distraction by their body energy. When you're engaged in thought your body is alert and attentive. Your eyes are active, you may have one or both hands placed by your head and you lean forward.

If you're participating in a meeting, attending a lecture or partaking in a dinner party and you're bored beyond belief, adopt the behaviours of someone who's engaged and interested. By putting some energy into your body and acting as if you're captivated by the conversation, you may find yourself becoming involved.

Resting your head in your hand, out of boredom or interest, requires hand to head contact, which is a reassuring gesture. Whether you're uninterested or contemplative, you subconsciously comfort yourself with this action. When you're bored or thinking, your head frequently rests in one or both of your hands. Rather than relying on this gesture alone, ascertain someone's mental state by looking at her eyes too.

Head resting on hand

When a person is thinking, she may bring her hand to her face, put her chin into her palm or extend her index finger up her cheek while her remaining fingers curl below her mouth. This gesture is particular to the evaluation posture (discussed in Chapter 9) and indicates that the person is thinking about what to do next.

If two or more people are in a discussion and one pulls back, you can bet that the person retreating is critical, cynical or in some other way negative about what the speaker is saying.

Tony and George were leading a discussion about the launch of a new product their business had developed. Tony tends to monopolise discussions, making it difficult for other members of the team to contribute. George, who is sensitive to others' reactions, noticed that their head of marketing was slumped in her seat, with her head propped in her hand. Her eyelids were heavy and her facial features were slack. Recognising that one of the team's most valuable players was about to doze off, George called on her to offer her suggestions, engaging her in the discussion and saving her – and others – from possible embarrassment.

Chin stroking

Chin stroking with the thumb and index finger is a gesture people use when they're deep in thought or making an evaluation. The index finger may also stroke the upper lip. If a man has a beard, he may even pull on it.

The eighteenth-century actor, Henry Siddons, in his book *Rhetorical Gestures*, says of the chin stroke, 'This gesture signifies the wise man making a judgment.'

Chapter 4

Watching Facial Expressions

. . . .

. . . .

*F*ace it. No matter what you say, if the look on your face doesn't match the words you say, people are going to believe what they observe, not what they hear. You know that from your own experience. Someone proclaims, 'I love you. All I want is your happiness. I'll do anything for you.' Sounds good to me. Only problem is that the downturned mouth, the deep vertical lines between the eyebrows and the tight jaw indicate that something's not quite right with this scene. The words are saying one thing while the face is saying something else.

Try as you may to hide your feelings, the curl of your lip, the twinkle in your eye or the flare of your nostrils gives the game away. No matter how hard you try to control your emotions, your facial features reflect your feelings.

One Sunday, Ted arrived at church in a foul mood. Life was not panning out the way he'd planned and he wasn't happy. Putting on his friendly face for the new vicar, he responded to her 'How are you?' with the single word 'Fine' accompanied by what was clearly a fake smile. (See Chapter 6 for more about false smiles.) Leaning close to Ted and smiling as she whispered into his ear, the vicar replied, 'Fine? You mean "F-I-N-E: fed up, insecure, neurotic and enraged"?' Pulling back and looking at the vicar with dropped-jaw and wide-eyed surprise and amusement, Ted replied, 'Yep. That about sums it up!' This time his smile was real.

Sometimes letting your facial expressions do the talking is more appropriate than blurting out your feelings. When being seen and not heard is a prudent choice, let the look on your face deliver your message.

Communicating Feelings When Words Are Inappropriate

Take a healthy measure of lips, teeth, jaws, cheeks, eyes and even your nose, and you can create a plethora of facial expressions. With more than 44 muscles in your face – 22 per side – you can communicate just about anything you want simply by appearance alone. And sometimes a look is all you need.

Say that you think the person sitting across from you is attractive, but you'd feel a fool coming out and saying so. The other person may feel a bit threatened or uncomfortable if you expressed your feelings out loud. So, what to do? You establish eye contact and hold it a little longer than usual, while giving a little smile. If you're really feeling up for a flirt, drop your chin a fraction or tilt your head as a silent invitation. Not a word's been spoken, yet a frisson is in the air (see Figure 4-1).

Women frequently indicate their interest by dropping the chin and looking up from under their eyebrows. Men tend to tilt their heads backwards, raising the chin.

Figure 4-1:
The tilted heads, eye contact, smiles and close, open body positions indicate mutual attraction.

The engine behind the expression

The facial nerve (cranial nerve VII) that controls your facial muscles is like a tree. The tap root is located deep within your brain's limbic system. From this root extend three branches, controlling facial responses to stimuli. The first branch regulates the tearing and salivating process. The second branch is responsible for transmitting taste messages. The third branch controls movements such as the smile, frown and squint. Because human facial skin is flexible and the muscles underneath respond quickly to brain impulses, you can communicate your thoughts, feelings and intentions through facial expressions without saying a word.

You may want to send a message telling someone that his behaviour isn't acceptable. A lowered brow, tightened lips and a slight shake of the head are usually enough to make your point.

A disapproving look may not always be enough to stop unacceptable behaviour. When Prince William was a four-year-old pageboy at his Uncle Andrew's wedding, his mother, the late Princess Diana, was seated near enough to her son to catch his eye, but not near enough to grab hold of him. During the ceremony, William became fractious and began playing with the other young attendants. Despite his mother's attempts to control his behaviour, including raising her index finger to her pursed lips, frowning and shaking her head, in a definite 'No' gesture, William took no notice. Finally, he turned his head sharply in the direction of his mother, frowned for all he was worth, pursed his lips and lowered his head – his endearing way of saying, 'No!'

The next time you disagree with someone and believe that it would be inappropriate to say so out loud, you can engage the other person in a bit of ocular one-upmanship. Establish eye contact and hold the person's gaze slightly longer than you would normally, with your lips tightly closed. Be aware that this expression can be perceived as aggressive if held for too long. If you're 'eye-balling' your boss, you may want to break eye contact first.

Recognising Facial Expressions that Reinforce the Spoken Message

As with all gestures, the expression on your face conveys your thoughts, feelings and intentions. Flash your eyebrows in recognition of someone whose company you enjoy, frown when reading your child's school report, grimace when your daughter comes home with the local ruffian, smile as a loved one approaches you, and you don't need to say a word to communicate your feelings. When you do choose to speak and your words reflect what your face is expressing, your message is clear. When your words are saying one thing and your facial expressions are saying something else, your listener responds to what he sees. For example, if you tell your son-in-law how happy you are to see him while your facial expression looks like you've been sucking a lemon, don't be surprised if he resists your efforts to play nice.

Open facial gestures – in which your eyes are engaged, your mouth is relaxed and your head is tilted with interest – invite conversation whereas closed expressions – pursed lips, a furrowed brow and squinted eyes – discourage interaction (see Figure 4-2). To indicate that you're keen to engage, establish and maintain eye contact, lean forward and let the corners of your mouth lift with curiosity. If you want to be left alone, avoid eye contact, pull away from the other person and let a frown settle on your features. You'll be on your own in no time.

If your gestures conflict with the words you're saying, your messages are mixed, leaving your listener confused.

Figure 4-2:
Pursed lips and a stern gaze indicate negative thoughts and emotions.

As well as sending messages through your body language, your voice also conveys your thoughts, feelings and intentions. To develop a voice that represents you at your best, start by breathing correctly. As you inhale, keep your chest still and allow your abdomen to expand as you fill yourself with nourishing oxygen. If in doubt about how to breathe properly, observe a baby at rest. His tummy rises and falls with each breath, while his chest remains still. After you've mastered that technique, hum your favourite tune to relax your vocal chords. (You can pick up tons of tips for creating a voice that commands attention in *Voice and Speaking Skills For Dummies* by Judy Apps (Wiley).)

When facial expressions and movements fail to match the spoken word your listener becomes confused. Your messages are mixed, leaving your listener wondering what you really mean. Figure 4-3 is an example of a person sending out mixed messages. While the pointed finger and furrowed brow suggest anger, the twinkle around her eyes and the upward curve to her lips indicate that she's not as angry as you may have first thought.

Figure 4-3:
When body language and the spoken word don't match, the message is mixed.

Because non-verbal behaviour makes powerful impressions, pick your gestures and expressions with care to convey a clear message.

Bill Clinton is known for his powers of persuasion. As a means of expressing his feelings and engaging with his listener, he employs a wide range of facial gestures, including the 'lower lip bite'. This gesture creates the impression that he cares deeply about his audience's concerns and can feel their fear and pain (see Figure 4-4).

Figure 4-4: Chewing on the lower lips demonstrates care and concern.

When you're not being perceived the way you want to be, consider your facial expressions. If your face is conveying one message and your words are saying something else, people looking at you are going to believe what they see more than what they hear.

Looking beyond the hang-dog expression

Some people are born looking sombre or sad — they can't help it. Their eyes turn down, their mouths curve south and their cheeks hang slack, rather like a bulldog whose facial parts suffer from the pull of gravity. The person with a downward-facing countenance has a look that spells 'miserable'. People with sombre expressions can be perceived as unfriendly, thoughtful or sad. Although they may be telling you how thrilled they are about their latest successful venture, their facial make-up says they're less than happy.

If someone with a sombre expression tells you how excited or happy he is, look to his eyes.

If they're engaged and the muscles around the outer edges are pulling upward, you can believe what he says. People with a perpetually sunny expression can be mistakenly perceived as frivolous or less serious. You need to take in the whole person before making a judgement.

Masking Emotions

If you've ever bitten your lips to keep from blurting out sentiments that would undoubtedly cause offence, if you've ever smiled when your heart was breaking or if you've ever frowned when you've wanted to laugh, you know what masking emotions is all about.

When people want to avoid expressing what's going on inside, they create the opposite facial expression with their pliable facial muscles and skin, and – hey presto! – they're masking their emotions.

I recently attended a friend's funeral. As I looked at the other mourners, I was struck by the similarity of gestures and facial expressions. All were tense, tight and controlled. Smiles of recognition were closed mouthed and tinged with anxiety. Some people licked their lips and chewed on them to prevent crying. Eyes were dull, many were moist, and all had a downward slant at the outer corners. Many clasped their hands in an effort to contain their emotions. Some put their arms around their partner's shoulders in a gesture of comfort. We were all doing what we could to contain our sadness, by controlling our gestures and facial expressions.

After the Falklands War, the then-British prime minister, Margaret Thatcher, was interviewed on television and asked why a British submarine had been instructed to torpedo the Argentine battleship, the *Belgrano*. Purportedly annoyed that she had to undergo the journalist's questioning, and knowing that it was important for her career that she was seen as informed, calm and in control, she explained that because the ship was inside the British exclusion zone the action was justifiable. Both she and the journalist knew that was a lie. The truth was that the ship was sailing away from the Falklands and was outside the exclusion zone when attacked. While Mrs Thatcher was making her false reply, her mask fell for a split second and she revealed a brief expression of anger. She gave a quick smile, which anyone looking carefully could detect was false from the lack of engagement in her eyes, followed by a momentary flash of anger. Her eyes protruded and her jaw thrust forward.

As quickly as the expression appeared, it was replaced by her masked expression. If you want to see the interview, check it out on YouTube.

A jutted jaw and protruding eyes indicate anger or annoyance.

Expressing a Range of Emotions

Whereas words are designed to divulge factual, provable data, body language exposes unspoken thoughts, feelings and intentions. Like it or not, whatever emotions you experience, thoughts you harbour or actions you're considering, you can count on your face to reveal them.

Showing happiness

If your grandmother was anything like mine, she'd tell you to 'put on your happy face' when meeting someone new because she knew that people respond positively to positive behaviour.

Facial displays of genuine, unadulterated, free-flowing happiness can't be missed. When you're experiencing pure joy, your eyes involuntarily twinkle, the laugh lines at the outside corners of your eyes deepen, your cheeks raise and, as your lips pull up at the sides and separate, you expose your teeth. No one can doubt your pleasure.

Insincere smiles are easily spotted. You need more than pulled-back lips showing off your pearly whites to convince someone that life's great. If your eyes aren't engaged with your mouth – that is, if your lips pull back in a smile and your eyes are dull, listless or averting the other person's gaze – you're sure to be labelled insincere.

A fake smile looks manufactured and unnatural.

When you're taking someone's photograph and you want him to smile, find another word – one that elicits a genuine smile – to replace 'cheese'. The word 'cheese' pulls back the zygomatic major muscles, resulting in a false smile and an artificial-looking photo.

If you're with someone who smiles at you and says he's happy, but a little voice inside tells you that something's amiss, listen to his voice. Then look at his eyes and cheeks for confirmation. To spot a genuine smile, observe the fleshy part of the eye between the brow and the eyelid. If it moves downwards and the end of the eyebrows dip slightly, the smile is for real.

Spotting the smile

In 1862, the French neurophysiologist Guillaume Duchenne de Boulogne published his studies of facial expressions. De Boulogne used electro-diagnostics and electrical stimulation to distinguish between genuine and false smiles. In addition to using the heads of people who had been executed by the guillotine, de Boulogne's principal photographic subject was an old man who had the rare condition of facial anaesthesia. This unfortunate condition made him the perfect subject for the scientist's investigations, because the electrodes used to stimulate the muscles were undoubtedly uncomfortable, if not quite painful.

With a hands-on approach, de Boulogne twisted and pulled face muscles from various angles and positions to discover which muscles controlled which smiles. He identified two kinds of smile that are controlled by two different muscle sets. The *zygomatic major* muscles, which run down the side of the face, are under your conscious control. These muscles are attached to the corners of the mouth and pull the mouth back, exposing the teeth while pumping up the cheeks. When you want to appear friendly or submissive, or show how much you're enjoying yourself when the opposite is true, you rely on the zygomatic majors to produce a false smile. The *orbicularis oculi* are the muscles that pull the eyes back, make them narrow and produce laughter lines that radiate from the outside corners of the eyes. The orbicularis oculi act involuntarily and produce a true smile.

Further research by Professor Paul Ekman of the University of California, San Francisco and University of Kentucky professor Dr Wallace V. Friesen reveal that the unconscious brain automatically generates genuine smiles. When you experience pleasure, the brain's limbic system, where feelings are processed, is stimulated, resulting in a smile in which the mouth muscles rise, the cheeks lift, the eyes narrow and the eyebrows slightly dip.

You can tolerate a lot of awkwardness in another person if his facial expression shows that he wants to get along with you. If he offers you an open smile and eye contact and tilts his head in your direction, he's indicating that he's doing his best to create an agreeable atmosphere.

Revealing sadness

Look at someone who's feeling blue and you can see that his facial features are slack and sagging. His eyes are dull and lifeless and the sides of his mouth are probably cast downward. Everything about his visage indicates sadness, despondency or despair.

When you're experiencing grief or sorrow, be prepared for your lips to tremble. Your eyes become moist, and you may cover your face with your hand to contain your feelings and block out whatever is making you feel sad.

Demonstrating disgust or contempt

To show disgust or contempt, narrow your eyes, wrinkle your nose and twist your lips into a grimace. Either drop your chin or lift it a fraction, and turn your head slightly to the side. People showing disgust tend to look down on the person or object of their contempt. In extreme cases they may lift their upper lip, which in turn makes the nose pull upward (see Figure 4-5).

Anne and her mother Jean were having a heated political discussion. Not surprisingly, Anne's views were in direct opposition to those of her mother. Finally, unable to win the argument or to convince her daughter of her misguided judgement, Jean, in a high display of contempt, wrinkled her nose, narrowed her eyes, tightened her lips and shook her head in disgust as if she'd just smelt an over-ripe stilton.

Signs of contempt are common in the business environment. Looks of disdain and scorn are tossed about the office floor with regularity when one high-flyer attempts to displace another.

Figure 4-5:
The pulled up nose, squinted eyes, raised upper lip and dropped jaw indicate disgust.

Nicola is extremely talented at spotting new trends in consumer behaviour. Although Tess, her boss, admires her perception, she also feels threatened by Nicola's youth, energy and ability to engage with senior board members. During meetings, Tess often responds to Nicola's observations and recommendations with pursed lips, a slight narrowing of the eyes, and a small turn of the head away from the younger woman.

Conveying anger

You've experienced the emotion, you know the feeling and you've worn the expression. Anyone in your vicinity recognises the signs. Before the big blow up, you probably stare hard at the source of offence without flinching. Your eyebrows pull down and inward, causing your forehead to furrow. Your lips tighten and turn down at the corners, or open stiffly as if in a frozen shout. You may also grit your teeth together. Some people flare their nostrils when they're very angry. Finally, if you're incandescent with rage, your face can turn white as the blood drains from the epidermis.

If your anger is about to get the better of you, inhale deeply through your nose, breathing deeply into your lower abdomen while keeping your upper chest loose and free of tension. Hold for a count of three, and then exhale slowly through your mouth. Deep breathing provides oxygen to the brain, enabling you to think clearly. The time it takes for you to inhale and exhale gives you a moment to regroup.

Distinguishing between surprise and fear

Expressions of surprise and fear are closely connected. In both expressions, the eyes widen and the mouth opens. The differences are subtle and found

---

Changing colours

According to zoologist Desmond Morris, facial colour as a part of the 'fight or flight' response is an indicator of rage level. If someone approaches you menacingly and his face is pale, he's more likely to attack than if his face is red. If the face is red, he's already experienced his deepest rage and has passed the point of attack. Although people think of those whose faces are red with rage as being the ones to fear, the reddened face is a sign of an internal struggle, frequently resulting in shouting and harsh language. Despite his threatening behaviour, the puce-faced individual is unlikely to do you real physical harm.

primarily in the attitudinal shape and position of the eyebrows, eyes and mouth. A few other telltale differences can also be identified.

Surprise!

An expression of surprise, unlike a fearful expression, is open and colourful. From the whites of your eyes and teeth to the redness of the inside of your lips and your mouth, which you expose as your jaw drops, a person can tell that you're genuinely surprised. Granted, not all people open their mouths, but the whites of the eyes show and the eyebrows rise in an arched position.

When you're surprised or startled, your eyebrows shoot up in an arch and horizontal wrinkles appear across your forehead. The whites of your eyes become more noticeable as you widen your eyes and your jaw drops, leaving your mouth in a slack position. (see Figure 4-6).

You may notice that someone who is genuinely surprised covers his mouth with his hand. This is an example of holding back an extreme emotion. Go to Chapter 9 for more information on how hand movements reveal feelings.

Figure 4-6: The woman is looking surprised (left) and fearful (right).

Boo!

The telltale signs of a fearful expression are

- ✔ A tensely pulled back open mouth
- ✔ Raised eyelids
- ✔ Exposed whites of eyes

When you experience fear, your eyebrows rise and pull together in a crooked curve. The centre part of your forehead wrinkles and, while your upper eyelids rise, exposing the whites of your eyes, your lower eyelids become tense and rise too. Finally, your lips tense and may pull back around your open mouth.

Revealing interest

When showing interest in what someone is doing or saying, you may find yourself cocking your head in his direction and nodding in agreement. Your eyes widen, taking in the information, and your mouth may be slightly opened.

The open position indicates interest. Whether the interest is romantic, intellectual, spiritual or just plain friendly, the look on your face is open. Your eyes are engaged, your head may tilt or nod and your body leans forward as if immersing itself in the subject. No blocks – such as lowered eyebrows, a jutting chin or a furrowed forehead – stand between you and the person who's caught your eye.

People nod when they're agreeing with what they hear. A slow nod shows that they're taking in what the other person is saying and are prepared to let him continue. A fast nod indicates that, although the person may be interested in what the speaker is saying, he wants to hurry things along.

Research into animal behaviour shows that, among others, birds, dogs and humans cock their heads when they're alert and listening. So if you want to know whether your dog or parrot is paying attention to you, see if he's cocking his head.

When evaluating what you're observing, you may raise one hand to your cheek with your index finger pointing upward and your thumb supporting your chin while your other three fingers curl in on your palm. When decision time arrives, you and your colleagues may find yourselves stroking your chins in a sign of thoughtfulness and contemplation. (Go to Chapter 9 to find out more about different hand gestures and what they mean.)

Chapter 5

The Eyes Have It

*B*ecause much of your face-to-face interaction with people involves looking at their faces, knowing what their expressions are expressing gives you insight into what they're thinking and how they're feeling. When in doubt, look to the eyes. The signals they send play a vital part in revealing emotions, thoughts and intentions. In fact, of all your body's parts, the eyes reveal your inner state most accurately. From their position in front of the brain's limbic system, they've got a direct line to your body's command centre. Your pupils – the dark disks in the centre of your eye – can't lie. When pleased with what they see, they enlarge. When they shrink in size, you're not happy. Eyes respond involuntarily to stimuli with little means of control. Of course, if you want to increase the diameter of your pupils to make yourself look more appealing, you can indulge in a bit of marijuana. Or perhaps not.

 Light affects the size of the pupil. The pupil contracts in bright light to limit the amount of light the eye absorbs and enlarges in low lighting to let more light in. Your eyes are the gateway to your soul. For better or worse, like it or not, they reflect your thoughts, feelings and intentions. The good news is, other people's eyes reflect their inner state, too.

This chapter looks at the role that eyes play in communicating your thoughts, feelings and intentions. You discover how to use your eyes to convey interest, command attention, show disapproval, signal submission, garner sympathy, create intimate feelings, demonstrate dominance and tell someone 'Enough is enough!' And because communication is a two-way street – eyes and all – I tell you how to decipher the eye signals that others send your way.

The Power of the Held Gaze

When two people establish and maintain eye contact in a comfortable way they create feelings of wellbeing and trust, foundation stones for successful communication. Sometimes, however, you may feel uneasy when looking at another person. Their eyes may be sending out messages of dishonesty, disloyalty, disappointment, unfriendliness, sadness, anger or despair. Whether the interaction is comfortable or not is partly to do with the way in which you do – or don't – look at people. The intensity and length of time someone holds your eye influences the meaning of the gaze. The following sections explain the different emotions or intentions that a held gaze can signify.

Dr Almeida is a psychiatrist. One of his patients, Nancy, a woman in her early fifties, was diagnosed with schizophrenia when she was in her late teens. For most of her life Nancy has successfully lived with her illness as a result of medication and psychiatric treatment. When Dr Almeida first met Nancy, he noticed how she stared at him for long periods of time without speaking. The look is unflinching and can be unnerving to people who aren't aware of the behaviours associated with mental illness. (You can find out more about behaviours associated with schizophrenia in *Schizophrenia For Dummies* by Jerome Levine (Wiley).)

When a person holds your gaze, she's telling you one of two things: she finds you attractive or interesting, or she's feeling anger or hostility towards you. How do you tell the difference? Look at her pupils: in the first case, they're dilated; in the second, they're constricted (see Figure 5-1).

Who's watching who?

Some people find establishing and maintaining eye contact difficult and avert their eyes when speaking. Others bore into their listeners with piercing eyes. Because of the connective quality of the eyes – the gateway to the soul, as the saying goes – it can be hard to gauge the other person's feelings and intentions. The exception to the rule is that the other person is avoiding you if she refuses to meet your eye. Research shows that when Westerners interact, they look at one another on average 61 per cent of the time. The speaker looks at the listener between 40–60 per cent of the time, and the listener looks at the speaker approximately 75 per cent of the time. People spend approximately 31 per cent of their time mutual gazing. This tells you that, if someone looks at you more or less than usual, something's going on that's impacting her response.

The average gaze for an individual in Western cultures lasts 2.95 seconds and the average mutual gaze is 1.8 seconds. In some Asian, African and South American cultures, as well as in the Middle East, prolonged eye contact is perceived as hostile or discourteous.

Figure 5-1:
Holding a gaze can demonstrate interest (left) or hostility (right).

Pupils, babies and the art of the deal

Confucius said, 'Look into a person's pupils. He cannot hide himself.' By observing the pupils of another person's eyes, you can tell whether or not she likes what she's looking at. If her pupils resemble warm drops of chocolate, you know that whatever she's responding to is having a positive impact. If they're steely and small, best move away fast! Dilated pupils show a favourable response; constricted pupils don't. In addition to responding to emotions, pupils respond to light. They enlarge when the lighting's dim and contract under bright conditions.

Consider these other fun tidbits:

✔ Research shows that most women's eyes dilate to their extreme when looking at images of other mothers and children. The next time you get a chance, observe a mother watching her newborn child and notice how her pupils enlarge.

✔ Newborn babies and young children appear to have larger pupils than adults. When in the company of adults, a child's or an infant's eyes often dilate in an unconscious attempt to look appealing and gain the adult's attention. This phenomenon is one that toy manufacturers (and cartoonists) recognise. To see for yourself, go into a toy shop and have a look at the best-selling dolls and cuddly animals: the eyes are designed with oversized pupils.

(continued)

(continued)

> ✔ The ancient Chinese gem traders were expert in watching their buyers' eyes when negotiating prices. If the pupils dilated, the trader knew he was offering too good a deal and had to negotiate harder.
>
> ✔ Courtesans and prostitutes were known to make themselves appear more enticing and desirable by putting drops of belladonna in their eyes to dilate their pupils.
>
> ✔ It is said that the reason the late Aristotle Onassis wore dark glasses when negotiat-
>
> ing business deals was to prevent his eyes from revealing his thoughts. Similarly, professional poker players wear sunglasses to hide their feelings about the cards they've been dealt.
>
> Unless you're prepared to use artificial means, like the courtesans did, pupil dilation is beyond your control.

Intimating interest

You can demonstrate interest in what you're doing or saying by fixing your gaze directly on the person or object you're addressing for slightly longer than usual. The length and direction of your gaze tells anyone who's paying attention that you only have eyes for who and what you're looking at. Focus your attention on another person and hold your gaze for more than two to three seconds and you imply that the person has grabbed your interest. To encourage her to look back at you, tilt your head and smile. (See Chapter 3 for more about head positions and Chapter 6 for tips on mouth movements.)

Liz went to an art fair with her friends, Frank and Peter. Their taste in art – South American contemporary with a twist – was very different from Liz's, whose preferences tended toward Monet and John Singer Sargent. Liz was uninterested in most of the paintings her friends were admiring. Not wanting to appear bored or dismissive of their taste, she forced herself to look at the paintings for longer than she would normally have done. Not only did Frank and Peter believe that Liz was enjoying the art, she discovered that by giving the work extra 'eye time' she began to appreciate it in a way she previously hadn't. Although she didn't want it in her home, she recognised how other people could value it.

If you struggle to establish and maintain eye contact and want to be perceived as a non-threatening and interested listener, focus your gaze on the triangular area between your listener's eyes and mouth.

Clinton's gaze

People who've met Bill Clinton report that he has a way of looking at you that makes you feel important and immensely interesting. He engages with his listener by establishing eye contact up front and lets his gaze scan slowly across your eyes and face as he speaks. You end up feeling that you are, for that moment, a truly significant and fascinating person.

Building rapport

When you want to build rapport with someone, research shows that you need to meet his gaze between 60–70 per cent of the time. So, if Kim likes Nick and wants to do business with him, she should look at him a lot. If Nick likes Kim too, they look at one another comfortably and before you know it, the deal's done! But what about those people for whom establishing and maintaining eye contact is difficult? No matter how genuine, honest and trustworthy they are, their lack of eye contact sends out avoidance signals.

Given the choice of working with a person who has to make an effort to look you in the eye and someone who's comfortable establishing and maintaining eye contact, who do you choose? Research shows that people prefer to work with others with whom they have rapport or a comfortable relationship. (For more about rapport and how to build it through body language, pick up a copy of *Neuro-Linguistic Programming For Dummies* by Romilla Ready and Kate Burton or *Persuasion & Influence For Dummies* by Elizabeth Kuhnke (both Wiley).) Even if you feel uncomfortable establishing eye contact, making the effort is worth the struggle. The more you get used to looking other people in the eye, the more comfortable, confident and trustworthy you appear, and the more successful your interactions are likely to be.

Andrew regularly has to make formal presentations at work. Although he's an outstanding presenter who's comfortable looking at his audience, when he's uncertain about his subject matter his eyes disengage and sweep around the room as if looking for an answer. Unaware of this habit, Andrew was surprised when he saw himself on video, transitioning from looking like a smooth operator to being in a pickle. Now when Andrew presents material he's not sure about, he pauses, smiles, breathes and forces himself to look at his audience before speaking. He finds when he does this that he feels more in control than before.

Creating intimate feelings

If you're gazing at another person and your eyes stray down his face onto other parts of his body, you're indicating an interest far removed from the world of business or a friendly 'hello'. When your eyes wander over someone's face and body, you're showing that you're attracted to him. If the look is returned, you may be onto a winner. If not, save your pride by reverting to the social gaze.

While both men's and women's pupils dilate when they find someone attractive, if a woman wants to increase the heat, she looks at the other person with a sideways glance. Referred to as the 'come hither' look (see Figure 5-2), it says, 'Come and get me'. If she doesn't want to be so obvious, she uses the social gaze and keeps her target guessing. (For more information on all the uses and meanings of sideways glances, check out 'The sideways glance' section later in this chapter.)

Figure 5-2:
The 'come hither' look commands attention and indicates sexual interest.

To show disapproval, disagreement and other negative feelings

Of course, not all gazes are warm and friendly. A steely-eyed gaze in which the pupils contract indicates displeasure. Beady little eyes, snake eyes and shooting daggers with the eyes are sure signs of dispute, disapproval or disagreement. If someone holds your gaze and his pupils are constricted, you can bet you're in his bad books. If, however, you're able to hold the gaze for several seconds longer than you normally would without looking away – an action indicating submission – you can send out your own message of disapproval.

Because your pupils contract when you're angry or in a negative mood, the eyes look harsh and unfriendly. Fake your smile and backslap all you want – if you're not pleased with what's going on and don't want to give the game away, you'd better put on your dark glasses to hide your feelings.

Showing dominance

A dominant person is the one in control, with authority. This person takes command, holds the power and influences others. Dominant people establish and maintain eye contact with confidence. Their eye movements are mostly slow and controlled and they're aware of their environment. They're comfortable looking at another person for an extended period of time, while being careful not to stare, which would just make them look slightly mad or rude.

The long hard gaze is a powerful pose and demonstrates dominance, whether you're looking towards someone or purposely cutting them out of your line of vision. People in control of the interaction demonstrate their dominance by choosing when and how long to look at someone. The following sections explain how dominance can be conveyed through the power of the gaze.

If you want to be perceived as dominant, strong and in control, slightly narrow your eyes. Donald Trump is a master of the beady-eyed glare. So are presenter of *The Weakest Link* Anne Robinson and actor Clint Eastwood, who has made the 'visor eyes' posture one of his trademarks.

Scenario 1: Being reprimanded

When you want to make a strong point, deliberately avoid eye contact to raise the other person's anxiety level. If you've ever been reprimanded by an irate boss or disappointed parent, you may recall how you felt when the person speaking refused to look at you. You knew that you were going to get the full force of her glare at some point; you just had to wait to see when.

When I was working as a hostess on a cruise ship, I was called into the cruise director's office early one morning. Scotty was a stickler for punctuality and I had been late for an event the night before. I knew I was in for it because I'd heard him shout at my colleagues on other occasions. What I didn't know was how intense the confrontation would be. When I entered his office he was sitting quietly behind his desk, staring out at the ocean with his back turned to me. With barely a glance in my direction, he told me to sit down. Continuing to look out of the porthole, he began to berate me not just for the previous night's transgression but for all my other failings as well. Unable to remain quiet and let him blow off some steam, I gave him excuses and argued back. Big mistake. He spun around in his seat and fixed me with a glare so forceful I felt as though I'd been slapped in the face and punched in the chest. His stare was so intense and he held it for so long that I was unable to meet his eyes. Scotty told me that I'd better watch myself and that he was keeping an eye on me. As he said those words, I looked up to see his eyes boring directly into mine. Not able to sustain the eye contact, I looked away. There was no question at that point who was in the dominant position.

If you find yourself disagreeing with someone and want to make your point, hold eye contact slightly longer than usual. Without saying a word, you leave no doubt that you, too, are feeling in control and should be taken seriously.

Scenario 2: In conversation

In conversation, the dominant person spends more time looking at the other person when she's talking than when she's listening. Whoever is speaking has control over the interaction. A dominant speaker watches her listeners to make sure that they're paying attention and aren't about to cut in. When the dominant person is in the listening position, however, she conveys her status by reducing the amount of time she spends looking at the speaker, indicating that she's not interested in flattering that person and is soon taking back the speaker's role.

Scenario 3: The unflinching stare

You can grab the attention of an adversary by looking her directly in the eye without flinching. Direct eyeball-to-eyeball staring can be deeply threatening. Just like children trying to stare each other out, you know that at some point you, or your partner, will break the contact because maintaining it is just too difficult.

My mother had an unnerving way of looking a person straight in the eye when she disapproved of his behaviour. Her mouth tensed, her eyes narrowed as they tightened around the edges and her gaze didn't falter. No one in the family escaped the stinging effect of her piercing gaze, which we referred to as 'The Look'. Unwavering, unflinching and undaunted, it elicited the following responses: we either attempted to stare our mother down, which we never achieved, or, unable to take the pressure, we averted our eyes in a downward glance. Either way, Mum won.

The Evil Eye

Belief in the Evil Eye derives from the feeling that people can be damaged by a prolonged stare. This superstition is still held in Mediterranean countries, and people often carry amulets and other good-luck charms to ward off disasters.

Fishermen commonly protect their boats from danger by attaching a pair of artificial eyes to the prows of their vessels as a means of out-staring a potential threat or enemy.

If someone is trying to bully you or put you off, look him straight in the eye, narrow your eyelids and focus directly on your target. If other people are around, let your eyes move slowly from one person to the next without blinking. Move your eyes first and let your head follow, keeping your torso still. The effect is unnerving. If you need a role model, Arnold Schwarzenegger in *The Terminator* is your man.

Using effective gazes in business situations

If you're uncomfortable looking people directly in the eye and you want to come across as a person to be taken seriously, keep your gaze in the triangular area between the eyes and the centre of the forehead. As long as your eyes remain in that space and you keep control of the interaction, the other person reckons that you're someone who means business. The following are other tricks that come in handy in business situations.

At last, a way to shorten business meetings!

One study showed that in presentations where visual aids are used, 83 per cent of the information is absorbed visually, 11 per cent through the audio channel, and 6 per cent through the other three senses. A study conducted at the Wharton School of the University of Pennsylvania found that in presentations that relied solely on the spoken word only 10 per cent of the information was retained. In order for a verbal presentation to be effective, key points must be repeated frequently. When a visual element is added to a verbal presentation, the retention rate increases to 50 per cent. By including visual aids in your presentations, you achieve a 400 per cent increase in efficiency. Further findings show that when visual aids are used in business meetings, on average they last 18.6 minutes as opposed to 25.7 minutes – equating to a time saving of 28 per cent.

Controlling a bore

Looking a tedious, dull and mind-numbing windbag straight in the eyes without flinching is a highly effective way of stopping her in her tracks. If you fix your eyes directly in the business gaze triangle without a flicker of an eye, you may be amazed at how quickly she comes to a halt.

The power lift

If you want to get your message across when you're presenting visual information during a meeting, guide the audience's attention to where you want it to look. A simple way of controlling your listeners' attention is to use a pen. Point to your material and verbalise what you're showing. Then lift the pen off the page and hold it between your eyes and those of your listeners (see Figure 5-3). This movement works like a magnet as your listeners lift their heads, look directly at you and, while both hearing and seeing what you're saying, absorb your message. While you continue to speak, keep the palm of your other hand open.

Figure 5-3: The 'power lift' controls where a person looks during a presentation.

The Wandering Eye: Breaking Eye Contact

Avoiding or breaking eye contact indicates a variety of things, including submission or discomfort. Although running away from unpleasant situations or feelings is instinctive, fleeing in panic isn't really an option in everyday life because, as humans, we aim to co-operate (unless, of course, the other person is threatening physical violence, in which case you run in the opposite direction as fast as your legs can take you!). On the other hand, at times avoiding someone's gaze gives you a great deal of strength, appeal and allure. It's all a matter of whose eyes you're avoiding and how you do it that creates the effect and determines the response. Here are the commonest reasons for avoiding eye contact, whether people do so knowingly or not:

- ✔ **To 'flee' from an encounter:** Evading someone's glance, gaze or stare is a defensive, protective action, a form of fleeing from an interaction that stirs up in you a 'fight or flight' response. When you think you're going to lose – whether you're in an argument or trying to gain someone's attention – you unconsciously withdraw from the encounter by pulling your eyes away.

  Looking away from another person, avoiding someone's gaze and averting your eyes makes you look smaller. People who feel uncomfortable unconsciously make rapid and frequent eye movements, indicating that they'd rather scuttle away than stay where they are.

- ✔ **To signal submission:** When you look away from a person who makes you feel ill at ease, you're relinquishing your power and handing it to the other person.

- ✔ **To avoid confrontation:** At the first whiff of confrontation, anxious people reduce the amount of time they spend looking at the person with whom they're disagreeing. When you're feeling anxious, your eyes search for escape routes where you can hide from what's going on rather than seek a solution. When it looks as if trouble's brewing between two people and you sense one of them is going to lose, don't be surprised to see the potential loser avert her gaze to remove the dominant person from sight.

- ✔ **To convey feeling uncomfortable:** People who are feeling ashamed, embarrassed or sad deliberately look away.

- ✔ **To catch another person's attention:** Pulling your eyes away from someone can show that you're interested in her. This behaviour is part of the flirtation process and encourages the other person to go after you. If you do withdraw your eyes for this purpose, make sure that you look back frequently. (For more about flirting techniques, turn to Chapter 13.)

The following sections discuss the ways in which many people avoid or minimise eye contact and explain what these different manoeuvres mean.

The eye shuttle

When you observe someone flicking her eyes back and forth, you can bet that she's subconsciously looking for an escape route. Notice that although her head remains still her eyes move rapidly from side to side. The action allows the person to take in everything that's going on around her and see where she can reposition herself without obviously giving the game away.

Philip was attending a conference where he saw Ed, a man he had met once before and whom he believed could be a potential client. Focusing on his own agenda, Philip made a beeline for Ed, who was already engaged in conversation with two colleagues. Philip re-introduced himself and, without being invited, joined in the discussion. What he failed to notice were Ed's eyes shuttling back and forth in search of the nearest exit. Although Ed wasn't interested in speaking to Philip, he's a polite guy and didn't want to embarrass him. While he smiled as Philip regaled the group with stories and remained where he was standing, his eyes didn't connect with Philip's as they scanned the room. Ed soon spotted another colleague and disengaged himself from the group, leaving his colleagues to deal with Philip, who never did do business with Ed, or his friends.

The sideways glance

The sideways glance carries several meanings, including interest, uncertainty or hostility. To determine which feeling is being conveyed, look at the rest of the person's body language.

When you look at someone out of the corner of your eye and add a slight smile while raising your eyebrows, as shown in Figure 5-4, it would be fair enough for the receiver to think that you're interested in her.

If you've ever spoken to someone who avoids looking at you while shooting glances out of the corner of her eye, chances are she's not very interested in you or what you're saying. It may be time for you to change tack in your conversation, or move on.

People tend to look towards things that interest them and look away from things that don't. Imagine that you're at a party. Your partner has gone to talk to friends, leaving you with a disagreeable guest. Try as you may, unless you're very polite and self-disciplined, your eyes stray in the direction of people or places you find more appealing. The brevity of your glances towards the other person signals your lack of interest in her.

If, during a conversation, the listener shoots a glance out of the corner of her eye and combines the action with downturned eyebrows and a furrowed forehead, you can bet that she's harbouring a critical, dismissive or hostile attitude.

Figure 5-4:
The
sideways
glance with
a smile
shows
interest.

The eye dip

Averting your eyes in a downward direction is a deliberate action designed to placate someone in a dominant position as well as an action designed to hide your feelings. In the first instance, by avoiding another person's gaze, you're giving her permission to take the dominant role in the interaction. In the second instance, you're holding the ace.

Dipping the eyes is also a way of demonstrating your reluctance to interact with someone. By dipping your eyes you're saying, 'If you want to connect with me, you have to make an effort.'

If you think that acting submissively is a weak or negative role to play, reconsider. Acting submissively can often put you in a real position of strength. And it's sometimes the best way to get what you want. Also remember that, if the manoeuvre is deliberate, you *choose* to relinquish control.

ANECDOTE

> ## Diana's dipping eyes
>
> Diana, Princess of Wales, was exceptionally adept at evoking empathy by dipping her eyes and lowering her head. This gesture is particularly appealing because it makes the eyes appear larger and makes a woman seem innocent and somewhat helpless. Both men and women respond in a protective way as long as they don't think they're being manipulated. Even as a young child, Diana used this gesture to good effect. Although initially she may not have been conscious of what she was doing, experience taught her that when she used her eyes in this fashion she engendered her public's empathy.

Other Ways Your Eyes Tell a Tale

Because your eyes reveal your thoughts, feelings and intentions – and you've got loads of them – they move in lots of different ways, exposing your internal state.

Winkin' and blinkin'

An engaging way to show a fun and friendly attitude is to wink. Winking also intimates that whatever you're talking about doesn't need to be taken too seriously. Similarly, people sharing a secret frequently share a conspiratorial wink. A wink carries many messages, so consider the context before deciding on an interpretation.

Sadly, not all interactions are fun and friendly. If you've got your doubts about the state of play, look to see how often someone blinks. On average, people blink between 6 to 20 times per minute, depending on their state of mind and the activity in which they're engaged.

Blinking longer than usual

If you've ever been in conversation with someone who, while speaking, blocks you out by shutting her eyes longer than she normally would, you know how annoying that action can be. Rather than blinking, these people close their eyes in an unconscious attempt to remove you from their sight. Some people find that closing their eyes helps them to think, focus and concentrate on what they're saying. Or, unfortunately, maybe they're bored by you or just aren't interested in what you're saying. Perhaps they feel superior to you. Hard to believe, I know, but possible. Whatever the reason, it can be interpreted as rude and off-putting.

I recently attended a workshop on, you guessed it, body language. I noted that occasionally when the facilitator was speaking she closed her eyes longer than felt normal. When one of the other participants pointed this out, she was surprised, having been unconscious of the habit. Upon reflection, the facilitator realised that she closed her eyes while speaking when not sure of what she was going to say next. She was subconsciously shutting out potential distractions while searching for an answer.

Blinking more often than normal

Many factors influence your blinking rate. Excitement, boredom, exhaustion and frustration all play their part. When you're animated, you blink more than when you're relaxed. You blink less when concentrating at your computer than when you're cheering on your favourite team.

The main purpose of blinking is to keep the eye surface moist, clean and healthy. Under normal conditions, the blinking rate is between six to eight blinks per minute. This can increase by four or five times when you're feeling under pressure.

When people lie, their energy increases and their blinking rate speeds up as they concoct their answers to difficult questions. However, just to confuse you, sometimes liars slow down their blinking rate.

Blinking less frequently than normal

When you're speaking and the listener is staring at you in a zombie-like fashion, you're probably boring her to distraction. A sure sign that you've lost her attention is the infrequency of eye blinks and the dull glaze that comes over her eyes.

While a lack of blinking can be a sign of boredom, hostility or indifference, it doesn't have to be. Confident people, for example, establish more and longer eye contact than people who are uncertain or are attempting to hide something. Although they blink less, they come across as interested listeners. (To find out more about how confident people use eye contact, refer to the earlier section 'The Power of the Held Gaze'.)

Lack of blinking can cause your cornea – the clear, thin, top layer of the eye – to become dehydrated. Your vision becomes blurry and you don't see as well.

Who's got a blinking problem?

Research shows that potential voters are more comfortable with candidates who look them squarely in the eye than with those demonstrating tics. During the 2012 debates between potential Republican presidential candidates, researchers investigated the corollary between candidates' blinking rates and voters' responses. During one debate, candidate Rick Santorum blinked at a rate of 61 times per minute, a more than 50 per cent increase on the other candidates, who blinked an average

27.8 times per minute. Although Mitt Romney's blinking rate averaged 33.9 times per minute, like the other candidates, this rate was tied to his comfort level. When rigorously challenged about his views on contraception his blinking rate accelerated. When he was confronted with a question to which he could give a standard response, his blinking rate decreased notably. The voters responded and Romney was elected his party's candidate.

Active eyebrows: The eyebrow flash

Since ancient times, people have initiated their greetings with the rapid raising and lowering of their eyebrows. Although this action can be so subtle as to be invisible to the naked or untrained eye, the gesture draws attention to the face in order to exchange clear signals of acknowledgement. Whether you're aware of it or not, when greeting another person, your eyebrows involuntarily rise. Except in Japan, where the movement is considered rude and has sexual implications (see Chapter 15), the eyebrow flash is universal and is even used by monkeys and apes to express recognition and social greeting. People who don't use the eyebrow flash when being introduced can be perceived as potentially aggressive.

Sit in a hotel lobby or at a bar and eyebrow flash everyone who passes by. You'll find that most people return the flash and smile. Who knows, they may even come over to talk to you.

Raised eyebrows don't always mean recognition, however. They can also mean the following:

- ✔ **Agreement:** When you agree with what someone is saying, you use the same gesture you use when you greet someone, the eyebrow flash.

- ✔ **Surprise and fear:** If you're surprised or scared, your eyebrows rise and stay in that position until the moment has passed.

Widening your eyes

The next time you get the chance, take a look at a baby's eyes. Notice that they're disproportionately large relative to the rest of her face. Unconsciously you respond to large eyes in a protective and nurturing manner. Large eyes make a person look more appealing, as any Hollywood starlet knows. Women create the look of submission by plucking their eyebrows to make the eyes appear larger. They then raise their eyebrows and eyelids, an action that particularly appeals to men. When a woman demonstrates submissiveness by widening her eyes, no man in her immediate vicinity stands a chance. His brain releases hormones stimulating his desire to protect and defend her.

If you want to appear innocent and attentive, open your eyes larger than their normal size. Unless the person being gazed at is aware of what you're doing, they're charmed by your likeable appearance.

You can make your eyes appear larger by raising your brows and lowering your lids, a technique that Marilyn Monroe used to maximum effect. (Sharon Stone and Kim Cattrall are pretty good at adopting this pose, too.) Most men and some women would, and still do, go weak at the knees when they look at photos of her with her lowered eyelids and raised eyebrows. People respond to this gesture because by maximising the space between the eyelid and the eyebrow the eyes appear larger, resulting in an innocent, sexy, mysterious or secretive look.

Flicking, flashing and fluttering

Fluttering your eyelids is usually associated with flirting. It's also a gesture you may find yourself using when you're on the spot and have to come up with a quick answer. Obviously it can also simply mean that you've got something in your eye causing an irritation, in which case, you probably rub your eye after fluttering for a moment or two. Flashing eyes – like Penelope Cruz's in *Vicky Cristina Barcelona* – indicate hot emotions such as anger or jealousy, although if you flash your eyebrows (refer to the preceding section) you're suggesting agreement or interest.

To flick your eyes over a person or an object shows a modicum of interest, which, depending on the response of the person or the amount of curiosity you feel for the object, can move into a longer gaze.

Chapter 6

Mastering Lip Reading

'*R*ead my lips,' said former President George H.W. Bush when running for office way back in 1988. Although your lips are the doorway to verbalising messages, they're equally adept at revealing thoughts, feelings, and intentions without uttering a word.

In this chapter you discover how the various lip positions, including a snarl, a pout and a lop-sided grin, tell the true story behind the spoken word.

Revealing Thoughts, Intentions and Emotions

The lips are made up of a complicated series of muscles running over, under, in and around the sides of your mouth (see Figure 6-1). Because the muscles are able to work independently of one another, they can pull and twist your mouth into weird and wonderful positions. One side of the mouth can mirror the other so that the whole mouth conveys the same message, such as when the sides of your lips turn up in a genuine smile of happiness or when they pull downward in disappointment or sadness. Your lips can also stretch in opposite directions, one side going up, the other side going down, indicating mixed emotions. The upper lip can rise in a sneer. The lower lip can tremble in fear.

The complicated series of muscles that control the lips include the orbicularis oris muscles, which sit at the sides of the mouth. Their function is to pull the lips back and push them forward. Other muscles controlling mouth movements include the elevators – such as levator labii superior – which lift the upper lip and the mentalis. This muscle, which sits at the tip of your jawline, pushes up your lower lip, causing your chin to wrinkle and making you look doubtful or displeased.

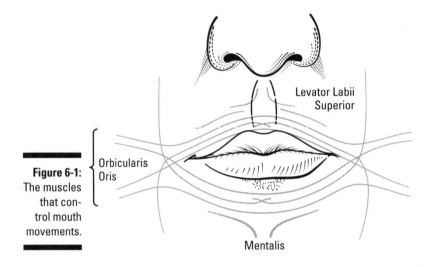

Figure 6-1:
The muscles that control mouth movements.

Levator Labii Superior

Orbicularis Oris

Mentalis

The unconscious tension in your lips indicates how you feel, regardless of what you say. You say you're feeling fine? Then why are your lips trembling? You say you're happy? Then why are your lips stretched across your mouth like a razor's edge? Whatever emotion you're experiencing – anticipation, pleasure, irritation – your lips are telling on you (see the *Body Language For Dummies* app for some examples).

Tight lips

Tight lips indicate tension. Now, don't be fooled into thinking that tension is always about negative emotion. Yes, your lips tense when you're angry and annoyed. They also tighten in anticipation when you're sexually aroused.

From the moment Amanda met Simon, she knew that he was the one for her. Not wanting to give her hand away too quickly, she worked hard to hide her feelings. Amanda said that whenever she saw Simon, she could feel a big grin wanting to burst forth across her face. In order to prevent this from happening she tightened the muscles around her mouth, pulling her lips together in a pursed pose. Unbeknownst to her, Simon could spot the sparkle of interest in her eyes and recognised the pleasurable tension Amanda's tightened lips were revealing. The good news was, Simon found Amanda quite cute too. (For more about how eyes convey messages, see Chapter 5.)

When you see someone whose lips are tight, tense or taut, you can safely bet he's holding back some kind of emotion, be it anger or attraction. When your own lips are trembling, you know that a feeling is about to burble forth. Whatever the emotion, tension is in the air.

Loose lips

Loose lips signal a relaxed state. They're also common to people who are depressed or sad. Lack of tension indicates that you've let go or, in some cases, given up. When your lips are loose, watch what you say. For want of a bit of tightness, you may give away your game.

Chewing on lips

When people feel anxious, they often chew on something such as a pencil, a finger or a lip. They may also fling themselves into the refrigerator, eating whatever they can find. Subconsciously, they're seeking the comfort of their mother's breast, that soft, warm place of wellbeing and security. The lip is the easiest object to chew on, because it's right there. You don't have to reach for an object and put it between your lips, you don't have to stick your finger in your mouth, you don't have to gorge on a take-away, you just have to engage your lips with your teeth to find comfort.

The three main lip-chewing gestures associated with anxiety are:

- ✔ **Lower lip bite:** The upper teeth bite down on the lower lip. The teeth rub against the lip, pulling it in and out of the mouth.

- ✔ **Upper lip bite:** The lower teeth protrude forward and catch the upper lip. The teeth may slide back and forth on the lip in a sucking-like manner.

- ✔ **Lip to lip bite:** The upper and lower lips come into contact, pulling inwards and resting tightly on the teeth.

In addition to showing anxiety, chewing your lips also signals self-restraint. As long as you're quiet about it, sucking on your lips is a useful way of keeping you from saying something that you may later regret.

Loose Lips Sink Ships

During the Second World War the American War Advertising Council created the phrase 'Loose Lips Sink Ships'. Seen on posters and heard on the streets, the expression advised people working in the armed forces and other citizens who might have information the enemy would find interesting to avoid careless talk.

People who feel embarrassed often chew on their lips as a way of holding onto themselves, even if only by the skin of their teeth!

Maintaining a stiff upper lip

The stiff upper lip is a real facial expression in which the upper lip muscle tightens as it contains underlying emotion. People who want to conceal their feelings tighten their upper lip to rein in their reactions.

The concept of maintaining a stiff upper lip dates back to the 1800s and is supposedly typical of the English approach to protecting private feelings and keeping emotions contained. The stiff upper lip comes in handy when you want to maintain your dignity.

When Oscar Pistorius, the disgraced South African Paralympic champion, was sentenced for the manslaughter of his model girlfriend Reeva Steenkamp, his defense team held their upper lips in a tight line. Some of the lawyers and courtroom observers, including the families of the accused and his victim, put their fingers to their upper lips in a gesture of restraint. The Blade Runner's lips turned down at both sides as his shoulders slightly rolled forward in a position of defeat.

A stiff upper lip is supposed to make you look brave. It can also make you look suspicious, however, because the expression is one of restraint. As with all gestures, consider the context before leaping to a conclusion about the meaning of an individual gesture or expression.

Holding back your feelings

The phrase 'keep a stiff upper lip' is symbolic of the British, and particularly of the young men educated in the English public school system during the time of the British Empire. 'Do your duty and show no emotion' characterises that era. The origins of the phrase can be traced to the United States, the first printed reference being found in the *Massachusetts Spy*, June 1815:

'I kept a stiff upper lip, and bought [a] license to sell my goods.'

Although that illustration doesn't explicitly refer to holding back one's feelings, it's similar to other nineteenth-century US references and the meaning is unmistakable. Here's one example, from the *Huron Reflector*, 1830:

'I acknowledge I felt somehow queer about the bows; but I kept a stiff upper lip, and when my turn came, and the Commodore of the P'lice axed [sic] me how I come to be in such company . . . I felt a little better.'

In 1963, the British humourist P.G. Wodehouse published a novel called *Stiff Upper Lip, Jeeves* – a quintessential English sentiment. In more recent times, public heroes have been permitted to demonstrate their emotions in front of their family, friends and fans. For example, footballers are frequently seen crying – or sulking – when they lose, while their fans share and support them in their grief. Before the Second World War that kind of behaviour would have been frowned upon.

Pouting, pursing and puckering

The pout is a comprehensive gesture. Depending on what the rest of your body is doing, pursing your lips can indicate disappointment, displeasure, frustration, sadness, sexual interest, thought or uncertainty. Whatever the reason for the pout, the facial movements are the same. In tandem, you contract your chin muscle and the side muscles – the labial tractors – of your lower lip. Your lips press together, your tongue rises against your palate and your pharynx constricts as it prepares to swallow (see Figure 6-2). Although you could argue that analysing the pout in this detailed way takes all the fun out of it, most people actually find it quite easy – so easy in fact that Hollywood starlets, small children, stroppy teenagers and disappointed mothers have mastered the expression.

One night when 18-year-old Cathy and her friends were out clubbing, they were trying to emulate Victoria Beckham's trademark pout. One of the girls quoted her mother's advice, 'You just put your lips together and blow' and bingo! For the rest of the evening the girls emulated their favourite celebrity.

When pouting as a sign of defence, the head drops down, eyes tighten and the forehead crinkles. When pouting for pleasure, the lips are soft, the face is smooth, and the eyelids drop to half-mast. For more about the power of the eyes, go to Chapter 5.

Notice how people's lips pinch at the sides and push forward when they're expressing disapproval, dismissal or disagreement. Look at the lips of people who are sexually aroused – they push forward in excitement, increase in size and redden.

For more information about the pout, skip to Chapter 13.

Pursed lips, in which the lips are puckered in a closed, rounded shape and pushed forward, indicate disagreement or calculated thought (see Figure 6-3). Lips in this position indicate that someone is considering his next move and calculating the consequences.

Figure 6-2:
The girl's pouts convey consideration (left), disagreement (centre) and sexual interest (right).

If you're out with friends or family and your partner starts to reveal some information you'd rather he not, purse your lips in a tight rounded 'O' and give him the Evil Eye. You may want to explain beforehand what the expression means to ensure he understands it when it appears on your face.

Figure 6-3:
Pursed or 'prune' lips indicate measured thinking.

If you're presenting a formal proposal or offering a simple suggestion and your listener meets your ideas with pursed lips, he's signalling mental resistance. Pause and invite his comments. Giving him the chance to air his opinions will make him feel acknowledged and then more inclined to listen to what you have to say. In contrast, of course, if you want to beat him at his own game, purse your lips right back. (For more about helping people understand your point of view, have a look at *Persuasion & Influence For Dummies* by Elizabeth Kuhnke (Wiley).)

Tensing your lips and biting back your words

When you feel your jaw locking and your lips tightening you're showing the world that you're pretty annoyed. Whether you pull back your lips baring your teeth, contain them in a razor-like line or push them forward in a puckered prune position, locked jaws and tight lips display anger, frustration, aggression or annoyance. When you tighten your lips and lock your jaw you're sending a clear signal that you're not amused and don't want to talk about it at the moment.

Graeme was invited to attend a senior leadership meeting at which several of the company's key decision-makers were present. Many of the points and positions that Graeme heard were in direct contrast to his sense of the business. Although with his own team Graeme expresses himself freely and encourages exchange, in the larger group, where it was clear that outside contributions weren't welcome, he found himself resisting sharing his opinions. At one point he observed his own behaviour, noticing that his mouth was in a tense line across his face, with his lips rolled inward and his teeth pressing down on them. The longer he held this position, the more negative he felt. For further insights into how body movements impact on mood, pick up a copy of *Communication Skills For Dummies* by Elizabeth Kuhnke (Wiley).

Changing thoughts and behaviours

When you've finished one thought or action and are revving up to start another, your lips close – if only fractionally – and open again as you change gears and take off again. In effect, you're closing one door and opening another.

Observe a person's mouth – whether he's the speaker or the listener doesn't matter. Notice him inhaling through open lips as he experiences a shift in mood, point of view or when an unexpected thought pops into his head. By paying attention to a person's facial movements, you can predict what's going to happen next.

Differentiating Smiles

Smiles carry a variety of meanings. While they're universally recognised as signs of pleasure, happiness and contentment, they also signal appeasement, and a secret bond. Studies conducted by Professors Marvin Hecht and Marianne LaFrance at Boston University indicate that the smile is a submissive signal and that people in subordinate roles tend to smile more in the company of those who are dominant or in superior positions.

Different cultures have different views about smiling. For example, the Chinese only smile among friends and family, while in Southern Europe something's wrong if people don't smile at you. You can find out more about cultural influences and body language in Chapter 15.

The next time you're among strangers, such as in an airport, shop or restaurant, smile at people whether you know them or not. Note their reactions. Your smile will generally be met by another. Research shows that smiling has a positive impact on others and facilitates relationships. As the penguins in the film *Madagascar* say, 'If in doubt, just smile and wave'.

The tight-lipped smile

When you stretch your lips in a straight line across your face without exposing your teeth, you're holding back information. Perhaps you're hiding your crooked teeth. Perhaps you're having to be polite to someone you don't like. Perhaps you've got a secret that you're bursting to share and know you mustn't. Whatever your reasons for keeping your lips shut and stretched, you're concealing, restraining or harbouring something.

Leonardo da Vinci's portrait of the Mona Lisa is a perfect example of the tight-lipped smile. When you look at her, you're aware that she's holding back something. And while she looks friendly enough, you know there's no way she's going to share her secrets with you. That's what's known as the tight-lipped smile.

Frequently you see photographs of masters of industry smiling with sealed lips. While they may look friendly, as well as calm, contained and in control – just the way we like our leaders to be – their closed mouths indicate they're withholding information.

According to one study, because the tight-lipped smile is contained, women interpret the expression as a sign of rejection and dismissal.

Liz recently had her photo taken for the company website. Like many people, she's uncomfortable posing for pictures, not liking the way her face contorts when giving a full-mouthed smile. The photographer suggested she think of her most private, pleasurable secret – something she wouldn't tell anyone, ever. Her sealed lip smile, in combination with her sparkling eyes, produced the best headshot she's ever had. She looks warm, inviting, in control and slightly mysterious. Her clients have commented favourably about the photo, wondering what made it so good. For more about the positive power of the eyes, refer to Chapter 5.

The closed-lip grin

The closed-lip grin, a close cousin to the tight-lipped smile, is another restraining or concealing gesture. Your pearly whites stay hidden behind your lips and your feelings remain private. The slight upturned corners of your mouth in combination with your closed lips and twinkling eyes indicate that something's giving you pleasure and you're not about to let on what that is.

Often when someone's flirting, teasing or being playful with another person he'll grin with closed lips, showing that although he's enjoying your company he's not sharing all of himself just yet. (For more about flirting behaviours, flip to Chapter 13.)

Peter was out with friends, celebrating a successful financial deal. Although he was happy to share some of the particulars of the arrangement, when one of the group asked him how much money he'd made, Peter's lips sealed shut in a closed-lip grin. Clearly, that was too much information to share.

Keeping your teeth covered when you're smiling indicates that you're hiding something (see the preceding section).

The lop-sided smile

When your muscles pull the sides of your mouth in opposite directions, one side going up and the other going down, you've got yourself in a twist. You're showing opposite emotions on either side of your face and the observer has to figure out what this lop-sided smile is saying. In Western cultures this type of smile signals sarcasm, embarrassment or irony.

In a lop-sided smile, one side of your mouth is moving upward in amusement while the other side's pulling down in restraint (see Figure 6-4). Consciously or not, when your mouth seeks this position you're showing two emotions – pleasure and your pain. Look to the actor Harrison Ford and the late Princess of Wales as your role models here. The lop-sided smile elicits protective responses in others. The side of the mouth going downward indicates sadness, anxiety or unease, while the side going upward shows the person's amusement, enjoyment and pleasure. Were you simply angry, disappointed or disgusted, both sides of your mouth would turn down. Were you clearly happy, both sides would pull upwards. The non-threatening lop-sided grin indicates a more complex feeling than does a simple smile or frown.

This provocative expression is particularly effective for eliciting someone's interest and luring them towards you.

Figure 6-4:
The lop-sided grin is compelling because it's both contradictory and mysterious.

The drop-jaw smile

This practised smile, in which the lower jaw releases downwards as the sides of the mouth pull upwards, is a favourite of politicians, film stars and celebrities. The expression conveys pleasure, surprise, excitement and interest. The actress Keira Knightley is a dab hand at the drop-jaw smile. She widens her eyes and drops her jaw while lifting her upper lip over her teeth. At the same time, she inhales, as if preparing herself for something wonderful to happen.

The turn-away smile

Turn your head down and away while looking upwards with your lips in a sealed smile, and you can capture the hearts of all who see you. This coy expression makes you look young, playful and secretive – an intoxicating combination (see Figure 6-5).

Figure 6-5:
A shy, coy smile is playful and enticing.

Unless their hearts are made of stone, men and women melt when someone smiles coyly in their direction. When you smile with closed lips and turn away others become enchanted by your powerful combination of warmth and vulnerability. Before they know what's hit them, they find themselves wanting to protect and nurture you. That possibility alone is enough to get you smiling.

According to Charles Darwin, the action of turning the head away from another person while looking at him and smiling creates a 'hybrid expression', one that's composed of two opposite meanings. The smile signals welcome whereas the motion of turning away conveys avoidance. The tension that's created by these two opposing actions is irresistibly appealing and more powerful than its individual parts.

The full-blown grin

A full-blown grin gives your face a good workout. The person at the receiving end smiles with you, basking in the sunshine of your expression. The muscles around your eyes crease and crinkle, and your teeth go on display as the sides of your lips stretch towards the tips of your ears. Your head pulls back, even if ever so slightly and, bingo!, you radiate the feel-good factor.

When you're watching someone smile, note where his head moves. A forward tilt indicates humbleness. A backward tilt tells you that the person's pleased and proud. (see Figure 6-6).

Figure 6-6:
Full-blown
smiles
indicate
humbleness
(left) and
pride (right).

Remembering that Laughter's the Best Medicine

Laughing and smiling go together like a horse and carriage. Some laughs burble up from the bottom of your belly, bursting forth with abandon. Others get stuck in your throat or your back sinus passages. Some land in your chest and all that escape are little bits of blowing air pushing through your nose like short trumpet blasts. Fortunately, your shaking shoulders and the smile spread across your face signal that you're laughing not choking.

Whatever kind of laugh you've got – a giggle, a snort, a snicker or a good old-fashioned hee-haw – the depth and freedom of the sound indicates how you feel about what you're experiencing.

Sometimes laughing is inappropriate but is still impossible to restrain.

Christina was in the university library, supposedly revising, when her mobile phone vibrated in her jacket pocket. She carefully removed it, so as not to be seen by the librarian, who was restacking the shelves close by. Christina opened the message from her friend, who'd sent her a joke. She read the text silently to herself until she got to the unexpected punch line, at which point a snort of laughter escaped from her nose before she could stop it. The librarian cast her a disapproving look, which made Christina's laughter increase. She finally had to hold her lips shut and squeeze her nose to keep any more sound escaping from her mouth.

Because of the contagious nature of smiling and laughing, make sure that the people you're smiling at and laughing with are the people whose company you enjoy.

Nancy is known for her sense of fun. Her laughter comes from the depths of her being and can fill a room with joy and hilarity. One night, she and a group of friends were having dinner at a local restaurant. Nancy's smiling face and cheerful laughter caught the attention of diners at several other tables, who found themselves laughing too. Eventually, a man from another group approached Nancy and begged her to let them all in on the joke as they were laughing so hard but didn't have a clue what they were laughing about.

Part III
The Trunk: Limbs and Roots

In this part . . .

- Explore how your posture reflects your inner state.
- Discover how your arms, hands, legs and feet give away your attitudes and feelings.
- Pick up tips for drawing attention to yourself and for rejecting signs of interest.
- Discover what the strength of your handshake reveals about you.
- Learn how the way you dress reveals more about the sort of person you are than just your taste in clothes!

Chapter 7

Taking It From the Torso

In This Chapter

▶ Recognising how your body speaks for you

▶ Finding ways to change your attitude

▶ Exploring the effects of posture

*T*he stance you adopt and the way you position your body reveal how you feel about yourself and others. Slumping into your hips, drooping your shoulders, and letting your stomach hang out isn't a particularly pleasing picture and reflects a poor self-image. The person who approaches you with head held high, an open chest and a firm stride is the one who gains your respect and positive attention.

In this chapter you find out how to get your muscles working with your attitude, to show the world just who you are.

Gaining Insights into the Impact of Posture

How you use and abuse your body determines how you feel about yourself and how others perceive you. Jobs are won and lost, reputations made and destroyed, relationships dissolved and cemented based on how the people involved present themselves.

Walk down the high street on a busy day and observe people passing by. Watch for those who appear to feel good about themselves. You notice that they move with ease. Their gestures are open and welcoming, with shoulders back and heads held high.

Keep watching people pass by and notice how the ones who don't seem comfortable with themselves move. Their heads are probably tucked into shoulders, arms folded across chests, and they move at a dreary pace. They look a sad and sorry lot. People who don't feel good about themselves hide in their clothes, their postures droop and you have little hope of getting a genuine smile from them (see Figure 7-1).

Figure 7-1:
Depressed
posture
collapses
in on itself.

Your posture, gestures and expressions reveal how you feel about yourself and determine how others relate to you.

Not only can you determine how others perceive you by the way you hold your body, you can also determine your own frame of mind. The way you present yourself reflects and influences your mood and attitude.

Evaluating what your own posture says about you

If you spend too much time slouching with a deadpan expression on your face and slumped shoulders, you'll appear inert and ineffectual. If, on the other hand, you hold yourself upright with an alert expression on your face, you look energised and ready for action.

To determine what your own posture reveals about your self-image or mood, follow these steps:

1. **Stand in front of a full-length mirror and take a good, long look at yourself.**

   Observe how you're standing, the position of your head and the look on your face. What message are you conveying?

2. **Turn away for a moment. This time decide how you want to be perceived.**

   Dominant, submissive, bored, angry, surprised? The list goes on. Carefully consider how you can convey that attitude by the way you stand and breathe, and by the look on your face.

3. **Turn back towards the mirror, having adopted the image you want to portray.**

   What do you notice? What are the differences and similarities between your first and second postures?

By being aware of the messages that your stance, gestures and expressions send out you can consciously determine how you're perceived. With time and practice, you automatically adopt the appropriate pose for the attitude you want to reveal.

Should you find yourself in a downbeat, miserable mood that you want to get out of, do the following:

✔ Inhale deeply from your diaphragm.

✔ Gently open your chest as if it were a treasured keepsake.

✔ Allow the crown of your head to lift from the base of your neck like a balloon tied to a string on a sunny day.

✔ Observe your surroundings.

✔ Continue to breathe gently, like a baby at rest.

✔ Settle into the moment.

If I'm not mistaken, by now you have a gentle smile playing around your lips, and the outer corners of your eyes may even be creasing with enjoyment.

Not feeling good about your body is okay as long as you act as if you do. Why? Because the way you act reflects who you are. If you behave as though you have a positive frame of mind, you feel that way. People want to spend time with you. When you enjoy yourself as you are, you make it easy for others to be in your company. And you may even find that by acting as if you feel good about yourself, you actually do.

Indicating intensity of feelings

People who are extremely agitated, exceptionally despondent or enormously cheerful reflect these moods, in part, by the way they hold their bodies. When your feelings are intense, it's like putting an exclamation mark at the end of a sentence. Intensity calls attention to itself. For moments of deep despair, your muscles relax, your body collapses on itself and you look like a forlorn rag doll. When you're filled with passion and excitement, your muscles tighten, your sinews become taut and your movements are forceful and concentrated (see Figure 7-2 and the *Body Language For Dummies* app for examples).

Figure 7-2:
The woman on the left is excited while the man on the right is laid-back.

Take yourself back to a time when your feelings were working at full tilt. Freeze frame that image of yourself. What do you observe? You see that your muscles are working in direct proportion to your thoughts, feelings and intentions.

Signs of emotion being acted out intensely are

- Fist-slamming
- Sharp finger pointing/waving/wagging
- Slouching
- Stomping
- Passionate hugging
- Uncontrollable crying
- Collapsing from exhaustion

As you read the words, you may recognise the feeling. Act out the gesture and the feeling intensifies. Add sound to the action, and the feeling becomes even stronger.

People nodding in agreement, as well as those shaking their heads in disagreement, often vocalise a humming sound. Someone who's annoyed may slam her fist and make a grunting sound as the fist hits the surface.

Alex was being groomed for partnership at a large city law firm. Although considered to be a bright and capable lawyer, Alex had some unresolved anger issues. During a practice role play for his interview, I purposely interrupted him while he was answering a question I'd posed. Angry with the interruption and without thought, he rose from his seat and clenched his fists while his facial muscles pulled his lips to a tight thin line. I had no doubt in my mind that Alex didn't like being interrupted. We looked at his actions and decided together that alternative behaviour choices would work more to his advantage.

If you're feeling tired and worn out, you may sigh as your body collapses in on itself. If you're feeling energised, you may make a short, sharp sound of enjoyment. If you want to intimidate someone, a low growl in the back of your throat shows that you're prepared to stand up and defend yourself. For more about the impact of sound and body language on communication, pick up a copy of *Persuasion & Influence For Dummies* by Elizabeth Kuhnke (Wiley).

If you're cuddling up with your partner and want to let her know just how much you're enjoying the experience, make a gentle purr or sigh as you snuggle in closer.

Revealing personality and character

Do you want to rule the roost or play a supporting role? Do you accept nothing less than crossing the finish line first or are you content being an also-ran? Your body's position, whether crisp and upright or limp and downtrodden, reveals what you think of yourself.

Imagine yourself as an iceberg like the one in Figure 7-3. Below the water line is what makes you tick. This inner core contains your sense of self and is the base from which your actions arise. Here you find your values and beliefs, your drivers and motivators, and your strengths and unique selling points (USPs). Above the water line is your outer self, what other people see and hear. The way you gesture, the way you carry yourself, your manners and mannerisms, plus how you choose to speak and dress, reflect who you are based on what's below the water line.

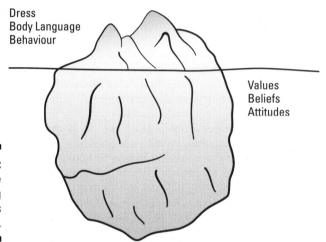

Dress
Body Language
Behaviour

Values
Beliefs
Attitudes

Figure 7-3:
The whole
iceberg
represents
all of you.

If your self-perception is that of a strong, forceful and dynamic character, your body is upright, stride purposeful and gestures focused and contained. Think of Leonardo DiCaprio in *The Wolf of Wall Street*. If you see yourself more as a simple, quiet, country type – along the lines of Martin Freeman in *The Hobbit* – your body may be more relaxed, your way of moving a bit easier and your gestures more fluid. And if you're Jack the Lad from southeast London, your body may strut and swagger, and your head movements appear quick and sharp.

If you don't like certain aspects of the way you behave, change your attitude. As your attitude changes, so do your actions.

Identifying the Three Main Postures

Although you have a repertoire of different postures you can adopt, you tend to prefer one to the others. You may prefer to sit, others may prefer to stand, whereas still others are quite happy to spend their time lying down. You can become so associated with one particular posture that people who know you well can recognise you from a distance by the way you use your body. Your posture is a clue to who you are and opens the door to understanding your character and personality. For example, the person who holds herself erectly has a different temperament to a habitual sloucher (see Figure 7-4).

Figure 7-4:
The woman appears engaged while the man seems uninterested.

The three main types of posture are:

✔ Standing

✔ Sitting (including squatting and kneeling)

✔ Reclining

Within this limited list, you can display your mood and temperament by the way you hold yourself and position your head, arms, and legs. People who slouch give the impression of being dull, uninterested or lacking in confidence. People who hold themselves upright appear to be engaged, energised and alert.

According to research by the American anthropologist Ray Birdwhistell, a person's posture reflects her past. People who've experienced prolonged depression may slouch and sag into their bodies whereas people with a positive outlook tend to hold themselves upright.

Standing

Some people are happy to stand. This position enables them to think and move more quickly than if they had to pull themselves out of a chair or get out of bed. At parties people tend to stand. Doing so enables them to walk towards someone they want to engage with and move away from someone they'd rather not get cornered by. Because moving toward and away from someone or something is easier when you're standing, this position is considered to be more active than sitting or lying down.

Participants at meetings frequently stand because people think more quickly and come to decisions more expediently than they do when given the chance to sit. It's the Let's Go position.

Kate attended a client meeting at an advertising agency in Denmark. When it was time for her and her client to brainstorm some ideas, they went to the Stand Up Room, which was designed for quick thinking and decision making. In the middle of the room was a tall stone table, provided for people to lean on and take notes. The table was the only furniture in the room. What Kate found was that, although it wasn't her preferred environment, she was able to make quick decisions and firm commitments.

Sitting

The seated position can be a less-energised position than standing. Because your body is bent in the middle, you may well collapse over your waist or flop back into your chair like a wilted flower if you're feeling a bit tired. Sitting is a more relaxed position than standing. The pressure is taken off your legs and feet and your buttocks take the weight.

Sitting postures convey different states of being depending on how your arms, legs and head are positioned. If you're tired you may unconsciously lean back into a chair, letting your legs and arms hang loose with your head tilted backwards. This is a sure sign that you're feeling worn out. At other times you sit upright, ready for action. Your back is straight, you're leaning forward and you look like you mean business.

If you go into your boss's office and notice that her body's hunched over her desk, wait to be invited before speaking. Her body language is telling you she doesn't want to be interrupted. If she raises a hand with the palm facing towards you, turn and leave. If, however, she beckons you in by turning her palm toward herself and wiggling her fingers, you may enter.

Although a relaxed sitting position aids thinking and reflection, be careful not to hold the pose for too long. You end up feeling drained and dejected.

The sitting erect position shows that you're focused in the here and now and that you're ready to take a decision or progress an action.

Libby was a focused student, obtaining a First as an undergraduate and further honours as she gained her Masters. She made a point of sitting in the front row during lectures, knowing that there she stood no chance of nodding off or demonstrating any signs of boredom or lack of interest. She felt that placing herself in the front row meant she was better able to concentrate on what the lecturer was saying.

Lying down

If you want to take some time for quiet contemplation, relaxation and reflection, you may find yourself wanting to lie down. This submissive pose is the ideal position for getting in touch with your feelings. You don't find the prime minister taking this position at a press conference, although leaders often sit in a supine position when considering their options.

As human resources director of a large firm, John found himself getting quite agitated before budget reviews, knowing that the partners would challenge him on his training and development expenditures. One quiet afternoon he found himself sitting with his feet on his desk, leaning so far back in his chair that he was almost prone. He felt clear-headed, relaxed and able to sort his feelings from facts. After he made up his mind how he was going to address the partners at the review, and felt confident in his choices, he sat upright in his chair and purposefully wrote his notes.

Changing Attitudes by Changing Posture

If you find yourself in a mood you don't like, change your posture. By changing the position of your body, your frame of mind changes too. If you find yourself in an enjoyable mood, notice the position of your body as well as your gestures and expressions. By being self-aware, you can keep the behaviours you like and eliminate those that you don't.

If you find yourself feeling glum and your slumped shoulders are revealing attitudes you may not want to share, physically change your posture and see what happens.

Plant your feet squarely underneath your knees and your knees under your hips, pull up from the waist, and open your chest as if it were a well-loved book. Let your head rise from your neck and shoulders, floating like a balloon on a string while your arms and hands reach forward as if to embrace

- A bouquet of your favourite flowers
- A lover
- Someone you don't like but nonetheless have to hug

You may notice some changes in the way your body moves according to how you feel about what you're embracing. You may feel changes in your mood, too.

In addition to changing your posture, you can also use visualisation to galvanise your spirits. To do so, visualise yourself at your most confident. What do you look like? How does your voice sound? What feelings are you experiencing? Notice what's going on around you. If other people are there, what are they doing? How are they reacting to you? Make your visualisation as real as you can. See yourself smiling, your eyes engaged, claiming your space, demonstrating likability and moving with purpose. Having created this picture of yourself in your mind, you can replicate it any time you're feeling self-conscious, insecure or lacking in confidence. For further information about visualisation techniques, take a look at *Neuro-Linguistic Programming For Dummies* by Kate Burton and Romilla Ready and *Confidence For Dummies* by Kate Burton and Brinley Platts (both Wiley). You can also find out more about visualising yourself as you want to be in *Persuasion & Influence For Dummies* by Elizabeth Kuhnke (Wiley).

Confident people don't always feel confident. They simply act as if they are.

Whistling happy tunes

In Rogers and Hammerstein's musical, *The King and I*, Anna, an English widow, with her young son, moves to Siam (now Thailand) to serve as teacher to the King's 26 children. Although somewhat overwhelmed at the prospect, and feeling less than confident, she knew that were she to show her fear, she'd lose her authority and the respect of the King. When they were about to embark, her son asked if she were afraid and, if so, how could she go through with this adventure. She said that, although she was scared, she would act as if she were brave. In the song 'I Whistle a Happy Tune', she sings, 'While shivering in my shoes, I strike a careless pose, and whistle a happy tune, and no one ever knows I'm afraid.' She knew that if she projected the image she wanted to create, people would respond to her accordingly, and all would be well. And it was. She gained the respect of the King, the admiration of his courtiers and the love of his children.

Using Posture to Aid Communication

I'm not saying that you can precisely ascertain what someone's thinking simply by looking at her posture. What I *am* saying is that you can tell a lot about people's state of mind by observing how they hold their bodies. Observing and registering what you notice about how people move and position themselves gives you an insight into how best to communicate with them.

Demonstrating your status through postural position

When you consider people in authority, you think of them in elevated terms. They don't have to be tall to show that they're top of the pecking order, they just have to carry themselves as if they were. Open and confident posture is the norm for individuals in high status positions. Conversely, people with lower status demonstrate their position by acting in a deferential manner. Their posture is closed and protective. (See Figure 7-5.)

Figure 7-5:
People's postures indicate where they lie in the pecking order.

Indira works for a large city firm. When she was put up for promotion, the male partners struggled when making their decision. Although Indira's capabilities were acknowledged as superb, something in her demeanour made them uncomfortable and uncertain. When Indira and I worked on her personal impact, she explained that she had been raised to show deference to people in positions of authority. Because of the hierarchical nature of the firm, she saw the partners as authority figures and behaved as she'd been taught. Her shoulders were slightly hunched, her chest somewhat rolled in, and her head slightly bowed. After practising specifically targeted exercises, Indira's posture changed, as did her self-perception. She now stands upright, makes eye contact comfortably and moves with authority. And she was made a partner.

Following are a few random bits of information about posture as a sign of status:

- ✔ When a person deliberately defers to you, she's showing low-status behaviour.

- ✔ In many Eastern countries, bowing is expected as a sign of respect.

- ✔ In the military, a sign of respect is standing to attention.

- ✔ You're more likely to hold your hands on your hips in the presence of individuals whose status is equal to or lower than yours. In front of someone whose status is higher than yours, your body language is symmetrical and contained.

Leaning forward to show interest and liking

According to Professor Albert Mehrabian of UCLA, people who like each other tend to lean in towards one another. The more you like someone, the more your body inclines in her direction. The forward lean is a sign of intimacy and affection.

By leaning towards another person, you're sharing space with her and showing that you want to be close. Accomplished interviewers understand the power of getting physically close to the person they're interviewing. After they've created a rapport with the person, they lean towards her to show trust. By respectfully moving into another person's personal space, you're demonstrating that you like her.

If you carefully observe a group of individuals interacting, you can tell their degree of attention, involvement, relative status and how they feel about one another by the way each one positions her body in relation to the others. People who are actively participating in the exchange lean towards one another. Those who are reflecting on what's going on pull back. The opposite of the forward lean is the backward lean, which indicates fear and displeasure. Someone who's not interested in or is bored with the conversation may slump and look in another direction. (See Figure 7-6.)

Figure 7-6: The woman's shrug, turned away head, and forward facing palms indicate her unwillingness to become involved.

If someone is really angry, not only does she scowl, she leans forward as well. If someone is filled with happiness, she smiles as her body moves forward. In both cases, the people seem to want to experience the emotion to the full. The expressions on the face reveal the emotion. The lean of the body reveals the strength of the feeling. Although facial expressions give more information about emotions, posture shows the degree of intensity.

Stand upright with your feet hip width apart, put your hands on your hips, lean forward and frown. Now stand in the same position, lean back and smile. This slight change of posture and facial expression allows you to convey two very different moods.

When you're at a meeting that's lost your interest, sit forward in your seat and rest your elbows on the table while you look at the speaker. This posture helps your energy level to rise and makes you feel more engaged.

Douglas was preparing for a job interview. He was feeling conflicted about the interview because he was leaving his current job not having progressed as far in his career there as he'd wanted to. During a practice session, he leant back in his chair, letting his chest droop and his head sink into his shoulders. When he saw himself on video, he realised the negative signals he was giving out. I encouraged him to sit towards the front of the chair and lean forward, letting his elbows rest on the table. When he saw himself again, he observed how much more interested, engaged and likeable he seemed.

Shrugging Signals

A child avoiding telling you the truth adopts the wide-eyed, head-pulled-back 'What? Who me?' look as she raises her shoulders in disbelief. The student who's called on by the lecturer to summarise the chapter that she hasn't read raises her shoulders in submissive apology. The person who wants to show a complete lack of interest gives a disdainful lift of the shoulders as she turns her head away. A submissive gesture, the shrug absolves the shrugger of any responsibility and indicates apology, disbelief and lack of interest.

A number of different shrugging styles depend on the attitude being conveyed and the individual performing the gesture. People from Mediterranean and Latin countries use their gestures freely, whereas Anglo-Saxons and Asians are more restricted in their use of physical movement. See Chapter 15 for more about body language across cultures.

Signalling lack of knowledge

You're at your first meeting of the day, feeling confident that you can answer any question your boss may throw your way. And then the unexpected happens and you freeze like a deer caught in headlights. You don't want to show your ignorance so you control your gestures. A well-trained observer, however, would spot the nano-second, micro-movement of your shoulders as your head momentarily drops into your rising shoulders like a turtle pulling its head into its shell.

An elderly couple approached Guy in London to ask him directions to Buckingham Palace. English was not their mother tongue and they struggled to understand Guy as he gave them detailed directions. Looking at them as he spoke, Guy was able to tell that they didn't understand what he was saying. They raised their shoulders and hands in bewilderment as they tilted their heads as if that would help them understand him better. By speaking slowly, using simple terms, pointing in the right direction and counting on his fingers how long it would take them to get there – if they didn't get lost – he hoped they understood him correctly. The final lift of the old woman's shoulders indicated that they had their doubts.

What makes a shrug?

According to zoologist Desmond Morris, the shrug comprises five elements, four of which are key to understanding the gesture. He labels these four *key elements* because they can, on their own, convey the message. The key elements for a shrug are:

1. **Hunched shoulders.** The shoulders are raised and lowered. Both shoulders are not required to convey the shrug. One shoulder hunching up on its own while the other remains still is an equally valid shrug.

2. **Hands twisted into the palms up position.** The palms of the hands face upward in an open position. A shrug can be successfully transmitted through the upward turning of one or both hands.

3. **Lowered mouth corners.** The head and body remain still as the corners of the mouth turn down.

4. **Raised eyebrows.** Like the full-bodied shrug, an upward jerk of the eyebrows can convey astonishment, indifference and bewilderment.

Any of these four individual gestures, taken on their own and in context, can be perceived as a shrug.

The one other element that goes into a full shrug is an *amplifier*, or supporting element. The amplifier in a full shrug is tilting the head to one side. This element taken on its own can't accurately transmit the message; it has to work in combination with one or more key elements to convey the point.

Conveying unwillingness to get involved

In addition to conveying misunderstanding, lack of knowledge and apology, the shrug can also indicate an unwillingness to get involved. Because of the submissive actions that make up a shrug – head pulled down into the shoulders, open forward-facing palms serving as a shield, raised eyebrows and a tilted head – the action indicates that you don't want to be drawn in.

Raising your shoulders is a defensive behaviour designed to protect your neck, one of your body's most vulnerable parts. By holding your open palms in front of you you're showing that, although you have nothing to conceal, you're also setting up a barrier between you and another person.

Rory is a secondary school chemistry teacher. Inevitably, at the end of lessons a mess of test tubes, beakers and other related items waits to be cleaned and put away in their proper place. When he asks his students who's responsible for the mess, without fail they raise their shoulders, palms and eyebrows as they turn away from him, signalling their denial of any responsibility.

To indicate that you want to remain neutral and uninvolved, raise your hand to shoulder height with your palm facing outwards and slightly shrug both shoulders.

Implying a submissive apology

Because the elements in the shrug – hunched shoulders, open palms, raised eyebrows and so on – are all submissive, the shrug is the perfect gesture to use when offering an apology.

A man of few words and the grand gesture, John had been in a foul temper for most of the day. Although Louise is usually quite patient and accepts her husband's moodiness, by late afternoon she was so frustrated that she burst into tears. Realising that he'd been out-of-sorts and treating Louise unfairly, John left the house, returning shortly with a large bouquet of tulips, Louise's favourite flowers. Offering them to her, he apologised without actually saying the words, 'I'm sorry'. The lift of his shoulders, his raised eyebrows, his slightly turned down mouth and his dropped head as he presented the flowers to Louise conveyed his apology.

Although this exercise doesn't convey thoughts, feelings or intentions, the shrugging gesture may bring you some relief when you're feeling tense or tired. Raise your shoulders up towards your ears and tighten them as much as you can. Hold that position for three to five seconds, and then release. Roll your shoulders in circles both backwards and forwards to complete the tension release. To avoid injuring yourself when doing this exercise, be careful not to overdo the tightening.

Chapter 8

Arming Yourself

. . . .

In This Chapter

▶ Shutting people out

▶ Letting someone in

▶ Disguising anxiety

▶ Sending signals through bodily contact

. . . .

*W*hether you're crossing your arms as a protective shield or opening them as a sign of welcome, the way you position your arms tells an astute observer how you're feeling and what you're thinking.

Certain postures elicit certain moods. Crossed arms hold your feelings in and keep other people's out. They show that you've set up roadblocks beyond which no person dares travel. Stay with this position for too long and you find yourself feeling shut off and negative. Unless, of course, you're cold, in which case holding your arms across your chest keeping the warmth in and the cold out makes perfect sense.

As for contact, touching can be a great tonic as long as you know who, when, where and how. Get touching right and the person with whom you make bodily contact feels engaged and connected; get it wrong and prepare yourself for a sharp smack.

This chapter shows you how you can read arm signals, appear self-controlled and increase your influence through physical contact.

Building Defensive Barriers

Any gesture that protects your body from an assault – be it real or imagined – is a defensive barrier. Ducking your head, averting your body, even tightening your lips and narrowing your eyes, are all examples of defensive behaviours.

As opposed to open gestures that welcome others in, these behaviours protect you and keep others out.

Crossing your arms over your chest

When you were a small child and feeling threatened and insecure, you may have hidden behind your mother's skirts or a solid piece of furniture. As you reached pre-school age, you may have created your own barrier by folding your arms tightly across your chest. During your teen years, you probably relaxed your grip and added crossed legs to the equation in order to appear more cool and less obvious.

The crossed-arms position is common throughout the world and communicates a defensive stance (see Figure 8-1). Not only does it serve as a protective guard against a possible attack, crossed arms also represent an inflexible position that tells you that this person's not budging. If you find someone attractive, for example, you keep your arms in an open position. Find someone aggressive or unappealing and watch your arms quickly cross over your chest.

You may also cross your arms over your chest if you're feeling anxious or are lacking confidence. Crossing arms is a common position to adopt when you're among strangers and is often seen in lifts, public meetings, when waiting to board a plane or indeed anywhere that you may feel insecure, apprehensive or intimidated.

People who say that they cross their arms over their chests because the gesture feels comfortable are right. Any gesture that matches the corresponding attitude feels comfortable. So, if someone feels negative, self-protective or in any way uneasy, even if he's not consciously aware of these feelings, it is quite common for that person to cross his arms. If he feels relaxed and is enjoying himself, he adopts an opened-arm position that reflects that attitude.

The meaning of the message lies with the receiver. Studies show that people react negatively to the crossed-arms position. Even if you're comfortable with your arms crossed over your chest, people observing you are going to interpret your attitude as defensive. So, unless you want to show that you disagree or don't want to engage, find other positions for your arms.

If you adopt the crossed-arm position when you're in a group of people, you soon notice other members of the group adopting the same pose. Although influencing people into assuming this position is easy, you may discover that you have difficulty in achieving open communication when the majority of the group has adopted this stance.

Figure 8-1:
The crossed arm position is a closed and protective one.

Most people adopt the crossed-arms position when they disagree with what's going on around them, as illustrated during a recent public meeting in our village. A landowner applied to the local council to turn his farm into a golf course. The villagers were divided in opinion over this change of land use and a public hearing was held. Those in favour of the change sat on one side of the room while those against the proposal sat on the other. At the start of the meeting, many of those who opposed the plan sat with their arms crossed over their chests. As the supporters spoke in favour of the proposal, more and more of the opponents crossed their arms. When the time came for those who opposed the plan to speak, the supporters crossed their arms. As the meeting progressed and people became more adamant and agitated, almost the entire gathering sat with their arms tightly folded across their chests. No constructive discussions took place at that meeting and the individuals present left feeling disgruntled.

An attitude can lead to a gesture or posture that reflects an emotion. As long as you maintain that pose, the attitude remains. Therefore, to get someone to change from a crossed-arms position, give him something to do or hold. Then he has to unlock his arms and lean towards you. This breaks his negative posture and creates a more open body position, which in turn leads to a more open attitude.

Blocking out information

Two groups of volunteers were asked to participate in an American research project in which the participants attended a series of lectures. The purpose of the project was to examine the effects of the crossed-arms position on retention of information and attitude toward the lecturer. The first group was instructed to sit in a casual, relaxed position, with their arms and legs in an open position. The second group was told to fold their arms tightly across their chests during the lectures. The study showed that the group with the folded arms had a more negative view of both the lectures and the lecturer and retained 38 per cent less information than the group that sat with their arms and legs uncrossed.

Gripped crossed arms

When you see someone fold his arms across his chest while his hands tightly grip his upper arms you're looking at a sure sign of restrained anxiety and apprehension. The person appears to be fortifying himself against adversity and holding on for dear life. People waiting in the doctor's or dentist's reception room are often seen sitting in this position, as are inexperienced air travellers who adopt the posture as the plane takes off and lands, indicating that they're in need of comfort or reassurance. Depending on their level of concern, they may grip their arms so tightly that their fingers and knuckles turn white.

Crossed arms and clenched fists

Cross your arms and clench your fists, and you look as if you're heading for a fight. This position demonstrates hostility as well as defensiveness, and can lead to aggressive behaviour. Don't be surprised if your jaw clenches and your face goes red too – individual gestures work in combination with others to convey thoughts, feelings and intentions.

If someone crosses his arms and clenches his fists when you're speaking to him, open your arms and expose your palms in a non-threatening, submissive way. This posture has a calming effect and the other person is more likely to drop his aggressive stance and discuss things in a reasonable manner.

The crossed-arms, clenched-fists posture is a sign of control and authority. Police officers who cross their arms tend to clench their fists as well to indicate that they're the boss and aren't to be trifled with. Interestingly, people who carry knives or guns, for example, seldom cross their arms because they already feel protected.

Crossed arms and thumbs up

A typical pose adopted by up-and-coming young men when engaging with their manager is standing with their arms crossed over their chests with their thumbs pointing upwards (see Figure 8-2). This position demonstrates both apprehension and confidence. Their uneasiness is conveyed through the crossed arms while the thumbs-up position demonstrates self-confidence and control.

Figure 8-2: Crossed arms with thumbs up are typical of young, high-flying males.

When you first meet a group of people, demonstrate your superior status and comfort – whether real or imagined – by keeping your arms in an open position. Shake hands firmly, stand at arm's length and keep your hands by your sides or in the power position with one hand resting in the other at waist height.

Because of the structure of women's upper torsos, they cross their arms lower on the body than men do. Girls entering puberty tend to adopt this protective position more frequently than do women.

Touching yourself: Hugs, strokes and more

The way you touch yourself gives observers clues as to how you're feeling. Most self-touching movements provide comfort and are the unconscious, mimed gestures of another person's touch, as if you've divided yourself into two people: the one who is providing the comfort and the receiver of the touch. Some of the more common self-touching behaviours include:

- **Hugging or stroking yourself:** When you were a child feeling distressed or upset, your parents, or whoever was looking after you, would hold you in their arms to comfort you. Now that you're an adult, when you feel self-conscious and insecure, and no one's there to reassure you, or it would be inappropriate to seek solace from another person, you hug or stroke yourself to provide your own comfort and reassurance. The most common self-touching actions are rubbing your neck, stroking your arms and fondling your face.

- **Half-hugs:** Because, when you cross both arms across your body, you show that you're feeling afraid or defensive, you may adopt the half-hug position instead. In this position, one arm crosses your body and holds or touches the other arm, creating a partial barrier. Women typically use this gesture more than men.

- **The fig leaf:** Both men and women hold hands with themselves in a barrier position to make themselves feel secure. Covering their 'crown jewels' they subconsciously protect themselves from a potential full-frontal attack (see Figure 8-3). Look at the line-up of footballers during a penalty kick and see where they place their hands and arms – as well they should!

The next time you see someone who's feeling lonely, dejected or in any way vulnerable, notice what he does with his hands. You'll see that he holds them in the fig-leaf position in an attempt to create feelings of comfort, protection and reassurance.

Placing objects in front of yourself

By placing a coffee cup, a clipboard or any other object between yourself and another person, you are setting up a protective barrier. These barriers are a subconscious effort to conceal any nervousness or insecurity you may be experiencing, whether you're aware of the feeling or not.

Figure 8-3:
The fig-leaf
position
provides
protection.

During a role play with a client in which she had to enter her boss's office, sit across the table from him and make a recommendation that she knew he wouldn't like, Chrissie clutched a pad of paper in front of her, clasping it tightly to her chest. Although she said that she had to carry the pad for taking notes, the way she held it clearly indicated that she was feeling insecure and threatened. So strong were her subconscious feelings that not even seeing herself on video convinced her that a different posture would create a stronger, more authoritative and professional appearance.

If you're at a function where drinks are being served and you're feeling insecure, hold your glass or cup in front of you with both hands. This action creates a subtle barrier, behind which you can seek refuge. As you look around the room, you're likely to see that almost everyone else is standing in the same position, indicating that you're not alone in your feelings.

Giving the cold shoulder

As you are undoubtedly a kind and thoughtful person who would never purposely insult anyone, this section is probably superfluous to your requirements. However, should you ever feel the need to display indifference or aloofness with the intention of giving someone a quick, sharp jab to his ego, turn your shoulder towards him, creating a barrier between yourself and your object of contempt. With a look of disdain, a downward turn of the mouth and the briefest of glances, the gesture leaves the recipient in no doubt of your scorn and derision.

Conveying Friendliness and Honesty

Open arms indicate a receptive, friendly and honest attitude. This position says that you've got nothing to hide and are approachable and amenable. It draws people to you, making them feel comfortable and at ease in your company. By leaving your body exposed, you're indicating that you're receptive to whatever comes your way.

Go to any sporting event and watch the players. The moment the winner sinks his final putt, crosses the finish line or scores the winning goal his arms open with the thrill of victory. The losers cross their arms in front of their bodies or let them hang dejectedly by their sides.

If you want to persuade someone to accept your viewpoint, hold your arms in an open position. Open arms indicate a confident, constructive attitude and create a positive impression. You're perceived as sincere, direct, and trustworthy, as long as your other gestures are equally open and forthright. (For more about body language and persuasion, refer to *Persuasion & Influence For Dummies* by Elizabeth Kuhnke (Wiley).)

Interpreting the gestures of the royal, rich and famous

During the Middle Ages people viewed royalty as all-powerful, a perception that extended to the belief that people who suffered from the glandular disease scrofula, commonly referred to as 'the King's evil', could be cured by the monarch's touch.

Just because someone is continually in the public eye doesn't mean that he's comfortable being on show. Celebrities, politicians and royals use subtle gestures intended to demonstrate how cool, calm and collected they're

feeling when inside everything's screaming, 'Get me out of here!'

The commonest gestures adopted by public figures involve an arm crossing over the body. Instead of folding both arms in an obvious protective barrier or grasping hold of one arm, the person touches a personal object he's wearing such as a watch, shirt cuff or ring. The gesture has no purpose other than to disguise nervousness. Here are a few other gestures you may have noticed:

✔ **Holding a handbag:** Queen Elizabeth II is rarely seen in public without her handbag. Yet unlike most women, queens and celebrities carry little if anything in their handbags. They have other people to do that for them. The accessory simply serves as a complement to her outfit and as a means of maintaining distance between herself and others. Holding the bag over her arm immediately sets up a protective barrier between herself and her public. When she's feeling nervous or insecure, the Queen can hide behind a handbag and pretend to fiddle with its non-contents.

✔ **Playing with a pocket:** Prince Charles has devised a way of slipping his right hand into his jacket pocket that's intended to create a relaxed impression. The astute observer realises that what he's really doing is hiding feelings or holding back an impulse. First, he turns up the flap of his pocket. He then fingers the flap before he finally places his hand inside. He often leaves his thumb protruding so that his entire hand isn't hidden. Leaving the thumb out of the pocket is a 'macho' gesture as demonstrated by tough guys who hook their thumbs over their belts or shove their hands into their trouser pockets leaving the thumbs exposed.

✔ **Fiddling with cufflinks:** Another gesture particular to Prince Charles is the cufflink fiddle. During public walkabouts he frequently adjusts his cufflinks as he moves towards his destination. This gesture allows his arms to cross in front of his body and serves no purpose other than to give himself a sense of security. Tony Blair, the former prime minister, would often adjust his cuffs before speaking in public. Roger Moore, when playing James Bond, also adjusted his cuffs before facing an adversary. These gestures are defence mechanisms, designed to reduce anxiety.

✔ **Tidying a tie:** Men in public view often straighten their ties as they move from one spot to another. This is particularly true when a man is about to make a formal speech or is simply preparing for what's coming next. This gesture is a symbolic way of making sure that everything's in place and nothing's on show that shouldn't be. For example, when Prime Minister David Cameron walks towards his destination having alighted from a car, he often straightens his tie. Doing so is his way of preparing himself for what's coming next, making sure that what's already looking good stays that way, and displacing any anxiety he may feel.

Touching to Convey Messages

Touching means many things to different people. It's a great way to offer comfort, create a bond and increase your influence. Some people use the gesture as a sign of reassurance, support and encouragement. Others use it as a signal that they want to interrupt you. Touching frequently occurs when someone's expressing excitement or is feeling festive. You also see people touch one another during a disaster or when they're listening to another person's troubles.

The act of touching isn't straightforward. Touch in an appropriate way and you come across as a caring, sharing kind of person. Touch incorrectly and you're perceived as an untrustworthy sleaze. Like most things, it's not what you do, it's how you do it. So heed this advice:

- ✔ **When to touch:** Neither the United States nor Britain are societies that encourage a vast amount of touching between individuals. People tend to relate a touch to a sexual advance when the intention may simply be to show support, express sympathy or demonstrate tender feelings. Different people respond differently to touching. Some people are natural touchers and freely give, and comfortably receive, hugs and kisses. For others, unsolicited touching is to be avoided at all costs. If in doubt, don't touch or let someone touch you.

  Before touching another person, pay attention to the kinds of contact he feels comfortable with. Until you know someone well, proceed with caution.

- ✔ **Where to touch:** A great deal of research has been conducted into where you're allowed to put your hands on another person and where you better not touch. The findings consistently conclude that your opposite-sex friends have more leeway about where they can place their hands on you than your same-sex friends. Unless, that is, you're gay or lesbian, in which case the opposite is true. Mothers are allowed more leeway than fathers.

- ✔ **Where not to touch:** Different cultures have different rules about touching. For example, what you may consider to be an affectionate gesture, such as patting a child on the head or ruffling a friend's hair, is highly insulting in Thailand. (See Chapter 15 for more about touching in different cultures.)

- ✔ **How long to touch:** Most parents instinctively know how long they may touch their children. For example, during a child's infancy both parents are comfortable bathing and changing the child. As the child grows older, the father leaves these activities to the mother. This occurs slightly earlier for his daughter than for his son. Eventually, too, the mother leaves her child to bathe alone (and hopes he does a good job of it).

If you're having a non-business related conversation with someone who you find appealing, allow your hand to touch his slightly while you speak. Also, when you're introduced and shake hands you may let your hand rest slightly longer in his than you normally would do. If you're uninterested in or are repulsed by the person, your touch is brief and uncommitted.

Touching plays an important part in superstitious rituals. The tradition of touching wood to ensure that anticipated good fortune isn't jinxed may stem from the ancient act of touching the sacred oak to appease the god Thor. Touching iron for good luck comes from the archaic belief that iron holds magical and supernatural powers.

Creating a bond

Consciously make physical contact with someone and you immediately establish a connection between the two of you. Parents touch their children, lovers touch their partners and doctors touch their patients. The power of touch is binding.

Engaging with other people through physical contact is something at which politicians and business people with sophisticated political skills are particularly adept. The double-handed handshake is a favourite of anyone seeking to connect with another person (see Figure 8-4). By using your right hand for shaking and your left hand for touching the other person's hand, lower arm or elbow, you demonstrate your desire to bond with that person.

Figure 8-4:
Shaking hands close to the body and touching the other person high on the arm indicates a desire to become intimate.

The next time you shake hands with someone you've just been introduced to, lightly touch him on his hand or elbow with your left hand as you repeat his name. Doing so creates a positive, memorable impression by making that person feel valued. Plus, repeating the person's name helps you to remember that the name is James, not John. Touching between individuals of equal rank and status occurs regularly. Patting a friend on the back, giving a chum a hug or squeezing a colleague on the arm are gestures that convey friendship and camaraderie.

The person doing the touching in a double-handed handshake is the top dog. If the other person touches back, they're each demonstrating their sense of personal superiority. For this reason, save the double-handed handshake and the touching with your non-shaking hand for people of equal or lower status to you. You may be perceived as overly ambitious or familiar if you touch someone of higher status this way.

At Max's annual rugby dinner the players were jostling about, punching one another on the arm, slapping each other on the back and draping their arms over each other's shoulders. The young men were comfortable with this level of reciprocal touching between equals. When the coaches spoke to the players they were seen patting the team members on the back, initiating handshakes and occasionally squeezing their upper arms. At no time did any of the players touch their coaches in a similar fashion. Unconsciously, the players were exercising their symbolic right to impose themselves on one another. In contrast, they demonstrated respect for their coaches' authority by limiting their degree of physical contact.

Get your timing right when touching others. Holding the touch for longer than three seconds makes someone wonder what your intentions are.

The longer the touch, the more intense the message. If you know the person you're speaking to well and you have a good rapport, you can feel comfortable touching that person at length. If you don't know someone very well, you're both likely to feel uncomfortable touching. Think of times when you've accidentally brushed up against a stranger or someone you didn't know very well. You probably pulled away quite quickly.

Demonstrating dominance

Something to remember about touching is that it's a hierarchical gesture. The person who initiates the touch holds the authority. The doctor touches the patient, the teacher touches the student and the priest touches the parishioner. A person of lower status who initiates touch with someone holding a higher position is considered impertinent.

At his annual summer office party, Nico, the company's CEO, circulated among his staff, placing his hand on the shoulders of many of the younger men and giving the female employees a squeeze on the upper arm in greeting. Not one of the staff members responded in a similar way. Whether they were aware of it or not, they knew it would be inappropriate and impertinent to reciprocate Nico's touch.

Your gender determines, to a large extent, what your touch means. A male boss who touches his female secretary does so as a sign of power and control. Woe betide the female subordinate who touches her male manager or the female boss who touches her male employee. Whereas a man's touch is perceived as paternal and powerful, a woman's touch is interpreted as a prelude to intimacy with sexual intent. Even in today's world of supposed gender equality, men struggle with the concept of women and power. Get over it, guys.

Avoid touching work colleagues. Laws govern behaviour in the workplace, which means you can receive a formal complaint for making a gesture that may be interpreted as inappropriate physical contact.

Research suggests that men perceive women as 'uptight' when they complain about men presumptuously touching them. As a disturbing commentary on society, female students and women working in restaurants, offices and factories are used to being touched by their male superiors and they're expected not to interpret these gestures as sexual advances. The research also shows that men may interpret a woman's touch as conveying sexual intent, whether this is the case or not. The findings demonstrate that if touching implies power or intimacy, and women are considered by men to be inferior in terms of status, a woman's touch is read as an intimate gesture, because power is not a reasonable interpretation. Sad but, according to the research, true.

Unless the people who are touching one another are of equal status, the person who is in a higher position is the one who, in theory, initiates the contact. In December 2014, during Prince William and the Duchess of Cambridge's visit to New York City, the American basketball player, LeBron James, put his sweaty arm around Catherine for a photo shoot. Perhaps he thought that being a champion, weighing in at over 17 stone and standing a good foot taller than the duchess afforded him superior status. Although the royal household made light of the incident, the press had a field day with this disregard of protocol, while James had no idea what the fuss was all about.

Reinforcing the message

Touch is a powerful gesture. Depending on how you administer it, touching can be a sign of love, support, anger or frustration. Say you're arguing with another person. The tension rises, cruel words are said and before you know it you're slapped across the face. This is an extreme example of reinforcing a negative message. The gesture supports what's been said and is a physical sign of anger, frustration, and desire to inflict pain.

Your little girl falls down and scrapes her knee. As she cries, you cradle her in your arms and stroke her hurt leg to soothe and comfort her. Here, the touch is a calming and placating action meant to reassure and to console.

In both cases, the touch reinforced the message. The type of touch determined the type of message being reinforced.

Savvy sales people, marketers and advertisers understand the importance of appealing to as many senses as possible, including the sense of touch, when selling to the buying public. You *see* the product and your visual sense is stimulated. You *hear* the product, like the snap, crackle and pop of breakfast cereal or the roar of a powerful engine, and your auditory senses are stirred. And when you *touch* the product, whether soft carpet or smooth leather, your kinaesthetic response reinforces the message that this product is something that you like the feel of.

If you want to appeal to someone, appeal to all of his senses.

If you're giving advice or information to another person, you may touch him on the hand, arm or shoulder to deepen your connection and reinforce your message.

Before touching another person, you need to establish a connection with him. You wouldn't touch a stranger any more than you'd invite a stranger to touch you. In a relationship between two or more people, the dominant person, or the one holding authority, implicitly has the permission to touch.

Notice people travelling in a crowded tube or train. Most draw into themselves to keep from touching the people sitting or standing next to them.

Jo went out to lunch with her friend Caroline who was having problems with her boyfriend. At one point during their conversation, Caroline was on the verge of tears. Instinctively, Jo reached out and gently touched Caroline's hand. She let her hand rest there until Caroline composed herself. Jo's touch felt reassuring and had a calming effect. By combining this gesture with a forward lean and speaking sympathetically, Jo was able to help Caroline relax and see things from a more peaceful perspective.

Inappropriately touching another person can be perceived as rude, threatening and intrusive.

The mother of the senses

An embryo, rocking in his mother's amniotic fluid, is sensitive to touch. At 9 weeks old, his fingers bend in a gripping motion when his palm is touched. At 12 weeks his fingers and thumb can make a fist. When the embryo's foot is touched on the back or sole, his toes curl in and fan out.

Increasing your influence

Out of your five senses (sight, smell, hearing, taste and touch), your sense of touch is your oldest and most responsive. Your body reacts viscerally to touch, leaning into the hand offering comfort and pulling away from the hand that harms.

If you touch someone on the arm or shoulder when you're asking him a favour, he may well agree. Grab someone by the arm to get his attention and he'll probably pull away.

So how can you tell if someone welcomes touch or is averse to it? Observe how he relates to other people and either welcomes or objects to being touched by them. People who touch themselves – for example, rubbing or stroking their faces, hands, arms and legs – would probably respond positively to your touch. A person who avoids self-contact and doesn't fiddle with figurines is telling you to keep your hands to yourself.

Embracing during greetings and departures

The next time you're at an airport, watch how friends and family members hug when they're arriving and when they're departing. What you notice is that when people hug upon arrival they maintain the embrace longer than upon departure. When they first see one another, the hug is intense and the embrace strong. The people are welcoming and bringing one another into their most personal space. The departure hug is shorter and less passionate. It's almost as though by the time the people are saying goodbye, they're having to let each other go.

Part of my duties as on-board hostess for Holland American Cruise Lines was to stand by the gangplank to meet and greet the passengers. At the same spot, a week later, we'd be saying our goodbyes. When the passengers first arrived there was little touching if any between us, as I welcomed them on board. I may have briefly shaken the hands of some. I definitely used my hands to guide others. By the end of the cruise, it was a different story. Embraces, hugs and heartfelt handshakes – we were new friends united. Having spent days at sea together, we'd established enough of a relationship to touch one another in a friendly fashion. For some, I even gave an extra little squeeze.

If someone pats you on the back when you're hugging him, he's giving you a signal that 'enough is enough' and he's ready to be released.

Chapter 9

Letting Your Hands Do the Talking

*S*cientific research shows that more nerve connections exist between the hands and the brain than between any other parts of the body. Unconsciously, your hands reveal your attitude towards another person, place or situation. By the way you position your hands, rub your palms and fiddle with your fingers, you're telling anyone who's paying attention what you're really thinking, feeling, and intending.

Watch how your hands move spontaneously in greetings, farewells and as you cement an agreement. Before you know it, your hands illustrate a point you're making and are effective in demonstrating both your sincerity and your annoyance. Whether you're expressing love, anger, joy or frustration, your hands hold the message.

In this chapter, you discover how you can use your hands to support the spoken word and add substance to your message. You find out how to position your hands to convey authority and dominance as well as demonstrate openness and submission. You see how other people reinforce what they mean by the way they mimic the actions or situations they're describing. You discover how to read a person by the way she shakes hands and, finally, you become aware of the telltale signals that the hands and fingers unconsciously reveal when you think no one is watching.

Up or Down: Reading Palms

Numerous experiments have been conducted to record how people respond to hand gestures. Research has shown that when a speaker uses the palm-up position, the vast majority of listeners react positively to what's being said. When the speaker delivers the same message with the palm facing downward, the positive response rate drops significantly. And when the speaker points her finger directly at the listener, the positive response becomes practically non-existent. The listener reacts negatively toward the speaker, tunes out what she's saying and makes personal judgements about her.

The open palm

The open hand is an ancient sign of trustworthiness. It's a positive position and is helpful for establishing rapport with another person. The open hand is also a submissive, non-threatening gesture. The next time you walk past a pleading street beggar, look at how her hand is positioned. Chances are the palm is facing upwards.

Showing honesty

Look at the direction in which a person's palms are facing. If she's being open and honest with you, one or both of her palms are facing up (see Figure 9-1). Oh, sure, con artists, professional liars and used car dealers know the tricks and use the open palm gesture when trying to convince you that they're genuine and sincere. You're not fooled because other gestures of honesty, such as an open facial expression, calm breathing and a relaxed stance, are missing and you thus sense that something's not quite right.

Making a connection

You often wave to someone you know when seeing her from a distance. Your palm is in the open position, facing front, rhythmically moving from side to side. This is a similar gesture to the one you use when waving goodbye. When you wave, you're almost reaching out towards that person with a desire to touch her. (Turn to Chapter 15 for more about waving in different cultures.)

A good way to make contact with a large group of people is to hold out one or both of your hands with your fingers spread apart and your palms facing upwards. This gesture, shown in Figure 9-2, acts like a magnet and pulls people towards you.

Figure 9-1:
The open
palm
indicates
honesty and
trustworthi-
ness.

Figure 9-2:
The raised
open palm
invites your
listener into
your space.

Saluting through time

Historians are uncertain about the origins of the hand salute. It probably dates back to late Roman times when assassinations were not uncommon. If a citizen wanted to see a public official, he was required to approach with his right hand raised to demonstrate that he didn't hold a weapon. A similar gesture developed for armoured knights who raised their visors with the right hand when meeting a comrade.

Traditionally, the British military saluted by taking their hats off as a sign of respect. In the early 1800s, the Coldstream Guards amended that gesture. Because of the wear and tear on the hats by constant removal and replacing, the soldiers were instructed to clap their hands to their hats and bow as they passed by their superiors. Other regiments quickly adopted this procedure.

By the mid-nineteenth century, the army salute took the form of an open hand, tightly closed fingers, palm to the front – the gesture that remains today.

The naval salute is markedly different from the 'open hand' army salute, in that the palm of the hand points downward towards the shoulder. This gesture can be traced back to the days of sailing ships, when the ship's timber was sealed with tar and pitch to protect it from seawater. To preserve their hands, officers wore white gloves. As it was considered highly undignified to show a dirty palm when saluting, the hand was turned to a 90-degree angle.

When you want to establish a sense of trust and honesty, let your hands remain visible. Otherwise, you may look like you're hiding something. (For more information on what this behaviour means, go to the later section 'Hiding your hands'.)

You can also use open-hand gestures to connect with your listeners, helping them to grasp an idea that you're explaining or showing them that you value their opinions:

- ✔ Say that you want to plant a thought in someone's mind without verbally force-feeding the idea. Bend your elbows at a 90-degree angle and hold out both your hands side by side, palms facing each other. Then slowly beat your open hands rhythmically up and down and watch the light bulb turn on as the listener sees the picture.

- ✔ The next time you're speaking and you want to hear what someone else has to say, turn towards that person with your palm open and extended in her direction. The gesture is as though you're giving her a gift. By handing her the chance to speak, she feels acknowledged and that you're interested in what she has to say (see Figure 9-3).

Figure 9-3:
The man on the left is acknowledging the woman next to him, while excluding the others.

Watch someone who wants you to come on board with her way of thinking. She's likely to hold both hands in front of her, palms facing her body as if she's holding a valuable item in her arms. If you find yourself using this gesture when you speak, you may also be attempting to grasp your own suggestion or idea.

The downward-facing palm

Turn your hand over with your palm facing downwards and bam! – you're projecting power and authority (see Figure 9-4). This position is used for giving orders where no room exists for discussion. Gesturing with your palm facing downwards says, 'I'm in control. Do as I say!'

You have to be careful when using this gesture, especially if your fingers are tightly closed because of its association with dominance and tyranny. Think of the Third Reich and the Nazi salute if you're in doubt. Hitler purposely selected this gesture, understanding its portrayal of strength, power and ability to intimidate others.

One of the stories Daniel James Brown tells in his book, *The Boys in the Boat*, concerns the 1936 Olympic Games in Berlin. At the opening ceremony Adolf Hitler entered the stadium and 110,000 Germans rose from their seats, jutted out their right arms and, with downward-facing palms, saluted him with precision and power. When the athletes marched past Hitler most offered some form of recognition, including dipping their flags and nodding their heads. A few teams presented the Olympic salute, which, unfortunately, closely resembled that of the Nazi Party, the difference being that the arm is extended to the right side of the body rather than straight out in front. Not to be intimidated into submission, when the Americans passed Hitler, void of expression they looked up at him, removed their hats and placed them over their hearts, as their flag bearer lifted their country's symbol high in an act of defiance.

If you want to calm a tense situation or ask for quiet, hold out both your palms slightly pointed downwards with your fingers slightly separated and gently beat them up and down. Make sure that your fingers are relaxed or you may just be fanning the flames of the fire!

Figure 9-4:
The downward facing palm conveys conciliation and control.

Closed-palm, finger-pointed

Close your palm into a fist, point your index finger and look out, world! You've just created a symbolic club for beating into submission anyone who's listening (see Figure 9-5).

Think back to a time when someone – a parent, teacher or boss – pointed a finger at you and shook it for all it was worth. Don't be surprised if the memory makes you cringe. You know just how threatening and aggressive this gesture feels. That's because it comes from our primate ancestors who shake their 'fists' before pummelling their opposition into submission with a right over-arm blow and a left upper hook. Pow!

While you're remembering annoying gestures you'd rather forget, what about the one where the speaker beats her pointed finger in time to what she's saying. Again, this action makes you feel as if you're being pummelled with a sharp stick and can evoke memories of being reprimanded as a child.

Figure 9-5:
The closed-palm and pointed finger are threatening and aggressive.

The finger wag moves rhythmically sideways, back and forth like a metronome. Another annoying gesture, this action is a silent 'telling off' and reminds you of just how badly you're behaving.

The finger jab, the wag's closest cousin, is like a stabbing motion and is quite intimidating. Not one of the most conciliatory of gestures, use it at your peril.

If you habitually point and beat your finger when speaking, make a conscious effort to practise the palm-up and palm-down, fingers-loose positions. You'll find that you can create a positive impact on people and a relaxed atmosphere.

Hands Up!

Second only to your face, your hands are your most visually expressive feature and can be equated to your voice because they talk so much. They serve as a substitution for words as well as supporting the spoken word by illustrating and amplifying what you're saying. For example, when you're giving directions to someone who's lost, you most likely use your hands to get her back on the right path. When you're emphasising a point, your hands move in time with your words. When you're describing a shape or a particular scene, your hands create a visual picture of what you're saying. These kinds of hand gesture make complicated explanations more comprehensible.

Hiding your hands

When you conceal your hands by putting them behind your back or shoving them in your pockets, you're keeping them from telling on you. Take yourself back to your childhood. You've just been caught with your hand in the biscuit tin. You quickly pull it out and stick it behind your back while saying, 'No! Honestly! I didn't take anything!' And all the time your hand stays hidden, twitching guiltily behind your back.

Fast forward to your life now. You've been out on the town with your pals, you arrive home as the sun's rising and your parent/spouse/partner asks you where you've been. Rather than owning up to whatever minor, or major, indiscretion you've committed, if you're a man you probably shove your hands into your pockets or cross your arms with your hands tucked neatly away while coming up with a good excuse and, if you're a woman, you busy your hands with a flurry of activities. Either way, your palms stay hidden.

The hand rub: Good for you or good for me?

When you rub your palms together, you're signalling a positive expectation. How quickly you rub them indicates who's going to benefit. The slow palm rub can appear devious or crafty and may leave you feeling a little uneasy. You can bet that whatever positive result may happen is going to happen for anyone but you. The quick hand rub indicates excitement, pleasure and enthusiasm. If someone is offering you an opportunity and is rubbing her hands together quickly as she speaks, you can feel assured that her proposal is good for you.

Consider these examples:

- ✔ A friend tells you how excited she is about a holiday she's about to take, a promotion she's been given or a fabulous idea she's just had. She may well quickly rub her palms together, with a big smile on her face.

  Once upon a time I lived and worked in Las Vegas. No, I wasn't a show-girl! However, I occasionally went to the casinos and observed the gamblers. I noticed that the people throwing the dice at the craps table would quickly rub them together – sometimes even giving them a kiss – before tossing them down the table. This action, along with the look of concentrated anticipation on their faces, indicated that they were expecting something positive to happen. Most of the time something positive did happen – for the casino, not the gambler!

- ✔ The car salesperson or estate agent sits you down and asks whether you're ready to pull out your cheque book, rubbing her hands slowly together as she does so. Meaning? Buyer beware!

- ✔ After taking all your relevant details about the purchase you want to make, the salesperson rubs her palms together quickly and says, 'I've got just the thing for you!' Here the message is that she expects the result to be to *your* advantage. And if it works out for you, it probably works out for her. Everyone wins in this case!

The folded hand

If you think that folding your hands together is a positive gesture because it looks contained and controlled, look again. Studies show that rather than demonstrating confidence, this gesture reveals frustration or hostility and signals that the person is holding a negative attitude. By folding your hands, you're indicating that you're holding something in them that you don't want to let out.

Sure, some people may say that they're just comfortable with their hands folded in front of their waists, resting on a table or in the fig leaf position protecting their private parts. And they may be. But because, like most gestures, this one is unconscious, you can be sure that more is going on than pure comfort.

The next time you're in a meeting and the speaker refuses to give anyone else a chance to talk, watch the hand positions of the rest of the group. They're likely to be in folded positions until someone finally interrupts, at which point their hands open as that person begins to speak.

If you're speaking with someone whose hands are clenched, you can bet that she's holding back some kind of negative emotion. Give her something to hold or a task to perform in order to get her to unlock her fingers and expose her palms. The longer her hands stay put in the closed position, the longer the hostile attitude remains.

The clenched hands

Think back to a time when you were really scared, nervous or holding back a strong negative emotion. Chances are that you were clenching your hands for all you were worth and your knuckles were white: the stronger the emotion, the tighter the clench. In addition to the strength of the clench, you can interpret where the clenched hands are placed.

In front of the face

Studies indicate that the higher the hands are held in the clenched position, the stronger the negative mood. So, if your boss is sitting with her elbows resting on her desk and her hands clenched in front of her face, she's probably going to be difficult to handle. By putting her hands near her mouth, she's indicating that she's holding back what she'd like to say. Be careful not to push her too far – she may unclench those hands and let the words fly out!

Annie is a fast-thinking, focused and determined businesswoman. She has numerous projects on the go at one time, all of which require her attention. She values her staff enormously and makes a point of having a few minutes of personal conversation with them all during the week. Most of them know that, although she's genuinely interested in their wellbeing, she also likes people to get on with their jobs. Evie, one of her employees, likes to chat and is a bit long-winded. When Annie sees Evie approaching her office, she puts her elbows on her desk and clenches her hands in front of her face, creating a barrier to keep Evie at bay as well as keeping herself from blurting out something she may later regret. Although Evie doesn't seem to read the signals, Annie's secretary knows that gesture is a sure sign of her frustration and annoyance and quickly interrupts the conversation to spare her boss further irritation.

In the mid-position

Say that you're working at your desk, frantically beavering away to meet a deadline and someone comes in for a chat. Although you're quite annoyed about being interrupted, you want to appear cordial and welcoming. You stop what you're doing, fold your hands on your desk in front of you and ask, 'How may I help you?' Folding your hands and keeping them at this mid-position signals that, although you're irritated, you're not yet ready to explode.

If the interloper is paying attention, she recognises that holding your hands in a clenched position means you're holding back a negative emotion. If she's smart, she suggests coming back at a more convenient time.

The fig leaf

A lot of people stand with their hands folded in front of their private parts. This position tells you that they're either comfortable standing like that or don't know what to do with their hands. They're probably subconsciously feeling threatened and looking for a position that offers protection. By putting their hands in front of their most vulnerable parts, they feel comfortable because they're covered. And, as a bonus, now their hands have something to do. Don't be fooled into thinking that this is a naturally confident position. The reason the position is comfortable is because it acts like a shield.

Letting the Fingers Do the Talking

If you look at the way people gesture with their hands when they're speaking, you can see that they often look like they're holding on to their words. These actions are based on the precision and power grips, which are the two ways you can hold on to an object. (See the *Body Language For Dummies* app for some examples.)

Your hands and fingers also grab themselves when you're feeling under pressure, frustrated or, conversely, wanting to demonstrate control or authority. Even as I'm searching for the right way to convey this message, I'm resting my elbows on my desk while I grip my palms in front of my face, watching the knuckles turn white. Finding no answer there, I put my fingers to my mouth. Again, no luck. I shift to resting my chin in my palms as I search for inspiration. Even Humphrey, my dog, can tell by the way I'm moving my hands that a struggle is going on here.

The precision grip

Hold something small between your thumb and fingertips. It can be a pen, a needle or a delicate piece of fabric. This is the precision grip, shown in Figure 9-6, which allows you to hold and manipulate an object precisely.

Now, when you're speaking and want to say something accurately or delicately, press your fingers and thumb together in a similar position with your palm facing towards you. Hey presto! Your listener understands that you're reinforcing what you're saying with great precision and accuracy.

Figure 9-6:
The
precision
grip dem-
onstrates
exactness.

To focus your listener's attention and be seen as authoritative, place your index finger against your thumb in the 'okay' gesture with your palm facing outward and your fingers softly rounded. This way you avoid intimidating your audience and you're likely to be perceived as thoughtful and goal-orientated. This gesture is a favourite of modern politicians. Gosh, what a surprise!

In some countries, the okay signal is considered rude. Before making any definite gesture, find out what's acceptable behaviour and what may cause offence. (You can read more about the use of the okay signal in Chapter 15.)

When you ask a question or are feeling uncertain about a point you're making or responding to, you may well find that your thumb and index finger are almost – but not quite – touching (see Figure 9-7). Funny how that happens, as if the fingers know that the answer isn't quite there. When the fingers do come together in a definite grip, the action is as if they've grabbed the information and are holding on to it.

Figure 9-7:
The thumb
and
forefinger
not quite
touching
show
hesitancy or
uncertainty.

The power grip

People who want to be perceived as strong, serious and forceful use their whole fist to make a point. This action is as if they're holding on to a strap on a fast-moving bus or hammering a nail into a block of wood.

You can use this gesture effectively in two ways. If you choose to deliver your message in a mild mannered way, leave your fingers bent, not fully closed. If, however, you mean business and are taking no prisoners, close your fingers into a fist and watch the fur fly.

Watch a public speaker or politician who deliberately wants to show just how much conviction and determination she has. Wow! Look at that tightly closed fist pumping up and down as if beating a big bass drum. Makes you wonder whether more than a bit of showmanship is going on.

A similar gesture is the air punch, where you beat the air with a tightly closed fist to give force to a strong statement. This gesture is also the one you can use when your team scores, your proposal is accepted or you win the lottery.

If you want to hold back the force when demonstrating the depth of your conviction, let your fingers and thumb curl inwards as if they're loosely grasping an object. When you're speaking and want to establish authority, let your fingers and thumb curve inwards as if they're almost but not quite holding an invisible object. Enjoy the ensuing sense of control and assuredness.

The power chop

Sometimes when you speak, you may feel so passionate that you find yourself using your hand like a weapon, jabbing, punching or chopping. Hopefully, you're just hitting empty air rather than a person or an object (see Figure 9-8).

Your listener had better take you seriously when you use these gestures because they're a sure sign that whatever you're feeling is pretty strong and you aren't going to accept any arguments or contradictions. In other words, you mean business!

Figure 9-8:
The chop conveys clarity and conviction.

To demonstrate real forcefulness when you're speaking and to underline your determination to swash-buckle your way through the obstacle course, turn your hand into a symbolic axe blade by positioning it sideways with your fingers held closely together. Now make strong downward chopping movements. Your hand and arm start acting like a meat cleaver and woe betide the person who gets in your way. Great Britain's Deputy Prime Minister Nick Clegg is particularly adept at using this gesture when making his points.

The scissors or double-chop motion is a great one to use when you're rejecting or disagreeing with what someone else is saying. Cross both your forearms in front of your body and make outward cutting motions with your hands. You're indicating that you don't want to hear any more by cutting off the conversation.

When my then teenage son Max was doing his best to convince me why he should be allowed to travel the world on his own, I wasn't about to be swayed. His passionate arguments were countered with my motherly wisdom. Not only did my words say, 'No', everything I was doing was rejecting his proposal. It was when I combined the double-chop motion with the finger shake that my daughter Kristina came in with the conciliatory palms down, gently beating gesture that reduced the tension and created a modicum of calmness.

The steeple

In his studies of body movements, Ray Birdwhistell noted that confident, superior types of people whose gestures tend to be minimal or restricted 'steeple' their fingers to demonstrate their confident attitude. You can achieve this position by letting your finger tips lightly touch like the steeple on a building.

This gesture is also called the 'power position' because people often use it in a superior/subordinate interaction. Lawyers, accountants and anyone in a position of authority frequently give instructions or advice with their fingers in these positions:

- ✔ **The raised steeple:** When the fingers are raised in front of the chest, the speaker is voicing thoughts or opinions.

  Use the raised steeple position judiciously. Taken to extremes, it can convey an arrogant 'know-it-all' attitude. If you tilt your head backwards when taking this position, don't be surprised if you're perceived as smug or arrogant.

- ✔ **The lowered steeple:** When you're listening you may find your fingers in the lowered steeple position. You look interested and ready to respond when you put your hands together like this. Women tend to use this position more often than the raised steeple.

Gripping hands, wrists and arms

If you want to project superiority and confidence, put your hands behind your back and grip one hand with the other. Look at prominent male members of royal families around the world. Observe senior military personnel, police officers patrolling their beats or the head of your local school striding through the corridors. Adopting this position of authority means they show no fear of exposing their vulnerable necks, hearts or stomachs to potential threats.

The next time you're in a stressful or uncomfortable situation, adopt the palm-in-palm-behind-the-back stance. Note how your feelings change from frustrated, insecure or angry to relaxed and confident.

As the grip moves up the arm, though, the meaning changes. You can bet that, if someone is gripping her wrist behind her back rather than just her hand, she's holding back some form of nervousness. This gesture is an attempt at maintaining self-control, as the hand holding the wrist or arm keeps it from hitting out. The farther up the back the hand goes, the greater the level of tension.

Gesturing with your thumbs

Gestures associated with the thumb convey dominance, superiority and in some cases aggression, so you won't find it surprising that in palmistry the thumb denotes strength of character and ego. If you've ever heard the expression 'under the thumb' you know the implication is that the person with the thumb is the one in control. Woe betide the person under the thumb, as according to ancient Roman history the thumb turned down served as a sign of imminent death. Here are some other interpretations of thumb positions:

- ✔ **Thumbs up:** This position generally denotes agreement. But be careful using it because in some cultures doing so is perceived as rude and highly offensive. (See Chapter 15 for more on cultural norms.)

- ✔ **Thumbs protruding from a person's pockets:** This gesture demonstrates dominance and self-assuredness. Although both men and women use this gesture, rare is the woman who adopts the position of holding her jacket lapel with the thumb exposed, whereas men often do.

- ✔ **Gesturing towards another person with your thumb:** When you use your thumb to point towards someone else, you're being dismissive, disrespectful or ridiculing the other person, especially if the gesture is accompanied by a sneer, a downward glance and a toss of your head (see Figure 9-9).

Christopher had the unfortunate habit of ridiculing Philippa, his wife, in front of their friends. When they were in company he'd often refer to her as 'the little woman' and gesture in her direction with a closed fist, using his thumb as a pointer. Although Philippa told him how irritating she found this gesture, as well as the accompanying remarks, Christopher took no notice. He did notice, however, when after several years of rude and disrespectful behaviour, Philippa divorced him.

Figure 9-9:
His thumb
gesture is
dismissive.

Analysing Handshakes

Shaking hands upon meeting is a tradition that creates a bond of solidarity. Our ancestors in their caves greeted one another with outstretched arms and exposed palms to show they were free of clubs and other life-threatening weapons. Scuttle along to the Roman period, where it was common to carry concealed daggers up one's sleeve. No surprise, then, that two men would grab each other's lower arms as a means of greeting and to check out the other's intentions.

As the handshake evolved it became a gesture to cement agreements, offer a welcome and bid someone a fond farewell. Therefore, make sure that when you shake hands the gesture is open, congenial and positive.

Deciding who reaches out first

Although shaking hands when meeting another person for the first time is customary, in some instances making the first move may not be appropriate. For example, if you've forced the meeting or the other person is uncomfortable in your presence it could feel awkward for you to extend your hand as a sign of trust and welcome. Yet if you consider the person you're meeting to be your equal and you're both glad to see one another, you simultaneously extend your hands in greeting.

When you show up at a customer's premises without having been invited, wait to see if she extends her hand in welcome. If you put your hand out first, she may feel forced to shake your hand, creating a negative feeling. If no handshake is forthcoming, give a small nod of your head instead.

Because some people aren't sure whether or not to shake a woman's hand in a business context, the woman should extend her hand first to show that she's comfortable with this greeting (see Figure 9-10). That way avoids wondering and fumbling.

Conveying attitude

Some people shake hands as if they're Attila the Hun about to put you in your place. Others remain passive and detached, barely offering you a fingertip. Still others present you with a cold, clammy hand reminiscent of a wet mackerel. How people shake hands tells you a lot about their thoughts and feelings about the person they're about to touch.

University of Alabama professor William Chaplin and his students examined the relationship between personality and styles of handshake. They found that extroverted and emotionally expressive people are inclined to shake hands firmly whereas neurotic and shy people don't. They also found that women who have an open attitude to new experiences use a firm handshake.

Figure 9-10:
The woman offering her hand first demonstrates her comfort and confidence.

The bone cruncher

Before you can stuff your hand in your pocket, the bone cruncher is there, turning your knuckles into pulverised paste. These people seem to have an overly aggressive attitude to compensate for their ineffectualness. The bone cruncher is to be avoided when it comes to shaking hands because you can do little to counter the action.

To avoid a potentially painful handshake, both men and women should avoid wearing rings on their right hands in a business context.

If you think that your hand has been purposely crunched, say 'Wow! That's one strong grip. You got something to prove?' You're letting the person know that you're on to her game. This has even more impact if other people are present observing the interaction. She's unlikely to play that trick again.

George lacks social skills and is unaware of how much pressure he puts into his handshakes. He unconsciously makes up for his social ineptness by putting an extra hard squeeze into his grasp. Women find it especially uncomfortable to shake hands with George and have been known to sport red welts after shaking his hand. One friend mused, 'If he does that when shaking hands, I wonder what happens when he kisses you?'

The wet fish

If you've ever been presented with a totally limp hand to shake, you know how unconnected it feels when your palms meet. People who refuse to commit to a handshake tend to be self-important and aloof. Granted, surgeons and concert pianists need to guard their fingers and are known for their soft handshakes. And people who have to do a lot of shaking also offer a relaxed hand in order to protect their fingers.

Some people offer the uncommitted handshake for other reasons. Some women think that it's appealing to present themselves as submissive to both men and women (see Figure 9-11). Very strong people sometimes offer a soft handshake as a way of highlighting their physical power. If a person is lacking in confidence, she also holds back from making a connection.

Figure 9-11:
The woman is enticing the man with her soft handshake and sensual movements.

The power shake

At times you may want to show that you have the upper hand, meaning that you're strong and in control. You can do this by making sure that your hand faces down in the handshake. Although your palm doesn't have to be completely turned over so that it faces directly downward, the slight turning still shows that you're the top dog.

Even if you're unaware of having placed your hand in the top position, you have the automatic advantage. Why? Because the hand down position is associated with dominance and control whereas the upward-facing palm conveys compliance and passivity. Even if you and the receiver are unaware of what your hands are doing, one position feels more dominant while the other feels submissive.

The double-hander

The double-hander is a favourite in the corporate and political arena. Through this particular handshake, the initiator aims to portray sincerity, honesty and a deep feeling for the receiver. By using it, you increase the amount of physical contact and by restricting the receiver's right hand you gain control of the interaction. Because the double-hander is like a mini-hug, choose your receiver carefully. Ideally, this handshake should only be used where a personal relationship already exists.

If someone thrusts her hand towards you, palm facing downwards, and grabs your hand in hers putting you in a submissive position with little chance of balancing the equation, what do you do? Allow the power player to take your hand with your palm facing upwards. Then, before she knows what you're up to, put your left hand on top of her right to create a double-hander. From this position you're able to straighten the handshake and gain control subtly and effectively.

Taking things in hand

In the double-fisted handshake the left hand is responsible for the following two points (see Figure 9-12):

✔ **The action conveys the level of intimacy between you and the receiver.** The higher up the arm your left hand goes, the more intimate the feeling. The meaning behind this gesture is complex. In addition to showing the degree of connection you want to demonstrate towards your receiver, the action also reveals the amount of control you exert.

✔ **By invading the receiver's personal space with your left hand you're staking rights on her territory.** Unless the receiver has positive feelings for you, this gesture can lead to feelings of suspicion and mistrust. If in doubt, don't use it – especially on your boss.

Figure 9-12:
The man
on the left
is showing
his power,
intimate
feelings and
control as
his left hand
moves up
the other
man's arm.

The leach

Some people just don't know when to let go. They grab your hand, shake it
and then hang on until you want to pry their fingers off. This is a subtle way
of demonstrating control. By prolonging the contact, they're engaging you for
longer than you may want. Interestingly, you'll probably allow the contact to
remain until you can think of a good reason to pull away, such as 'Excuse me,
I'm about to sneeze!'

The space invader

Whether you're pulling someone into your territory when shaking hands or
invading her space by plunging your arm into her terrain, a power play is
taking place and you hold the power.

In the first instance, you propel your arm forward, forcefully grip the receiver's
extended hand and simultaneously go into a quick reverse thrust. As you yank
her into your space, you huddle over the handshake until you're ready to let it
go. If you pull someone into your personal space, you create a handshake on
your terms.

Be aware of the amount of force you apply or you may find the other person falling on top of you as you pull her in. That's what you call getting the relationship off on the wrong foot!

If you invade the other person's territory, you extend your arm fully, forcing her to retreat. Her arm ends up in a cramped position while your extended arm fills her space.

The firm shake

If you want to create a sense of mutual respect and equality, make sure that when you shake hands with another person both your palms are in the vertical position, your fingers are wrapped around one another's hands and that you apply the same amount of pressure. Your hands should meet in no-man's land, halfway between your space and the other person's.

Taking the left side advantage

The next time you look at a photograph of two leaders standing next to one another, see which one looks more dominant. Chances are that you perceive the person on the left side of the picture to have the edge.

If the photograph shows them shaking hands you can easily see that the hand of the person on the left is in the upper position, making her appear more powerful and in control. Savvy politicians are aware of the impact of this body position and jockey to place themselves to the right of their colleague, or adversary, in order to come out on the left in the photo.

To gain the left side advantage to make yourself appear as if you're calling the shots, position yourself to the right of the other person. If you want to increase your power play, place your left hand on her back while shaking hands. Although the other person may feel annoyed by your obvious manipulation, you can smile warmly, knowing that you've got the advantage.

Displacing Your Energy

If you ever notice yourself drumming your fingers, pulling your earlobe, touching your face or scratching your head when you haven't got an itch, you're experiencing displacement activities. These are easy to spot because they're the small, inconsequential gestures you make when you're feeling inner turmoil or stress.

Drumming for relief

If you're in a meeting and someone's drumming her fingers on the table, pay attention. Those digits are speaking. Bored, frustrated or even irritated – the percussionist is impatient.

Stephen works for an international law firm. He recently found out that his colleagues call him 'Thumper' because of his constant finger drumming during meetings. Stephen reveals his state of mind by the tempo of his finger tapping. When he's bored, he drums the four fingers of his right hand in quick succession. When he's thoughtfully considering a suggestion, he quietly taps his middle finger. When he's prepared to conclude the meeting, he knocks his knuckles on the table. Without his saying a word, his colleagues know what Thumper's thinking.

Fiddling for comfort

Notice what you do the next time you feel anxious. Chances are that you'll fiddle with an object. You may jangle your keys, twist a ring on your finger or adjust your clothes. You may also touch yourself by picking at your nails, tugging your earlobe, rubbing your cheek or running your fingers through your hair. The purpose of these actions is to ease nervous tension.

When people are feeling anxious, they focus their excess energy on themselves as a way of providing temporary relief. These actions are sometimes referred to as 'adaptors' because they help you adapt to your internal tension. Adaptive behaviours are mainly focused on the head and face. Unconsciously you may find yourself stroking your face, running your fingers over your lips or rubbing the back of your neck when you're feeling upset. These hand gestures are reminiscent of those your mother may have used to comfort you when you were a child.

Hand to nose

When your hand goes to your nose you may be harbouring a fear or falsehood. Whether you're telling a deliberate lie (as if), having a dishonest thought, pretending to be brave when you're totally terrified or simply feeling a moment of self-doubt, the hand going to your nose signals discomfort.

The act of self-touching signals a need for reassurance. Rubbing the nose, giving it a quick wipe or a simple scratch are responses to the tingling sensation caused by heightened blood flow to the nose when you're feeling stressed.

Feeling the heat

In a 2012 study of the effect of mental states on body temperature, researchers at the University of Granada, Spain concluded that body temperatures adjust according to a person's physical, mental and emotional status.

Lying leads to an increase in temperature in the nose and the area around the eye's inner corner. The tingling feeling that comes with the temperature change makes her want to wipe it away.

To identify if someone's feeling under pressure, observe her hand-to-face gestures.

Hand to cheek

The hand to cheek gesture indicates boredom, disinterest and fatigue (see Figure 9-13). Resting your hand on your cheek is like resting your hand on your pillow. Before you know it, you may be nodding off into dreamland. In meetings, lectures and restaurants you see people resting their heads on their hands as negative feelings creep in.

Figure 9-13: The woman's hand-to-face gestures show that she's doubtful (left), is evaluating (centre) and is unengaged (right).

If you're speaking in a public forum and you notice that heads are resting in hands, change what you're doing. The change catches your listeners' attention and saves you the humiliation of heads and hands collapsing into an embarrassing heap.

Hand to chin

The chin resting on the top of the hand is a sign of thinking: the person is concentrating on something. The thumb under the chin with the index finger pointing up the side of the face signals that an evaluation is being made. Like Rodin's *The Thinker*, you see that the person is pondering.

When you scan papers and magazines, observe the postures public figures adopt. Politicians, businesspeople and others who want to be seen as thoughtful are frequently photographed in the evaluation posture, with their hands resting on their thumbs and their index fingers pointing up their cheeks. The pose indicates that the person is weighing up the merits of the argument and considering her options.

Biting fingernails

People working in intelligence are told to observe a suspect's mannerisms. Mannerisms are a sure sign of a person's inner state and are more difficult to disguise than facial features. Mannerisms are so entrenched that eliminating them is hard, whereas facial features can be fairly easily changed. When assessing another person, look to her hands for clues to her personality.

Doctors examine a patient's fingernails with the same amount of care and attention as they look at the face and the eyes. Any irregularity, including shape and colour, is evidence of physical poor health and psychological stress and anxiety.

Nails bitten or picked to the quick lead to brachyonychia, a condition in which the width of the nail plate and nail bed is greater than the length. If any of the nails, especially the thumb, have been sucked they may show teeth markings. These are signals that someone is experiencing extreme tension. You start to doubt that she confines her stress behaviours to nail-biting alone. Former UK Prime Minister Gordon Brown's fingernails look like they're chewed regularly.

Chapter 10

Standing Your Ground

*A*t times in your life, you've had to take a stand and make a firm decision. You probably planted your feet firmly on the ground and got on with what you had to do. At other times you've been able to take it easy, wandering from one pillar to another.

You've stamped your foot in anger – or known someone who has – you've rubbed your ankle up against another's as well as your own, and you've stood with your weight on one leg in boredom as well as bounced on your toes in excitement.

In this chapter, I look at the different types of stance you adopt depending on your mood and circumstances. You also discover what the swinging foot is saying, as well as the pointed toe.

Showing Commitment and Attitude through Your Stance

The foundation for a firm stance is to stand with your feet evenly placed under your hips and with your weight equally distributed between them. What you choose to do with that foundation depends on what you want to show and how you want to be perceived. How you hold yourself reflects the effects of life experiences as well as social position.

You can identify someone's status from the way he stands. Kings don't slump, at least not in public. The petty officer stands to attention when his superior enters the room. The servant bows at his master's will.

The person who slouches, who lets his head droop, his shoulders hunch and his feet turn inwards shows submission, a lack of commitment and indicates that he's withdrawing or holding back. Conversely, people who place their weight evenly between their legs, with their feet firmly planted under them, look confident and self-assured, providing their other body parts are working in harmony with the feet and legs. When standing in this position, don't be surprised if you find yourself holding your head high, with your chest open and stomach in. Presto! You're standing like a winner.

Straddle stance

The straddle stance is a stable position and the one most favoured by those who are showing dominance. It requires that your legs are straight, and that your feet are placed hip width apart, with your weight equally distributed between them.

While men tend to adopt the straddle stance more frequently than women, male or female, tall or short, people adopt this stance when they want to demonstrate power and dominance.

Macho messages

A resolutely immovable posture, in which someone has planted his feet so firmly that no room exists for budging, tells you that he's standing his ground (see Figure 10-1). He's also showing you who's boss by filling more space and presenting his private parts.

Body language and your best you

Amy Cuddy is a social psychologist and associate professor at Harvard Business School whose TED Talk, 'Your body language shapes who you are', has already garnered over 22.5 million views. Cuddy's research proves that adopting a confident posture – even when a person isn't feeling confident – affects testosterone and cortisol levels in the brain and, as a result, improves his likelihood of success. The message is simple and powerful: if you want to change other people's perceptions of you and even your own body chemistry – change your body position. For further information about Cuddy's research and how its findings can have a positive impact on your life, go to www.dummies.com/extras/bodylanguage.

During his last year at junior school, Tommy, aged 12, was in the school's winning rugby team. At the party after the match, a group of boys stood in a circle, talking among themselves. As proud winners, each of them had adopted the straddle stance, demonstrating his machismo. Even at such a young age the boys were strutting their stuff.

Figure 10-1:
The straddle stance conveys messages of dominance and power.

If you're feeling defeated and want to change your mood, adopt the straddle stance – also known as the Superwoman pose – with your head held high and your shoulders back. By adopting this powerful position, you can create the matching feeling.

Threatening signs

Throughout history and across cultures, phallic displays have been considered signs of dominance. By standing with his legs apart, a man unashamedly shows his crotch to anyone who's looking, declaring himself to be The Terminator. Exposing himself in this way, even though he may be fully covered, demonstrates that, as far as he's concerned, he's the boss.

You can tell if two people are ready to fight or are merely sussing each other out in a friendly manner. If they stand face to face with their feet apart, their hands on their hips or their fingers and thumbs tucked into their belt loops or the tops of their pockets, they probably don't like one another very much and are looking for trouble. If, however, their bodies are turned slightly away from one another, they're simply sizing each other up in a friendly interchange.

A dominant male baboon exposes and flaunts his erect penis as a means of signalling to other male baboons his power and status. Men in New Guinea proclaim their position in the community via the size and decorative features of their penis sheaths. European men in the fifteenth and sixteenth centuries wore codpieces as a sign of virility and social status.

In the most recent version of the James Bond film, *Casino Royale*, Daniel Craig strides out of the ocean wearing a swimsuit that unashamedly draws the eye to his crotch. The light blue colour of the swimwear, combined with Craig's ice blue eyes and his well-endowed and highly toned body, highlights the character's strength and power.

Parallel stance

The parallel stance (shown in Figure 10-2) is a subordinate position where the legs are straight and the feet are placed closely together. You may well take this position if you're called up in front of the headteacher, reporting to your commanding officer or standing in front of a judge, awaiting sentence.

Figure 10-2:
The parallel stance is a sign of uncertainty and submission.

Feet placed closely together reduce the foundation for standing and make the stance more precarious. You can easily push someone over from this position if you were to catch him off guard. People who aren't sure about their position on a subject unconsciously adopt the parallel stance. Standing with their legs closely placed together they're indicating that they feel hesitant or tentative. A wider stance provides a broader and firmer foundation. Unbalancing a person who's standing with his legs separated is much harder (see the preceding section).

To experience the contrasting sensations, attitudes and impressions that result from standing in the straddle and parallel positions, try the following exercise:

1. Stand in the straddle stance for 60 seconds.

2. Note how you're feeling, what you're thinking and what you'd like to be doing as you stand in this position.

3. Stand in the parallel position for 60 seconds and repeat Step 2.

What differences do you notice when you're adopting the two stances? How can you use these differences to suit your needs?

Buttress stance

Built against or projecting from a wall, buttresses are architectural structures designed to reinforce the wall to which they're attached. The word suggests support, as in one person buttressing another person's argument.

In the buttress stance, you place most of your weight on a straight supporting leg, allowing your other leg to serve as a buttress. This non-weightbearing leg can be straight or bent. Whichever it is, the foot most likely points away from where the rest of the body is facing.

Although people adopting the buttress stance say they're just resting comfortably, the position signals that the person wants to move. The stance bears a close resemblance to the act of walking. Just before moving, you shift your weight to one leg in order that the other is free to take a step. Although you may not choose to move from the buttress stance, your legs are positioned so that they easily can. This position conveys a cleverly disguised message: you're prepared to go.

If you see someone repeatedly shifting his weight from one foot to the other while engaging with you, he either has to go to the toilet or is signalling that he's had enough of your company.

Preening and posing

From the Middle Ages to the middle of the nineteenth century, men of elevated position and high social status adopted a stance that conveniently displayed the inner part of the leg – one of the body's erotic zones. Gentlemen and posers would bear their weight on one leg, presenting the other with the inner thigh facing. The fashion designs that saw men's dress move from hose to tight breeches, accessorised with fine shoes, permitted and encouraged men to indulge their desire to preen and pose, showing off their legs and their masculinity. Today,

celebrities know how to position their legs to display them to their best advantage, turning their feet outward to reveal their inner thighs, the softer and most erogenous part of their legs. On the red carpet at the 2012 Oscars ceremony, Angelina Jolie created a media frenzy when she exposed her inner right thigh, all the way up to the top. This celebrity move earned her a Twitter feed – Angie's Right Leg – accruing more than 12,000 followers within hours as well as numerous hashtags.

Scissors stance

Think of your legs as the two blades of a pair of scissors. Cross one over the other, keeping your knees straight and you're in the classic scissors stance. This is an obvious defensive gesture, because the person is doing his best to protect his most precious parts without resorting to putting his hands over them. (For physiological reasons, women find it easier to adopt the tightly closed scissors position than do men.) People also adopt this position when their bladder is about to burst.

When one leg is crossed over the other and one of the two knees is bent, the position is called the 'bent blade stance'. Someone standing in the scissors stance or the bent blade stance is demonstrating his immobility, both physically and mentally. His locked feet, reflecting his locked mental state, are placed in such a way that a speedy departure is impossible without a vigorous uncoiling of legs and feet.

Crossed legs, especially in the standing position, relay varying messages:

- ✔ **Negativity, defensiveness and insecurity:** Crossing your legs is a defensive position. The gesture often accompanies the crossed arm position, reinforcing the barrier. If legs only are crossed, the suggestion is more submissive than defensive. Cross the arms and you're looking at a protective stance.

- ✔ **Commitment and immobility:** A person standing with his legs crossed when in conversation is showing that he's committed to the interaction and has no intention of leaving.

✔ **Submission:** The crossed-leg position comes across as submissive because the stance conveys no sign of impatience.

✔ **Vulnerability:** Standing in a position from which you can't easily move makes you appear vulnerable (see Figure 10-3). When women take this stance, they often dip their heads and look up from under their brows, adding to the impression of defencelessness.

Figure 10-3:
The scissor position makes the woman look vulnerable.

If someone tells you that he's standing with his legs and arms crossed because he's cold, see how his hands and legs are positioned. Someone who really is cold tucks his hands into his armpits or hugs himself. His legs are stiff, straight and pushed tightly against each other.

Entwining your legs

Some gestures are particular to men and others are particular to women. Women more than men twine their legs, locking the toes of one foot around the ankle of the other. While the purpose of the position is to offer security – think of how good it feels to be wrapped up in a warm blanket – the stance highlights insecurity and resembles a tortoise in retreat.

Moving with your mind

Research shows that the body's movements reflect the mind's state. For example, people meeting in a group for the first time usually stand with their arms and legs in the crossed position. As rapport develops and they become more comfortable with one another, they release the closed pose and open up their bodies in a predictable pattern. First, they uncross their legs and place their feet in the parallel pose. Then they unfold their arms and hands, allowing them to become animate. As their comfort levels rise, they move from the parallel stance to an open position in which the feet are slightly apart and facing the other person. Similarly, indicators of someone who has withdrawn from the conversation are crossed arms and legs. A person standing or sitting in this position is unlikely to be convinced by anything you may say or do.

If you want to unlock a woman from the entwined leg position, take a friendly and low-key approach to her in order to get her to open up.

Kelly, a new member of the marketing team, was making her first customer presentation. Feeling excited and scared, she stood in front of her boss, her colleagues and the clients in her pencil skirt and three-inch heels. Without realising what she was doing, she tucked her right foot behind her left ankle, creating a pole-like position. Although she was seeking security, the position was precarious and did nothing to steady her nerves. When she noticed how she was standing, she placed both feet firmly under her and found that she felt more confident and was able to speak with greater clarity, credibility and conviction.

Reflecting Your Feelings in the Way You Position Your Feet

Because your feet are the farthest point from your brain, your grey matter has less control over them than it does, say, over your hands or facial expressions. You're less aware of where your feet are facing and what they're doing than you are of your eyes, which are about as close to your brain as they can get.

Pointing towards the desired place

Humans evolved with two legs, the purpose of which is to move forward towards what you want and away from what you don't want. The direction in which your feet point tells the observer where you want to go. We've all experienced talking to someone who'd rather be somewhere else. While his face is smiling and his head nodding, his feet are pointing away from you (see Figure 10-4).

Figure 10-4:
The woman is indicating that she'd like to leave, while the man wants to hold her attention.

When the feet, head and torso are pointing in the same direction you're demonstrating an open, or dominant, attitude.

Your feet act as pointers, signalling where your mind is going. Like a magnet, they point in the direction of someone who appeals to you.

Sabine is a vivacious, attractive woman to whom men flock. At a recent party, she was flanked by a group of three men who struggled to take their eyes off her. Each man stood with his front foot pointed toward her, silently indicating his interest. As her feet shifted from man to man, she was unaware that she was reeling each of them in like a fish on a line. Sabine was constantly smiling and her body was in an open position, demonstrating her ingenuousness and warmth.

If you're in conversation with another person and notice that he doesn't seem entirely engaged with you, sneak a look at where his feet are pointing.

Mike and Susan were at a party. It was late and Mike was tired, bored and wanted to be in his own bed watching television. While he and Susan were saying their goodbyes, Mike couldn't understand why he was having so much difficulty getting his wife to leave. Had he looked, he would have seen that while they were saying goodbye to their hostess, Susan's feet remained pointed towards her, whereas Mike's feet were heading towards the door.

Fidgeting feet

Fidgeting feet are a good indicator that someone is feeling impatient. The feet say they want to flee and so are forced to fidget until the time comes to walk or run. If you're standing, you may repeatedly tap your foot to indicate your impatience. If you're sitting with your legs crossed, you may twitch the hanging foot up and down or back and forth.

To appear calm on the outside when everything inside is in a panic, breathe from your diaphragm, adjust your stance and let your feet take root.

Knotted ankles

Whether you're sitting or standing, if you've knotted or twisted your ankles together, the signal you're sending is, 'I'm holding back'. Locked ankles reflect a closed, insecure or negative attitude, suggesting ambiguity or revealing a lack of confidence. Unless you're the Queen, who frequently sits with knotted ankles, they're definitely not a sign of someone who's feeling confident and in command.

People who say they're comfortable sitting with their ankles tightly crossed probably are. Their bodies are reflecting their mental state and no tension exists between the two. Whether they confess that they're comfortable because their actions are reflecting their attitude – which according to the signs may be nervous, anxious or defensive – depends on how comfortable they are admitting their emotional state.

Observe the differences in how men and women sit in the crossed ankle position. Men often clench their fists, resting them on their knees, or tightly grip the arms of the chair. Their legs are splayed, exposing their open crotch. Women tend to hold their knees together, with their feet often placed to one side, their hands resting in their laps side by side or with one placed on top of the other.

In the army, if someone tells you to 'keep your heels locked' the message is, if the subject doesn't concern you personally, don't talk about what you don't have to.

Signs of holding back

Studies of body language by Gerard Nierenberg and Henry Calero, in which they pay particular attention to the participant's ankles, show that people very often lock their ankles when holding back information.

Trained in-flight airline personnel are told to look at passengers' feet to spot those who are feeling shy, reserved and apprehensive. Someone sitting with his ankles locked at take-off is feeling anxious. When the cabin staff offers him a refreshment, he tends to unlock his ankles and move forward to the edge of his seat. If his ankles remain in a locked position, however, the crew is aware that he wants something and is holding back asking for it.

Studies into the behaviour of dental patients show that more men than women immediately lock their ankles when sitting in the dentist's chair. Men also grip the chair's armrests or clench their hands together around their groin area. Women, too, clench their hands, leaving them to rest on their mid-section.

Research with law enforcement and government bodies reveals that most people being interviewed knot their ankles at the start of the questioning. The reason for this is as likely to be based on fear as on guilt. Defendants sitting outside a courtroom waiting for their hearing are three times more likely than the plaintiffs to have their ankles tightly crossed and tucked under their chairs in an attempt to control their emotions. Nierenberg and Calero's research into the human resources profession reveals that most interviewees lock their ankles at some point during an interview, indicating that the person being interviewed is holding back an emotion or thought. Using appropriate questioning techniques, the questioner can get the other to open up and reveal valuable information.

Finally, Nierenberg and Calero's research shows that patients who are being wheeled into an operating room with their ankles crossed and their hands clenched, tend to be un-reconciled with what's coming next.

Twitching, flicking or going in circles

If you suspect someone of lying to you or holding back information, look at his feet. Research on deception reveals that a person who's asked to lie shows more signs of fraud below the waist than above. Are his feet twitching, flicking or going around in circles?

Hand and eye movements are under conscious control. Because they're close to your brain and a main source of communication, you're more aware of what they're doing than you are of your legs and feet, which, no matter how short you are, are still quite far from your brain.

Leaking information isn't restricted to deception. For example, people showing interest in another person use their bodies to reveal what their minds are thinking and their mouths mustn't tell. Say that a man is speaking to a woman

Letting your feet do the talking

Research by Paul Ekman and William Friesen on deception behaviours shows that when a person lies he produces more ruse signals below the waist than above. Because people are more aware of what their hands and eyes are doing they can consciously control their actions. Although the legs and feet are also under conscious control, they are mostly ignored and often out of sight. They are therefore a more accurate source of information. A focus group watched recordings of people, who, unbeknownst to the group, were lying.

The group was then asked to determine if the people on the tape were lying, or telling the truth. The evaluators answered more correctly when they were able to see the lower part of the body. The findings showed that liars pay more attention to what their hands, arms and faces are doing because they know that that's where people look. Because their lower extremities are out of the way, liars forget about them and are betrayed by miniature muscle movements in their legs and feet.

he finds particularly attractive. He's very likely to stand with one foot pointing toward her with his legs apart exposing his groin area and to hold his arms in a splayed position to make himself look larger and fill more space. If the woman doesn't find him attractive and wants to give him the brush-off, she holds her legs together, faces her body away from him, folds her arms and makes herself appear as small as possible.

Walking Styles

Some people slump and drag their feet. Others add a lively bounce to their step. Still others swagger, shuffle or canter along a path. However a person walks, he's being true to his internal thoughts, feelings and intentions. Alternatively, he's presenting an image of what he wants you to believe. The way people walk tells you a lot about their plans, attitude and general state of being.

How you walk reflects both your physical and mental state. Vivacious, young and healthy people walk faster than those who are older, depressed or infirm. The energetic walker swings his arms high, both in front and behind, sometimes giving the appearance of marching. For the most part, young people have more muscle flexibility than older people and can move faster, giving the appearance of energy and excitement.

If you find yourself feeling depressed and dragging your feet as you walk along, increase your tempo. A quicker pace increases your energy and lifts your spirits.

Chapter 11

Playing with Props

. . . .

In This Chapter

▶ Projecting your self-image

▶ Putting glasses to good use

▶ Performing the rituals – make-up and dressing

. . . .

*E*very moment of every day, you project an image of yourself just as
others do. People use a plethora of props, such as hats, pens, glasses
and make-up, to create an image. Mention props to an actor and her eyes
come alive. She knows that these inanimate objects are her friends. Props
can create an image behind which you can hide or through which you can
reveal your character.

As you observe someone and the way in which she accessorises herself, you
can figure out what that person is like. Your success rate depends on your
level of sensitivity, and your ability to recognise and interpret what other
people's choice of props, or accessories, is revealing.

In this chapter I look at how the way you handle your props reflects your
thoughts, mood and intentions. I also consider the choice of props, and how
you use them to create a perception. Finally, I ponder the power behind the
prop.

Using Accessories to Reflect Mental States

How people use their accessories – glasses, pens, briefcases and handbags,
for example – indicates their internal state. The pen clicker at a meeting,
the traveller rifling through her bag and the celebrity hiding behind her
sunglasses all reveal to you through the way they play with their props how
they're feeling inside.

The girl props her sunglasses on her head, her brother wears his baseball cap backwards, their mother perches her reading glasses at the end of her nose as she examines her children's behaviour and their father at the sink noisily snaps a teatowel. Coy, defiant, domineering, annoyed – each person is telling you their state of mind.

Regardless of the purpose for which props are designed (glasses for reading and protecting your eyes from the sun, briefcases and handbags for holding personal and work items, and pens and pencils for writing), how you handle them reflects your internal state. You put things near and in your mouth when you feel in need of reassurance – chewing on fingers, pencils and arms of glasses, for example. You check your briefcase and handbag repeatedly to set your mind at rest. You throw things in annoyance. Your moods are revealed by the way you handle your props.

Showing inner turmoil

According to zoologist Desmond Morris, putting objects in or near the mouth is reminiscent of a baby seeking comfort at its mother's breast. Any gesture, no matter how small, in which you place an object against your lips or mouth (see Figure 11-1) is an attempt to relive the sense of security you felt as a suckling babe, and is a sign that you need comforting or reassuring. In other words, chewing on the arms of your glasses and chomping on a pencil indicate that all is not at peace in your world.

Some tension-relieving activities you may observe include:

- **Adjusting clothes:** This action indicates that the person is feeling uncomfortable. If you see someone making adjustments to her clothes when none are needed, you're correct in thinking that she's feeling tense.

- **Biting fingernails and cuticles:** This action is similar to the sucking behaviour of infants and provides reassurance. The action is also related to the gesture of putting your hand in front of your mouth to prevent you from expressing a thought or an emotion.

- **Playing with objects:** Jingling change in pockets, clicking a pen or fiddling with jewellery are deflecting signals indicating nervousness. Touching the objects provides sensory comfort, similar to holding a favourite toy when you were a child.

- **Running fingers through hair:** When you're feeling tense and agitated, you may find that your hand goes to your head and your fingers run along your scalp. This is a comforting gesture, reminiscent of the hair ruffles or strokes you may have received as a child.

✔ **Shaking a shoe:** Nervous energy building up like a pressure cooker has to come out somewhere. Although you may look calm in your upper torso, if you're nervous, anxious or excited, a jiggling foot gives your game away.

Check out the *Body Language For Dummies* app for some examples of these tension-relieving activities in action.

Figure 11-1:
Sucking on an object signals a need for reassurance.

Pausing for thought

When you need to take time to think something through, you may find yourself rolling a pen between your fingers, taking a sip from your coffee cup or doodling in your notebook. These behaviours provide comforting sensory stimulation. Sipping and chewing actions provide the reassurance you found as a suckling baby. Behaviours that involve a form of stroking are comforting.

When you see someone remove her glasses slowly and deliberately, and then repeatedly wiping the lenses (when they aren't particularly dirty), you may be right in thinking that she's stalling for time. If she then sucks or chews on the earpiece, she's indicating that she's seeking reassurance.

Studies conducted by Gerard I. Nierenberg and Henry H. Calero, pioneers in the study of non-verbal behaviour, show that some people deliberately remove and clean their glasses as many as five times an hour. Video-recordings of intense negotiation sessions show this gesture happening frequently. The people performing this action usually wanted to stall for time while considering whether they'd ask a question, request clarification or raise more opposition. Nierenberg and Calero also discovered that a person sucking on the earpiece of her glasses during negotiations subconsciously implies that some form of nourishment, probably in the form of more information, is required.

If you have a tendency to speak first and listen later, put something into your mouth to keep you quiet. This can be the earpiece of the frame of your glasses, a pencil or a glass of water. This action gives you time to think about what you're going to say before blurting out something that you may later regret.

Through the Looking Glasses

Glasses can enhance the eyes, framing them provocatively. They can hide the eyes when the lenses are tinted. They can open the doorway to communication and they can act as a road block. Some people wear glasses with non-prescription lenses for these reasons. They don't need them to improve their vision; they wear them to project an image.

Because of the number of people who wear glasses, this section on the signs to watch for can help you see things more clearly.

Stalling for time

Someone wanting to gain time before making a decision takes her glasses off, cleans the lenses and puts them back on again. Others take their glasses off and suck on the earpiece. This latter gesture frequently appears at the close of a negotiating session when someone's been asked for a decision. When the person puts her glasses back on, at this point she's indicating that she needs or wants more information. When someone takes her glasses off and cleans the lenses immediately after asking for a decision, the best thing to do is hold fire.

Scrutinising the situation

If someone peers over the top of her glasses at you, don't be surprised if you feel scrutinised. Peering down on another person conveys a critical or judgemental attitude. The glasses underscore or highlight the action.

The act of looking down on another person is intimidating, aggressive and indicates intense feelings. The person being looked at is put in a lower, sub-servient position to the person doing the looking (see Figure 11-2).

Figure 11-2:
Peering down on people can make them feel uncomfort-able.

If you wear glasses and want to pin someone down without climbing on top of her, drop your glasses on to the lower bridge of your nose and peer over them long and hard. This is a guaranteed way of making the person you're looking at feel put on the spot.

Granny-style glasses, which many people use for reading, naturally make you look over the top of them when you lift your eye from the page. This inadvertent gesture elicits negative responses, which may not have been your intention.

Sunil had recently joined a well-established team and was working outside of his comfort zone. At his performance review, he was surprised to receive feedback from peers and subordinates indicating that he was perceived as condescending and confrontational. Exploring his behaviour patterns, we noticed that rather than removing his reading glasses and looking his colleagues straight in the eye, he looks down on them over the top of his glasses. This intimidating behaviour was winning him no friends. Recognising the negative impact of his behaviour, and needing his glasses only for reading, he now makes a habit of taking them off whenever he's speaking. While he initially felt vulnerable and exposed without his glasses, he now understands that he connects better with others when he removes such barriers.

Controlling the conversation

You can use your glasses to control a conversation. Think of yourself as a conductor. When you want the attention to be on what you're saying, put your glasses on. When you want to demonstrate that you're listening, take them off. To indicate that the conversation is over, fold your glasses and put them away.

Showing resistance

Some people take their glasses off quickly in a flash of annoyance or slowly with much deliberation. Both gestures are sure signs of resistance to what's occurring. Someone rejecting a proposal may throw her glasses onto her desk.

To relieve the emotional tension, you need to change your approach so that the other person puts her glasses back on. Then the two of you together can see the situation more clearly.

Appearing cool

Sunglasses belong in the sun, not in nightclubs and meetings. Their original purpose was to protect people's eyes by blocking out light. Some celebrities and wannabes use sunglasses to keep other people from getting too close to them, and others say they wear them to protect their eyes from flashing lights. Your eyes are one of your primary means of communication. Speaking to someone who's wearing sunglasses is a bit like speaking to the Wizard of Oz. You can hear the person, but you can't see her.

Perching your sunglasses on your head creates the impression of being cool and youthful. When you park your sunglasses on your head you give the appearance of having a huge pair of doe-like eyes with enticingly enlarged pupils, mimicking the positive effect that big-eyed babies and cuddly toys have on a person.

Wearing spectacles in the office

Studies show that people wearing glasses in a business context, whether male or female, are perceived as intelligent, knowledgeable, conservative and genuine. The heavier the frames of the glasses, the more frequently these descriptions were reported. Business leaders who wear glasses tend to choose heavy frames, which may be why, in a business context, glasses can be seen as power props.

Highly decorated frames that make a fashion statement are not taken seriously in a business environment. Glasses with oversized lenses, such as those favoured by Elton John in his early days, overly decorated, coloured frames or any frames with rhinestone-encrusted branding say that you're more interested in fashion than business. In an office environment, such glasses can quickly and drastically reduce your credibility.

Frameless glasses, or those with thin, spindly frames, hold less authority than heavier-framed glasses. Because they make the wearer appear more accessible than heavy frames, frameless versions may be preferable for social situations or when you want to portray a 'good guy' image. Wear your heavier frames when you're presenting the year-end financial results, when you want to look serious, knowledgeable and in control.

Contact lenses make the pupils of your eyes appear large and appealing, moist and dilated. Your eyes look soft and sensual, which, although appropriate for a social situation, may not always be suitable in your average business context.

The perception of women who wear both glasses and make-up (discussed in the following section) is that they're smart, self-assured, urbane and outgoing.

Making It Up as You Go Along

One of the benefits of being a woman is that, unlike a man, she can enhance her image by applying make-up without drawing undue attention to herself. Whether going out on a Saturday night or coming into work on a Monday morning, the woman who has taken the time to apply her make-up appropriately is going to get noticed – and for the right reasons.

Not for women only

Archaeological finds in Iran have revealed that approximately 10,000 years ago both men and women were avid wearers of make-up. Early examples of facial cosmetics were made from colourful stones, animal skin, shells, bones and teeth. Men and women of the Kermani tribe used white powder made from lead or silver as a foundation, highlighting their cheeks with a red powder made from the hematite stone.

Both men and women wore make-up with enthusiasm. Men applied their cosmetics with such care that it was often difficult to tell them apart from the women. Surena, the fifth-century BC Iranian chieftain known for his bravery and fearlessness, used to decorate his face for battle with such finesse that even his enemies were surprised.

Although it is well-documented that men regularly wore make-up, little proof existed that the same was true for women until masks and statues were discovered in Khuzestan. These masks had eyebrows that were elongated and painted black. The lips and cheeks had a rose tint and a painted line extended from below the eyes to the eyebrows.

As personal adornment became more important, water, which the early cave-dwellers used for viewing themselves, was no longer a satisfactory solution. The Iranians discovered a material that, when melted, shaped, polished and formed into sheets, accurately reflected a person's likeness. These early mirrors were also highly decorated, often with beautiful mythological images.

Make-up at the office

Studies consistently show that business women who wear make-up advance further and faster in their careers than women who don't (perhaps because, sadly, men are still doing most of the promoting). This isn't to say that a woman should apply her make-up with a trowel for the office environment. Save that for clubbing and hot nights out. Make-up is meant to enhance a woman's image and to be applied in such a way that the wearer looks healthy, not overdone.

Cosmetics for play

At times, a guy and a gal want to put on the Ritz, strut their stuff and show the world what they're made of. Most women, and a few men, apply make-up to enhance what they've already got. They exaggerate their leisure-time look by making their lips more prominent, emphasising their eyes and gearing their clothes and accessories towards fun and frivolity.

Dressing the Part

You can't ignore the importance of your appearance and personal presentation if you want to succeed. Dressing appropriately for your shape, colouring and the part you're playing demonstrates that you care about how you present yourself. You feel confident when you know that you're well turned out. You look credible. People are drawn to the positive energy you exude when the clothes fit and the colours flatter.

Your choice of accessories and how you put them together reveal how you perceive yourself and how you want to be perceived. If you can afford to invest in high-quality items, do. They don't have to be the most expensive products on the shelf, although cost and quality often go hand in hand. What they do have to be is appropriate for the environment and reflective of you at your best.

Women's accessories

Forget about fashion and follow the styles that work best for you. Although leggings and smocked tops can look great on women at play or working in creative industries, they're out of place in a corporate environment. The same goes for short skirts and low-cut tops. These items draw attention to the wearer, which is fine for a date but not the office. The sexual messages they convey are better left outside of the office where the focus is meant to be on the task.

Excessive jewellery is also out of place at work if you want to head up the ladder. Dangly earrings are distracting, as are a wrist full of bracelets and fingers covered in rings. Stick to a few classic pieces if you want to be seen as professional. Forget that advice if you're a Vivienne Westwood fashionista however, and pile it on!

One of my first clients was a woman in her mid-twenties working as a designer for an international chemical company. Being a creative type, she went to work wearing dangly earrings, long skirts and lacy blouses. She was good at her work and couldn't understand why she wasn't getting the promotions she believed she deserved. Part of my job was to help her understand the impact her choice of clothing was having on her career. Working in a male-dominated industrial environment, her clothes and accessories were out of place. Recognising how her flawed judgement was holding her back, she agreed to leave the clothes that she believed reflected who she was at home and wear more simple and tailored clothes to work. Although she fought this change in principle, she discovered that she had several different styles of dress that she felt comfortable wearing and that reflected her at her best.

Dressing the First Lady

Much has been made of Hillary Rodham Clinton's dressing habits. Seen speaking in Congress wearing a pink blazer over a black top that rode low on her chest with a subtle V-shape pointing downwards to her bosom, the punters took note. Not that Ms Clinton was pouring out of her top like a bar-room chanteuse – she was simply nodding her head to her femininity and sexuality. Not one known to acknowledge comfortably her style and image, it was a slight surprise to see her bare this part of her body. During her husband Bill's first term in office in the early 1990s, she was photographed wearing a black Donna Karan shoulder-revealing gown, named by Karan the 'cold shoulder dress'. Karan noted that regardless of a woman's age, her shoulders remain sensuous and appealing. Throughout the Clinton years, the First Lady wore clothes that were feminine and stately, never sexy. Her second inaugural gown was by Oscar de la Renta, originally designed with cap sleeves and a wide neckline. After Clinton's alterations, the dress had long sleeves and a high, Victorian-like collar. In December 1998, at the peak of the Monica Lewinsky scandal during which it was revealed that her husband had had an affair with an intern, Hillary appeared on the cover of *Vogue* wearing another de la Renta gown, with long sleeves and a boat neck, looking bold, glamorous and regal.

Samantha Cameron, wife of British Prime Minister David Cameron, and United States First Lady Michelle Obama have become style-setters, as they take their clothing statements seriously without turning into fashionistas. And the clothing choices of Catherine, the Duchess of Cambridge, sell faster than hot cakes.

Men's accessories

The environment that you work and play in determines what's appropriate to wear. Gold chains hanging around your neck are fine if you're a DJ, bartender, rock star or gangster. If, on the other hand, you're working in industry or the professional or corporate world, leave the jewellery at home.

Accessories need to be clean and in good repair. A frayed belt, scuffed shoes and battered briefcase look unkempt, as if you can't be bothered to look after them. You're sending out the message that you don't care about your possessions enough to maintain them. This lack of attention to detail may suggest that you're lazy and can't be bothered to look after your own things.

Too much pattern on a tie confuses the eye and may draw negative responses. Wear clean and simple silk ties to the office to project a professional image.

If you want to advance in your career, dress appropriately for your body shape and colouring. Making an effort with your personal appearance, and dressing appropriately for your environment, is a vital career skill. Whether you're working in advertising, the music industry or investment banking, if you want to move up the corporate ladder, look at the people who have the jobs above you and note how they dress. You can also turn to an image consultant to help you find the shapes and colours that suit you best.

Part IV

Putting the Body into Social and Business Context

Find out more about Body Language at www.dummies.com/extras/bodylanguage

In this part . . .

✔ Find out where to place and position yourself in the boardroom for greatest effect.

✔ Uncover how to read and reveal signs of interest and dismissal in the dating arena.

✔ Learn how to engage with a possible romantic partner.

✔ Discover body language pitfalls and behaviors to avoid.

✔ Utilise tips that can improve your relationships, both at home and in business.

Chapter 12

Being Aware of Territorial Rights and Regulations

*I*f you've ever bumped into a stranger on the high street, been squashed on a rush hour tube or been kissed by someone you'd rather hadn't kissed you, you've experienced space invasion. Unless invited, it feels a bit creepy when someone gets too close, whereas it feels so much better when the distance is right.

In this chapter, you look at the different areas of space around you. You find out why what feels comfortable at ten paces feels differently at one. You also discover why cohorts sit side by side and adversaries sit face to face. Finally, you discover how the way that you position yourself, whether upright, supine or simply off kilter, impacts on your gestures, movements and the impression you make.

Understanding the Effect of Space

The way you fill and move within space impacts on your thoughts, your feelings and the way that others perceive you. People who know where to position themselves in relation to someone else control the interaction. They know when to get up close and personal, and when to back off. They know the different implications between standing so close to another person that you can feel that person's breath, and standing so far away that you have to squint to see one another. By knowing where and how to place yourself in relation to another person, you can consciously control that person's perception of you.

Territorial perimeters aren't just a matter of manners. Foreign invaders, rival gangs, trespassers, burglars, pushy bullies and aggressive drivers all know that their invasion into another's territory can be met with varying degrees of resistance. Zoologist Desmond Morris sees humans as competitive as well as co-operative creatures. As humans strive for dominance, systems must be put in place to avoid chaos. Territorial perimeters, whereby everyone knows and respects one another's space, represent a co-operative system.

A man is said to be king of his castle. As reigning sovereign, whether your castle is a flat in the heart of the city, a country farmhouse or a caravan, you know that you've the right to be dominant in your own territory. And everyone else has the right to be dominant in his. When someone enters your space without being invited, you may feel a little edgy. Whether someone is subject to fighter planes attacking from above or his mother bursting into his room, the person whose space has been invaded is probably going to fight back.

Although you may feel perfectly calm, confident and comfortable in one environment, your feelings may change in another. Say that you work in your own office. You feel comfortable and in control of your environment because you're in familiar surroundings. Then you're called into your boss's office. Suddenly, the comfort level changes. You're now entering someone else's territory and the control shifts from you to the person whose space you've penetrated. Your body language changes from dominant to submissive without you even realising it.

Knowing Your Space

Humans have circles of space around them, which range from no space at all (touching) to too far away to touch. As with animals, humans protect their territory by following accepted codes of behaviour. Whereas birds sing to proclaim their dominance over a particular part of a hedgerow, and dogs lift their legs to stake claim to a lamppost, humans indicate through their body movements what they perceive to be their territory, and to what degree others may penetrate it.

The five zones

In his book, *The Hidden Dimension*, the American anthropologist Edward T. Hall, defines *proxemics* as the study of the human use of space within the context of culture. Understanding that cultural influences impact upon how people move within their space, and the amount of space a person is comfortable with, Hall divides space into five distinct areas. The relationship you have with another person determines how near you allow that person to come to you. (You can find out more about culture and space in Chapter 15.)

Hall demarcates five concentric spatial zones that affect behaviour:

- **Close Intimate (0–15 centimetres/0–6 inches):** This space is saved for lovers, close friends and family members. Close Intimate is a position for the most intimate behaviours, including touching, embracing and kissing.

- **Intimate (15–45 centimetres/6–18 inches):** Lovers, friends and relatives are welcome in this space. The distance is comfortable and secure. If a stranger, someone you don't know well or someone you don't like enters this space you feel uncomfortable, and your body reacts protectively.

- **Personal (45 centimetres–1.2 metres/18 inches–4 feet):** For most Westerners, this distance is the most comfortable for personal conversations. If you step too far into the space, the other person may feel threatened. If you stand outside of the space, the other person can feel rebuffed.

- **Social (1.2–3.6 metres/4–12 feet):** When you're in a business-based interaction with shop assistants and tradespeople, this area is where you feel most comfortable. If you stand within the inner ring, you're perceived as being too familiar. If you stand outside the outer ring, you're perceived as rude and stand-offish.

- **Public (3.6 metres +/12 feet +):** If you're speaking to an audience in a formal setting, the distance between yourself and the first row is in the public space. Any closer and you feel intruded upon; your communication feels cramped. Any farther away and you feel distanced from your listeners, making it harder to connect with them.

The distance between two people reveals their relationship and how they feel about each other.

Other territorial positions

In addition to your space bubble's five concentric circles, you have another set of territorial positions, private and personal to you. You have:

- **Inner space:** Your internal thoughts and feelings.

- **Immediate outer space:** Friends, family, close colleagues.

- **Public arena:** The larger world in which you interact with an assortment of people.

People who enjoy their own company and prefer to keep to themselves have few requirements. They live quieter, simpler lives than those who surround themselves with people and fill their time with social activities. People who live lives that involve lavish entertaining need space to accommodate all the individuals and the accompanying accessories that go with a socially active life. Their personalities require a broad expanse of space.

A person who has many people taking up much of his time occasionally draws into his inner space for quiet contemplation. Executives, politicians, busy parents and professionals – as well as the ubiquitous celebrity – need time alone to recharge their batteries. Big personalities fill their space with their movements. For example, they hold their arms farther from their bodies than do quieter people. Their gestures are definite and they move with purpose. People whose personalities are more internally directed use fewer and smaller gestures. (See Figure 12-1.)

Figure 12-1: Big personalities require more space than quieter people.

Space also works in proportion to status. Presidents, senior partners and chief executives require a copious amount of resources, including space, in a practical sense and to fulfil both their own and others' expectations regarding status.

Reality TV?

The media has brought strangers into our lives to such an extent that some people believe that they know, or have a personal relationship with, actors and performers. Actors frequently tell stories of being treated as if they were the character they portray rather than themselves. Actors playing doctors are often approached by fans asking for medical advice. The fans infiltrate these actors' private space based on their perceptions of them garnered from their public space.

Television comes directly into a person's private space and brings its characters with it. People believe that they have a relationship with an actor because they've spent time together in the home.

Growing up in Palm Beach, Florida, a town of great opulence and wealth, Paula often saw 12-bedroom mansions occupied by a family of four. The size of people's homes reflected their status – large homes indicated large incomes and large personalities. Small homes indicated lower income and lower status. Paula's mother's two-bedroom house cosily accommodated her, her mother and her younger sister. Paula's mother was divorced, living on a limited income, didn't entertain much and had little use for a lot of space. Half a mile away was the winter home of the late President John F. Kennedy. His home was huge in comparison, with high walls surrounding the property and bodyguards circling the grounds. The president's position of power, status and authority came with more needs than those of a young divorcee on a restricted budget.

You can tell a person's status by how much personal space he requires. The more space expected and offered, the higher the status.

How you manage your space determines how others respond. By being clear about how far a person may come into your territory, you make it easier for others to recognise your boundaries and behave accordingly.

Using Space

Whether you're protecting your property, demonstrating dominance or showing submission, the way that you move in your space indicates your attitude. Touch an object and you're saying, 'This is mine.' Turn away from it and you're saying, 'No, thanks.'

Demonstrating ownership

When you use your hands to lead and guide another person, you're taking control. Your behaviour becomes dominant and protective as you touch what is yours and what you value. When you lead another person by the hand, when you guide someone by placing your hand on his back or when you stand close to your partner and put your hand on his upper arm, you're demonstrating that you own or are in control of that piece of property.

Victoria Beckham, Emma Thompson and Angelina Jolie are masters of the proprietorial pose. When they stand close to their husbands and place a hand on their man's chest or upper arm, the signal says, 'Private property. Keep off.' Prince William is also frequently seen placing his hand on his wife's lower back as he guides and protects her.

Following Millie's acceptance of his marriage proposal, James has struggled to keep his hands off his soon-to-be wife. When they're with their friends and families, James holds Millie's hand, places his arm around her and guides her through crowded rooms with a gently placed hand on her lower back. Likewise, Millie places her hand on James's upper arm and chest and frequently leans her body into his. Clearly James and Millie consider that they belong to one another.

If you want to intimidate someone, touch an object that belongs to him. By entering his territory without an invitation and touching what's his you're demonstrating dominance.

If someone you don't know comes to your home or office, you can demonstrate ownership and dominance by leaning against your door frame in a proprietorial manner.

Showing submission

Entering a foreign environment frequently causes people to feel uncomfortable and to act in a submissive way. They wait to be invited to sit, refrain from touching objects in the space and contain their gestures. As soon as they feel at ease, their body language opens up.

Michelle's boss, Nick, suggested that she and I work together to develop her influencing skills. A potential high flyer, Michelle's body language was letting her down. Rather than projecting confidence and credibility by owning her space, she ducked her head, hunched her shoulders and pulled into herself. She came across as doubtful and insecure. When Michelle recognised the impact of her body language, she took the necessary steps towards change.

If you purposely want to show submission, close your body by pulling your arms in close and keeping your hands to yourself. If, on the other hand, you want to convey dominance, use expansive gestures.

Guarding your space

In addition to clarifying ownership of people and possessions, people jealously guard the space that immediately surrounds them. Humans create an invisible bubble around themselves within which they function. Placing objects between yourself and others, spreading your arms across your desk and wrapping your arms around yourself are all ways of guarding your personal space.

In normal circumstances, most people respect one another's personal territory. Sometimes, however, space invasion is unavoidable. When someone invades your territory without your permission, you feel uncomfortable. No problem if you know the person and have invited him in. Not so good if you neither know him nor want him there. Fortunately, even when your personal space is invaded, you can still find ways to limit the intrusion as much as possible. Consider these examples:

- Turning your head away
- Avoiding eye contact
- Pulling into yourself

At the end of the first day of the conference, Liz and Ben were discussing business over dinner. Matt, a larger-than-life character and conference attendee, saw Liz and Ben and tried to gain their attention. The closer he came to their table, gesturing grandly in recognition, the more the pair kept to themselves. They turned their bodies towards one another, leaned their heads closer and continued their conversation without ever making eye contact with their colleague. Later they saw Matt sitting by himself, by which time they were ready to invite him to join them for coffee.

Wait to be invited into the Close Intimate zone to avoid causing offence, discomfort or embarrassment.

Revealing your comfort level

How near, how far and at what angle you position yourself in relation to someone else indicates how relaxed you feel with that person. Sitting comfortably among friends, you probably sit close to one another. Your body leans towards them, and your eyes are engaged. Among people you'd rather avoid, your body angles away. You avoid eye contact and pull back. You're making it clear that you don't want to connect.

Putting distance and objects between yourself and another person can make for an awkward conversation. Stand too far away and you may come across as stand-offish. Get too close and you may be perceived as intrusive. Some people like to put objects and distance between themselves and others. It makes them feel protected and gives them the opportunity to observe someone from afar. Others like to get up close right away. They want to burrow in and connect.

If you turn your shoulder on another person, you're showing him that you don't want to know. Your shoulder acts as a barrier, keeping the two of you at arm's length. When someone turns his back on you, he's shutting you out.

When Mary arrived at the conference centre where she was scheduled to speak, she was surprised to discover that, rather than speaking in a small meeting room as she'd expected, her session had been moved to the large auditorium. As the delegates entered the room, they sat at the back and slumped in their seats, leaving rows of empty chairs between Mary and themselves. When Mary encouraged them to come to the front of the room, they declined, stating that only directors and senior managers sit in the front rows. Mary stepped down from the stage, walked to the middle of the auditorium and spoke from there. By meeting them on their territory, she built trust with the delegates and was soon able to get them to come to the front of the room. When she got them to pretend to be directors, they laughed and sat up with a sense of pride. (For more about building trust and creating rapport, pick up a copy of *Persuasion & Influence For Dummies* by Elizabeth Kuhnke (Wiley).)

Your personal space is bound to be infiltrated at times, such as on a crowded bus, in a packed lift or at a busy bar. Except for those who enjoy pressing the flesh, most people make an effort to pull apart in crowded conditions. If there's no way out, you're okay as long as only shoulders and upper arms make contact. If someone goes further, feel free to scream!

Giving the cold shoulder

The origins of the expression 'giving someone the cold shoulder' are disputed. It may have come from the practice of providing welcome guests to one's home with a hot meal and grudgingly giving unwelcome visitors a cold shoulder of mutton, if they were lucky. In Sir Walter Scott's *St Ronan's Well* (1824), the writer remarks: 'I must tip him the cauld shouther, or he will be pestering me eternally.'

Maintaining your personal space

For a country lad now living in the big city, crowds and confined spaces are a challenge. Comfortable with big skies, lots of land and quiet forest shelters, the concrete jungles of major metropolitan areas require an attitude adjustment. Skyscrapers are a far cry from wide open spaces.

When defining your personal space consider the amount of space you need to feel comfortable. To identify when you transition from feeling comfortable to feeling constrained, look at your gestures: when you're feeling free, your gestures are more fluid.

The next time you're at the doctor's, or hairdresser's, or are waiting at the boarding gate for a flight, observe where people sit. Normally, you find a row or more of chairs. The first person to sit usually plops himself down at one end or the other. The next person to enter sits halfway down the row. Both are at a socially comfortable distance from one another – neither too close to appear invasive nor too far away to seem stand-offish. The third person sits at the free end, the fourth between the middle and end position, and so on until eventually someone is forced to sit next to another person.

When people queue in Britain, they envelop themselves in an invisible space bubble. Each person has his own bubble and, on a good day, everyone respects each other's territory. Interestingly, crowded conditions, such as those found on the rush hour bus, tube or train, lead people to ignore one another. According to psychologist Robert Sommer, in crowded conditions people imagine that someone invading their personal space is inanimate. Therefore, no need exists to relay any social signals. Individuals stand or sit still when they're ignoring their surroundings. The larger the crowd, the less individual body movement. People's faces take on a blank and expressionless look indicating that communication is not being sought. They avoid eye contact by staring at the ceiling or the floor.

Considering Seating Arrangements

Seating positions should never happen by chance. When planning a dinner party or a special event, good hosts spend a great deal of energy deciding where their guests should sit. The position in which you're placed reflects your status, and impacts upon people's perception of you.

If you're at a dinner where place cards aren't in evidence, notice who's drawn to sit next to whom. Where people place themselves in relation to you signals their attitude toward you, their view of themselves in relation to you and the level of co-operation you can expect from them.

Before you seat yourself, or direct people to where you want them to sit, think about the individual interactions you want to facilitate.

Speaking in a relaxed setting

Sitting with the corner of a rectangular table between you and another person encourages relaxed, friendly conversation (see Figure 12-2). You can clearly see one another and open room exists for gesturing. The corner of the desk serves as a subtle barrier in case something's needed. This position also denotes an even division of space with both people on an equal footing.

Figure 12-2: Sitting in the corner position diffuses tension and promotes a positive attitude.

Co-operating

When you work on a task with another person, or if you find that you and someone else think along the same lines, you're more than likely to find yourselves sitting side by side (see Figure 12-3). Most people intuitively sit in this configuration when they're working on a joint project with someone else. This position enables you to look easily at your partner and get a revealing close up of their facial expressions and body movements. Make sure you're not invading the other person's space. Unless, of course, you've been invited. When you introduce a third person to the seating arrangement, things get interesting. To begin with, where you place yourself in relation to the other two determines how everyone at the table is perceived. By sitting next to person number one – establishing the co-operating position – or at his side with the corner of the table between you, you're showing the new kid on the block that you and person number one are aligned. From this position you can speak to and ask questions of the newcomer on the first person's behalf. In sales, this position is called 'siding with the opposition'.

Figure 12-3:
Sitting side
by side
creates
feelings of
cooperation.

Whenever you're influencing people, always aim to see their point of view, to make them feel at ease in your company and to ensure that they feel good about working with you. You gain more co-operation by sitting in the corner, or co-operative position, than you do by placing yourself in the combative position, in which conversations are shorter and sharper. (You can find out more about strategic positioning and persuading in *Persuasion & Influence For Dummies* by Elizabeth Kuhnke (Wiley).)

Laying it on the table

Different table shapes and sizes affect mood, intention and outcomes. If you want to create an informal relaxed atmosphere in which people feel equally powerful and prominent, place them at a round table. Square tables are usually found in the company cafeteria and are good for having short, direct conversations. A rectangular desk is effectively used for business activities, short conversations and reprimands. If you want to offer a dominant position to a favoured few, seat them at the ends of a rectangular table. Whichever table you pick, make sure the high-status individuals sit facing the door, not with their backs to it.

Combating and defending

Placing yourself across a table from another person sets up a barrier and a hostile, or defensive, atmosphere. Standing or sitting directly face to face with someone else indicates that a challenge or confrontation may be imminent. If you find yourself in this position, don't be surprised if you fold your hands at chest level. You're just preparing yourself for what's coming next.

In a business scenario, if you want to set up a challenging or competitive atmosphere, sit people directly across the table from one another. On the other hand, in a social situation, such as at a dinner party or in a restaurant, this is a positive position because it enables conversation.

If you want to reprimand someone or demonstrate who's boss, sit directly across your desk or table from him. If you want to be perceived as an active listener, fair-minded and unlikely to show favouritism, come out from behind your desk.

Keeping to yourself

If two people don't want to interact with one another, they sit diagonally across the table, at the farthest ends of the table. This position is typical in a library, when two people share a reading table.

The expression 'diametrically opposed' comes from this seating position and implies lack of interest, indifference or hostility. If you want to keep the discussions open between you and others, mind the gap and come a little bit closer.

Creating equality

King Arthur's Round Table empowered his knights with equal authority and status. No one was in a lesser, weaker or more dominant position than anyone else. Each knight was able to claim the same amount of table territory as his compatriot, and everyone could be seen easily. The circle is considered a symbol of unity and strength, and sitting in a circle promotes this effect.

Although the model of King Arthur's Round Table promotes equality, who sits where in relation to the perceived leader denotes positions of status and power. The position in which people place themselves affects the dynamics of power within a group. The people sitting on either side of the person of higher status (and holding the most power) hold the next level of power, the individual on the right of the high-status person being granted more power than the individual on the left. The farther away from the high-status individual, the more diminished the power. Whoever sits directly across from the person with the highest status is placed in the competitive position and is most likely to be the one who causes most trouble.

To connect with other people and involve them in a discussion, stand or sit in an open position and look everyone in the eye as you speak.

You can identify the distribution of power within a family by its dining table, presuming that family was free to choose any shape of table it wanted. Families that encourage their members to share their opinions and points of view prefer round tables. Families with an authoritarian at the helm opt for rectangular tables.

Orientating Yourself

Stand up, and you move and think one way. Lie down, and you move and think in another. Depending on whether you're standing to attention or slouching in your chair, you find yourself thinking and behaving differently. How you position yourself determines and sends out signals of how you view the world. The world, in turn, responds in its own way to the signals you send.

Horizontally

Someone who's lying out flat or slumped over his desk or curled up in a ball risks insulting his colleagues and companions. If these people expect you to demonstrate polite attentiveness, you're going to have to change your posture and show that you're alert.

If you're extremely dominant, or among exceptionally good friends in an informal setting, you can get away with being horizontal. In the first case, you don't care what people think and say, and in the second case you know that you're safe with friends and trusted family members.

People in a supine position find that their thinking process is expansive – their thoughts are free to meander and flow. In an upright position, thoughts are sharper, clearer and more coherent. You need both styles of thinking in order to explore all possibilities fully.

People's posture has become increasingly relaxed. Before the Second World War, people behaved more formally. Their clothes were structured and restrictive. After the war, fashions changed. With the advent of jeans, track suits and leggings as wardrobe staples, people's gestures and body placements reflect the new, relaxed atmosphere. Individuals can now move with more ease and less restriction than their forefathers could because of the flexibility and freedom their clothes permit.

To carry out this little exercise, you need a partner. Ask the other person to lie on the floor while you stand over him, accentuating the height difference. Give the person lying on the floor as loud and powerful a telling off as you can. Change positions, with you now lying on the floor looking up at your partner standing over you. Repeat the reprimand. Don't be surprised if your formerly forceful voice now lacks authority.

Vertically

A person positioning himself lower than you is demonstrating his subordinance. Someone standing above you is sending dominant signals. Whether you position yourself high or low, you're telling people where you stand in the pecking order. Kings and queens are referred to as 'Your Highness'. Crooks, robbers and other unsavoury characters are labelled 'low life'. People talk about the 'upper classes' and the 'lower classes'. The higher up you go, the more perceived status and authority you have. The lower down the scale, the less influence you wield.

Lowering yourself

In order to make himself appear small and deferential, a man removes his hat or tips his head when meeting someone in a position of higher authority. Women curtsey in a sign of deference and respect when meeting royalty. Men and women genuflect or bow their heads upon entering a church, and kneel for prayer. Beggars sit on the ground. When their eyes look downwards, they're at their lowest.

Short people suffer the indignity of being looked down upon. Because they're shorter than others, their credibility often gets overlooked. Short women are particularly susceptible to interruption and being talked over in meetings. In order to make up for their lack of height, short people must gesture and behave with strength, command authority and demonstrate gravitas. Filling their space by standing up, holding their arms slightly away from their bodies and gesturing with clarity and focus creates an image of confidence, control and commitment. High heels and lipstick help, too. (See Chapter 11 for make-up tips.)

The more subordinate a person feels, the lower he positions his body. When a student or employee enters your office and you sit while he stands, you're demonstrating your power. The commanding officer doesn't rise when the junior lieutenant enters the officers' mess.

Conversely, sometimes lowering yourself can raise your status. When you flop into a chair in front of the neighbourhood bully, you're demonstrating that you're at ease in that person's territory. By touching his belongings and behaving in unrestricted ways, you're indicating that, although someone else may have a claim on the environment, you're more than comfortable taking over. This behaviour can be perceived as dominant or even aggressive.

Japanese businesses instruct staff members to bow at different angles, depending on the status of the customer. A customer who's 'browsing' receives a 15-degree bow whereas the customer who's buying is awarded up to a 45-degree bow. (See more about cultural influences on body language in Chapter 15.)

Elevating yourself

An Olympic gold medallist stands on a podium above the other medal winners and the judge sits above his court. To live in the penthouse is to live above, and look down upon, the crowd. People in 'high places' are looked up to and seen as superior. It would be most unusual to find the senior partner's or chief executive's office in the basement.

Clients frequently ask me how they can project an elevated image when they're not tall. One female client who is barely 5 feet in her stocking feet tells me that she pretends that she's tall. Instead of straining and struggling to gain attention, she puts her efforts into visualising herself as a tall, slim woman, who fills her space and commands attention. By acting the part, she radiates the appearance. And she always wears high heels at work!

Because of the nature of their work, many of my clients appear on television. One of my shorter male clients consistently received feedback that, although he was knowledgeable, on camera he lacked credibility and gravitas. Reviewing his tapes, I devised a strategy for future public appearances to assure increased authority and presence. If he had to stand behind a lectern, it was to be low enough for his chest to show. Cameras were to be angled to give him the appearance of greater height. I coached him in speaking directly to the camera so that his viewing public felt that he was speaking to them individually and he wore dark, single-breasted suits that elongated his body. His television performances have improved dramatically, and he demonstrates increased comfort and gravitas.

Think tall

Except for movie stars, who tend to be small although the screen makes them look big, tall people experience more success, better health and longer lives than short people. Research teams lead by University of Florida Professor Timothy A. Judge and Professor Daniel M. Cable of the University of North Carolina analysed data from four independent projects in the United States and the UK, following approximately 8,500 participants from their teens through adulthood. These and other related research projects show that tall people have greater self-esteem and social confidence than shorter people. Tall people are perceived to be more authoritative and in command. The physical action of looking up towards someone elicits feelings of respect. The person in the limelight responds with feelings of confidence. Looking down on another person instils a sense of superiority on the viewer's part and submission on the person being looked at. These findings show that women who opt for high heels and short men who slide lifts in their shoes understand the power and impact of height.

Asymmetrically

If you're sitting at your desk and your left elbow is resting on your table top while your right hand is placed on your hip, you're sitting in an *asymmetrical pose*. Unlike a symmetrical pose in which corresponding body parts mirror one another, the asymmetrical position is two different poses indicating two different mindsets. Straight, symmetrical posture is clear in its intent. Asymmetrical positions hold intrigue. Because of its complexity, asymmetrical posture reveals more about a person than symmetrical posture, in which the two sides of the body reflect each other.

Someone standing stiffly upright, with his mouth closed and his eyes staring straight ahead is giving little away. Someone whose body has fluidity and movement is interesting and expressive. When your torso and limbs are in contrasting positions, your body is more expressive and effusive than when in a poker-like position.

Balancing the asymmetrical body

Studies of neuromuscular therapy and yoga provide insights into how humans stand, sit and gesture. The bottom line is that your body movements impact on your ability to live a healthy and balanced life. Yoga practitioners aim to create harmony by synchronising their body's outer shell and their inner soul. They call this synchronisation 'the dawning of the light of the spirit'. The diagonal pull of gravity that results from activities such as carrying heavy bags, sitting on one buttock, lifting heavy boxes and hoisting children onto a shoulder puts your body into asymmetrical positions. Some sets of muscles work overtime, while other sets slacken, leading to discomfort, misalignment and a body all akimbo.

In his poem, 'Boy and Top', Mexican poet and Nobel Laureate Octavio Paz writes, 'Each time he spins it / It lands, precisely / At the centre of the world.' Like a top, the body has a centre of gravity that it continuously seeks as your body's muscles work to keep you aligned. Because no one is perfectly symmetrical, your muscles pull in one direction or the other, side to side, front to back, away from, or towards, your centre. Any misalignment in the body causes one part to overstretch while another part underper-

forms. As the muscles pull and contract, they create an illusion of symmetry in an effort to create balance.

Back pain is common for couch potatoes and marathon runners alike. When the upper-right thoracic muscles contract because of a slight curvature of the spine, the lower-left lumbar muscles also contract because they're pulled in a counter direction. So that's what's happening! Pilates, ballet and yoga are safe forms of exercise for stretching and strengthening the muscles. As the practitioners say, 'First you lengthen, then you strengthen.' No matter what your age, marital status or financial worth, a fit, firm and flexible body can be yours.

Chapter 13

Rating, Dating and Mating: Courting with Your Body

*T*ry flirting without using body language. Go on, give it a go. Surprise, surprise! It can't be done. You simply can't convey romantic interest without the body getting into the act. To play a really successful game of flirtation, your body has to speak what your mouth mustn't say.

When you're feeling good about yourself you focus your eyes, position your mouth and manoeuvre your shoulders, hips and hands in ways that send out signals saying, 'Check me out! I think you're hot!' After you get a person's attention, you shift gears to hold onto your target's interest and move the attraction to another level. Having captured and conquered the unsuspecting or equally interested party, your body moves in new ways demonstrating comfort, ease and familiarity. Observe how long-term lovers anticipate one another's actions by the way they move in sync with their partners.

How you move your body exposes how ready you are for a bit of romance, how attractive you feel and how interested you are in another's advances: some courtship signals are deliberate, others are unconscious. In this chapter, I explore the wide, wild world of courtship behaviour and explain how it can put a big smile on your face.

Attracting Someone's Attention

Watching people when they're in the company of someone they find attractive is fascinating. The stomach gets pulled in, whether it needs to be or not, slumping is exchanged for an upright stance, displays of health and vitality are conveyed through a lively walk, muscle tone becomes heightened and a youthful appearance replaces the ravages of time or too many late nights.

Men stand taller, thrust up their chins and expand their chests, making them look like the king of the jungle. Women tilt their heads, flick their hair and expose their wrists and necks, demonstrating vulnerability and submissiveness (check out Figure 13-1).

When you find another person attractive, your eyes dilate and you can do nothing to stop it (check out the later section 'Recognising dilated pupils: A universal sign of attraction' for details). If things go to plan, the recipient of your gaze unconsciously responds in a similar way and the excitement begins.

Figure 13-1:
Both individuals are expressing sexual tension and interest in one another.

Vicky is a particularly attractive woman. A former model, she's remained trim and fit, wears just enough make-up to highlight her perfectly formed features and moves with purpose and energy. One day, Vicky and I went out for lunch. As we walked through the restaurant, I noticed a man tracking her while continuing his conversation with his partner. Although he didn't move his head, the muscles around his mouth raised, he slightly adjusted his seating position while expanding his chest, his eyes widened and he watched her out of the corner of his eye until she passed. After she was out of his line of vision, his body reverted to its original position and he continued his conversation as if nothing had happened.

Richard went for a walk one day after work. Worried about business and feeling overwhelmed by his responsibilities, he walked slowly, looking at the ground in front of him with his arms across his chest, hunched shoulders and a bent head. At one point he looked up and noticed an attractive middle-aged woman coming towards him with a smile on her face and a bounce in her step. Without thinking, he adjusted his posture to reflect hers by lifting his chest, squaring his shoulders and establishing eye contact. His energy heightened and he began feeling lighter and more positive as he noticed the woman continuing to smile at him. Before he knew it, he was smiling back. Although tempted to stop and engage her in conversation, he thought of his wife and young family at home and walked on by with a hint of a grin and feeling more willing and able to face life's challenges, as he reflected on his and the mystery woman's brief flirtation.

Putting a spring in your step, a twinkle in your eye and a smile on your face makes you look attractive, feel appealing and come across as hot.

When you're rating someone's attractiveness and in turn are being rated, messages that convey interest, keenness and compatibility are relayed through posture, gestures and facial expressions. Regardless of age, fitness and capabilities, no one's immune to checking out other people.

Here are some things to keep in mind as you go courting:

✔ **Women usually make the first move:** Research shows that 90 per cent of the time women initiate the first move in the mating game. I can hear my mother now: 'Nice girls don't show that they're interested. They wait for the man to make the first move.' Well, apparently not. Women go for it. Men simply respond. Through a series of subtle expressions and movements (including covert smiles, eye contact and gestures that accentuate their femininity), women send out signals of interest. If a woman's a good flirt, the man in her sights thinks that he's taking the lead although in fact he's merely dancing to her tune.

The rating, dating, mating ritual is a complicated process, rather like ballroom dancing in which you follow a series of steps, moving in time with your partner. If a woman is to succeed in the ritual, she has to count on the man to decode the signals she's sending out. For a man to succeed in this game, he has to recognise, interpret and respond to the signals correctly. When a man deduces that a woman's interested and shows his interest too, the woman gives him the green light to move to the next stage. Unless she's just a tease, in which case walk away.

✔ **Men aren't good at reading the signals properly:** Men tend to misinterpret friendly behaviour for sexual interest because men have 10 to 20 times more testosterone than women. *Testosterone* encourages dominant behaviour, increases sexual interest and rises in the face of a challenge. Heightened levels of testosterone can make a man hunger for an evening of lust, when all the woman had in mind was dinner.

✔ **Availability counts more than beauty:** Men pursue a woman who may not be the most sexually attractive as long as she conveys her availability. A beautiful woman with all the right physical attributes is left on the shelf if she doesn't appear to be interested. In a contest between looks and signals, signals win hands down.

Going courting: The five stages

When you see someone you want to get to know better, you go through a predictable pattern of courtship. The first order of business is to get that person's attention:

Being sexually appealing *and* available

Research consistently shows that men are attracted to healthy-looking women who demonstrate sexual availability. Both men and women are drawn to athletic bodies. Men see such a body as a sign of good health and an ability to provide them with children. Women see lithe and muscular bodies as signs of power, signalling the men's ability to provide for and protect them.

Men are drawn to women with childlike faces, including doe eyes, petite noses, bee-stung lips and full cheeks. These facial characteristics elicit fatherly, protective emotions in most men. Women tend to prefer men with mature faces that show they have the ability to protect and defend. Strong jaws, large brows and a prominent nose appeal to most women.

The good news for women is that, although good looks may initially give her a slight edge over her competitors, a woman doesn't have to be a natural beauty to attract a handsome man. What she needs to do to bag her prey is display availability signals. Although you may need surgery to create a tilted nose or a rose-bud mouth, and you can't always count on the results being what you hoped for, all a woman has to do to signal her availability is find out and practise the signals.

Granted, some women may be disturbed, if not appalled, to know that modern men are initially more attracted to a woman based on her looks and her sensuality than on her ability to discuss world affairs, balance a cheque book, play the piano or stuff a turkey. But modern research concurs with what painters, poets and writers have alluded to for thousands of years – a woman's ability to make a man feel excited and filled with a sense of mystery appeals more to him than any family trust fund or intellectual capabilities she may possess.

1. Eye contact.

The woman looks across a crowded room. She spots someone she finds attractive. She waits for that person to notice her. She looks the person directly in the eye for 3–5 seconds and then looks away. The object of her interest watches to see what she does next. She establishes eye contact again, and then at least one more time. When a man sees a woman who catches his eye, he glances at her body first. After he makes eye contact with her, he slightly narrows his eyes and holds the gaze somewhat longer than he normally would, indicating his interest.

2. Smile.

The woman flashes a fleeting smile or two – a hint of a smile with a promise of things to come rather than a toothy grin. The man needs to respond to this signal or the woman thinks that he's not interested and moves her sights. If interested, the man establishes eye contact with the woman and lifts his chin slightly as he smiles, inviting her to engage with him.

3. Preen.

The muscles of both men and women become slightly tensed. Her posture straightens, accentuating her physical attributes. If seated, she crosses her legs to show them off. If she's standing, she shifts her hips and tilts her head to expose her neck. She plays with her hair, runs her tongue over her lips and adjusts her clothes and jewellery. A man may straighten his stance, pull in his stomach, push out his chest, adjust his clothes and touch his hair. Both point their bodies towards one another.

4. Talk.

The man walks over to the woman, making it look as though he's the initiator, and offers her a few chat-up lines. Having given him permission to approach by the signals she's sent through her body language, a woman then waits for the man to begin the conversation.

For a man, initiating a conversation with someone you find attractive can be a minefield. Here are a couple of tips to help you navigate it safely:

- If you misread the signal and sense that you're about to be ignored or rebuffed, pretend that you just want to ask the other person about unrelated subjects, such as the time, what she's drinking or who won the evening's football match. You may sound a bit of an idiot but at least you aren't given a brusque brush off in response to a clumsy pass.

- If, after a few minutes of speaking, the woman yawns, frowns or sneers, she's clearly not interested. If she crosses her arms, puts her hands in her pockets and avoids your gaze, you may as well walk away.

5. Touch.

If a woman is interested in a man, she may create an opportunity for him to touch her arm lightly. When both people are happy with the touching process, they increase the amount. When people aren't interested in taking things further, they avoid touching. If you're going to touch someone, begin by touching her on the arm, which is less intimate than touching someone on the hand. If she doesn't pull away when you touch her on the arm, you can progress to her hand. If she continues to allow you to touch her, you may place your hand on her back or around her waist. A woman who doesn't want to be touched pulls away.

You may not have thought that so much choreography exists in the initial stages of courtship and the steps may seem incidental. They're not. Without going through these five stages, which may only take a few moments at most, the courting ritual stops before it begins. (Check out the *Body Language For Dummies* app to see these stages in action.)

Highlighting gender differences

People who want to attract the attention of the opposite sex emphasise their gender to make themselves sexually attractive and appealing. Women pout, arch their backs and lean forward, bringing their arms close to their bodies to push their breasts together to create a deep and appealing cleavage (see Figure 13-2). Men stand tall and expand their chests. (Check out the later section 'Showing That You're Available' for more on male and female courting gestures.)

Unless you want to be perceived as a hot totty or aggressively on the make, keep your gestures muted in the early stages of the courtship process. Otherwise you may find your signs of possible interest being interpreted as signals of immediate availability.

Walking, wiggling and swaggering

The way you walk reveals your interest. Both men and women take on youthful characteristics when seeking the other's attention. They create the impression that they possess an unlimited source of energy by the way they vigorously bounce along. Unlimited energy can be sexy because it indicates the promise of being a tireless mate.

When a woman wants to indicate her interest, she rolls her hips and swings her arms further back, exposing her soft and supple flesh. Because women have wider hips than men, as well as a wider crotch gap between their legs, they're able to walk with a rolling motion that draws attention to the pelvic

Figure 13-2:
By arching her back, pursing her lips and pushing her breasts forward, the woman's showing she wants the man's attention, while his open stance indicates he's open to her advances.

area. Men, being built differently, can't emulate this walk and find the difference sexually appealing. If you've seen the film *Some Like It Hot* you're sure to remember the scene where Marilyn Monroe walks down the railway platform, while Jack Lemmon and Tony Curtis stare at her undulating bottom in awe. As Jack Lemmon says, this remarkable movement was 'like Jell-o on springs'.

Women in advertisements and commercials – especially those advertising fashion and beauty products – are often directed to roll their hips and lead with their pelvis to draw attention to the products they're promoting. The women watching want to emulate the model's movements while the men watch in wonder. Whatever the reaction, the movements create increased product awareness leading to increased sales, which is the bottom line for the ad agency and the client.

Some men swagger, thinking that it makes them look strong and domineering. They swing their arms across their bodies, elbows bent, hands at waist height, turning their arms inward showing just how manly they are. However, men who swagger tend to come across as boastful and arrogant, while men who stride with purpose, with a firm and relaxed gait, appear confident and assertive.

When Igor, a personal trainer and bodyguard, walks into a room, no one doubts his confidence and ability to assert himself. A former world champion extreme fighter, and serving member in both the Russian Army and police force, this man means business. Quiet in speech and manner and demonstrating a no-nonsense attitude, Igor commands respect *and* attention. The women at his gym openly flirt with this muscled-man, behaviour that confuses him. Unconsciously cracking his knuckles and flexing his pecs, he doesn't understand why women half his age find him attractive. I wonder what he'd do if he knew that women twice his age find him attractive, too. A fit and firm body is a sign of strength. What woman – or man, for that matter – isn't drawn to that!

Filling the space

Men adopt dominant positions by sitting with their legs apart and their arms opened to show they need lots of space for their frames to fit into (see the example in Figure 13-3). They shift their bodies, change their positions and use their hands frequently to emphasise what they're saying. When some men feel insecure, they become more expansive in their gestures, whereas others pull into themselves.

Women accentuate their femininity by moving slowly and pulling their gestures towards themselves. They give the appearance of needing less space than men, making them appear little and subservient. Submissive gestures such as tilting their heads, entwining their ankles and crossing their legs as well as touching their hair and face indicate not only that they're ready, willing and able, but also that they're seeking protection and comfort.

The next time you're watching a televised awards ceremony, notice how the women on the red carpet move. They revel in showing their sensuous shoulders, drawing attention to their breasts as they do this. Women cross their legs, one in front of the other, to give them a slimmer look than if they were to stand with their legs hip width apart. This position also squeezes the upper thighs, making the woman (and anyone paying attention) more aware of her vaginal area.

Is she hobbling or flirting?

Besides wearing high heels to make themselves look taller and more powerful, women wear heels to make themselves appear more feminine. The higher the heel, the stronger and more vulnerable the look. Men are in awe of women who can stride out in 6-inch Jimmy Choos without missing a beat, as well as captivated by the wily ways of a femme fatale in Louboutin wedges. Whether aware of what they're doing or not, in order to balance themselves women in high heels arch their backs and push out their bottoms, creating a wiggle to their walk that men inevitably notice. The late, great Marilyn Monroe is purported to have chopped three-quarters of an inch off the heel of her left shoe to create her famous wiggle.

Figure 13-3:
The man fills his space and draws attention to his crotch by sitting in the spread eagle position.

Discovering other 'is he, isn't he' clues

The clothes you wear and the way you wear them advertise your sexual availability. How much of your body you show and which parts are on display, as well as your facial expressions, also send signals regarding your attraction to someone and willingness to move forward in a relationship:

- ✔ **Clothing:** In addition to protecting you from the elements, your choice of clothing signals what you want to reveal about yourself. In response, people make assumptions about you based on what you wear. Clothes that draw attention to your sexuality indicate that you're prepared to be noticed. Low-slung or tight jeans draw the eye to the wearer's genitalia and tight-fitting tops enhance the chest.

- ✔ **Facial expressions:** Women use lively and animated facial expressions demonstrating interest, vitality and energy, whereas men tend to be more controlled, reflecting a desire to convey dominance, restraint and power.

Kim's a woman who knows the power of her body. She rocked up at a recent fancy dress party wearing a skin-tight pink dress and black strappy high heels that would make Beyoncé blush. Kim's fit, firm and curvaceous figure encased in passionate pink, her full red lips, glowing skin, tousled hair and painted nails exuded sexuality and ensured that every man and most women looked at her with awe and appreciation.

Showing That You're Available

Having established that you're interested in the other person (as I describe in the earlier section 'Attracting Someone's Attention'), you need to show that you're available. Some of your gestures are studied and deliberate; others are completely unconscious. They all have the effect of showing that you're in place and ready to go, whether you know it or not.

Although men and women use the same basic preening gestures – such as touching their hair, smoothing their clothes, pointing their bodies in the other's direction and increasing eye contact – a few subtle differences are worth noting.

Unlike most of the mammal population where the males rank number one when it comes to sexual advertising, in the world of *homo sapiens* women take the lead. Their clothes, hairstyles, make-up and fragrance choices advertise their femininity. Whether a conscious choice or not, an interested and available woman sends signals designed to lure a partner into her fold.

Peeping at the many female courting gestures

The list of female sexual behaviours is long and moves right down her body from her head to the tips of her toes.

Tossing her head and flicking her hair

When a woman sees someone she finds attractive, she tosses her head or runs her fingers through her hair, often consciously. Whether her hair is long or short, the gesture is a subtle way of showing that she cares about her appearance and is making an effort to look appealing. An added benefit of this movement is that it exposes her soft underarm, a highly sensual part of a woman's body that most men find irresistible (see Figure 13-4).

Canting her head

A head tilted to the side gives an appealing and helpless look. By exposing the neck, a vulnerable part of the body, the head-cant is an ideal courtship signal because it implies that the woman trusts the man so much that she's prepared to display a defenceless part of her body to him.

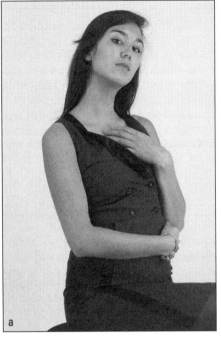

Figure 13-4: By drawing attention to her soft flesh, the woman demonstrates vulnerability and willingness.

a

b

The origins of the head-cant can be traced to infancy. A baby rests its head on the parents' shoulders when being comforted. The head-cant is a stylised version of the infant's gesture and unconsciously sends out an appeal for protection. Without knowing why, men feel a sudden surge of compassion, probably because the woman looks so vulnerable and helpless that the pose appeals to their masculinity.

Showing her neck

A woman uses two ways to expose her neck to make herself look appealing. In one she raises her chin slightly; in the other, she turns her head so the man can get a clear view of her neck. By showing her soft skin on a vulnerable part of her body, she makes herself look helpless and sexy, which is a lethal combination that no hot-blooded male can resist.

Dipping her head

A woman can make her eyes seem bigger, and herself seem smaller, by lowering her head when she's looking up at her lover. The result is that she looks vulnerable and in need of protection. Women also lower their heads when they're flirting because a lowered head is a sign of submission. The late Princess of Wales made this pose popular and it continues to be copied by women across the globe as they recognise the (paradoxical) power of submission.

Pouting and wetting her lips

Full lips are seen as a female characteristic and are considered full of sexual promise. When a woman pouts, the size of the lips increase, as does the man's interest. When she licks her lips she's indicating her readiness. The number of derma-fillers on the market for enhancing thin lips and creating the Angelina Jolie effect is proof positive of the power of the pout.

The facial bone structure of men and women is vastly different. During the teen years, as testosterone increases in men, their features become stronger, larger and more pronounced. Women's facial features change only slightly. Owing to more subcutaneous fat, their faces seem full and childlike, particularly their lips.

Touching herself

Women have a much larger number of nerve sensors than men, making them more sensitive to touch. A woman may leisurely stroke her neck, throat and thighs, drawing attention to those parts of her body, signalling to a man that if he plays his cards right she just may let him caress her in a similar way. By touching herself, a woman can fantasise about how it would feel if the man she fancies were the one doing the touching.

Often you're not aware that you're touching or stroking yourself. The gesture is an unconscious action in response to your interest in the other person. Women who *are* aware of the effect this behaviour elicits become adept at performing self-touching actions to call attention to themselves.

Susan had been dating Dennis for several weeks when she invited him to her house for dinner. This occasion was the first time Dennis had visited her house, and from the moment Susan opened the door to him she began to feel a tingling sensation throughout her body. She found him powerful, sexy and exciting and anticipated that, by the time dessert was served, he'd be stroking her body. During the meal, Susan caught her reflection in the dining room mirror, noticing that as she leaned in towards Dennis she was stroking her bare shoulder with her middle finger and the hollow at the base of her neck with her thumb in anticipation of what she wanted to happen.

Putting on a Clara Bow

A fiery-haired legendary silent film star of the 1920s and 1930s with a free-spirit encapsulating charm, charisma and sex appeal, Clara Bow was the original 'It' girl, having starred in the 1927 film *It*. One of the most duplicated features of all time is the actress's cupid bow-style lips, always enhanced with a splash of bright red lipstick.

Lips, labia and lipstick

A woman's labia are in proportion to the thickness of her facial lips. According to zoologist Desmond Morris, women 'self-mimic' their outer genital lips by making their facial lips wet by licking them or using lip gloss, thus creating a sexual invitation.

When a women is sexually aroused her lips, breasts and genitals enlarge and become redder as blood flows into them. The use of lipstick dates back 4,000 years to ancient Egypt when women painted their lips to mimic their sexually aroused and reddened genitalia. Modern research shows that when men look at photographs of women wearing different lipstick colours, they're consistently drawn to the bright reds which they describe as the most attractive and sensual.

Exposing her wrists

The underside of the wrist is considered to be one of the most erotic places on a woman's body because of its highly delicate skin. A woman showing interest and availability reveals this smooth, soft skin, increasing the rate of frequency as her interest grows (see Figure 13-5).

Figure 13-5:
By exposing her wrists she's signaling her availability.

Fondling cylindrical objects

If you find yourself fondling any object that remotely resembles a phallus, you're acting out what's going on inside your head. The same is true for someone else if you notice them stroking a firm, upright object. The scene in *Ghost*, in which Demi Moore and the late Patrick Swayze work a mound of wet clay on a potter's wheel is an erotic, emotive and classically graphic example of the sexual arousal that can be ignited by fondling a phallic object. Don't be surprised if a person you're speaking with fondles a personal item of yours while you fiddle with your earring, pen or the stem of your glass. The stimulus is too much to resist and he has to respond in a similar way to show that he's paying attention and wants to possess you.

Sliding a ring on and off your finger can show a desire to have sex with the person you're speaking to.

Glancing sideways over a raised shoulder

A woman who raises her shoulder is performing an act of self-mimicry, as her smooth shoulder emulates her rounded breasts. By turning her shoulder towards a man, holding his gaze with slightly lowered eyelids just long enough to get his attention and then quickly looking away, a woman can drive a person to distraction (see Figure 13-6). If he's interested, that is. This gesture tantalises him and suggests a peep show, which most men find hard to resist.

Putting her handbag in close proximity

A woman's handbag is her personal domain. Even most married men live in terror of entering this most forbidden territory. Because a woman treats her handbag as if it were a personal extension of her body, she sends a strong signal of sexual intimacy when she places her bag close to a man.

If a woman finds a man attractive, she may deliberately stroke and caress her bag in an inviting manner, tantalising and teasing her male admirer.

A woman who places her handbag close enough to a man for him to see or touch it is sending out signals that she's attracted to him. If she keeps her bag away from him, she's creating an emotional distance.

Pointing her knee in his direction

Watch the direction a woman's knee points when she sits with one leg tucked under the other. If a man is at the end of the sight line, you can bet that she finds him interesting. From this relaxed position, she's able to flash a bit of thigh and gain her target's attention.

Figure 13-6:
By raising
her
shoulder,
she's
highlighting
her other
curves.

Dangling a shoe

If a woman is sitting with a man and dangles a shoe off the end of her foot she's sending out the message that she's relaxed and comfortable in his company. In addition, the foot acts like a phallus as it thrusts itself in and out of her shoe. Many men become unsettled by this gesture and they don't know why.

If you want to test a woman's comfort level as she swings her dangling shoe off her pedicured toes, say or do something that unsettles her or makes her anxious and observe how quickly that shoe goes back on her foot.

Entwining her legs

Men consistently rank the leg twine as the most appealing sitting position a woman can take. Women consciously use this gesture to draw attention to their legs. When one leg is pressed up against the other it gives the appearance of highly toned muscles, which is the position the body takes just before engaging in sex.

Women who want to snare their bait and demonstrate their own interest slowly cross and uncross their legs and gently stroke their thighs as an indication of their desire to be caressed.

Dakota Johnson, Jennifer Lawrence, Madonna, and Beyoncé rank amongst the great female thigh rubbers. The image of them stroking their inner legs is enough to make grown men whimper and females sigh in wonder.

Examining the few male courting gestures

Compared with the vast number of courtship signals women have at their disposal, men have a sad and paltry few. In their effort to attract a woman, men often rely on their power, money and status as a means of flexing their muscles. Men's idea of a sexual invitation is to rev their engines, flaunt their wealth and challenge other men.

This isn't to say, however, that men don't preen when a potential partner comes into view. In addition to pulling in his stomach, expanding his chest and lifting his head like a conquering hero, a man smoothes his hair, straightens his tie, adjusts his clothes and flicks real or imaginary dust from his lapel.

If you're a man and you want to see whether a woman finds you attractive, tidy up your appearance by wearing a smart suit or a jacket and tie. A loosely knotted and slightly off-centre tie elicits a nurturing response in a woman. She instinctively reaches out to make the necessary adjustments, brushing your shoulder or lapel just in case a bit of fluff needs removing. If she's drawn to you, she wants to make you look like the well-put-together man she wants you to be.

The most sexually aggressive posture a man can display is to hook his thumbs over his waistband, into his belt or into the top of his trouser pockets. With his arms in the ready position and fingers pointing subtly to his genital area, men take this stance to stake their claim or show other men they're not to be trifled with. If a man uses this gesture in front of a woman, he's indicating that he's both dominant and virile (check out Figure 13-7).

If a man is looking at you with his thumbs in his pockets and his fingers pointing toward his crotch, with dilated pupils, a longer-than-usual gaze and one foot pointed toward you, consider yourself targeted.

Figure 13-7: A man whose fingers point towards his crotch is drawing attention to his source of power.

Recognising dilated pupils: A universal sign of attraction

If you've gazed longingly into another person's eyes you certainly know how powerfully the eyes convey the message, 'I find you incredibly attractive.' What you may not realise is that your pupils dilate when something arouses and stimulates you. As you can do nothing to control this reaction, give up playing hard to get because anyone paying close attention sees your pupils enlarging and knows that they're in with a chance.

Penile enhancements

In the fifteenth century, the male codpiece came into being (refer to Chapter 10 for more details). The purpose of this not-so-subtle item of clothing was to display the purported size of the man's penis, which determined his social status. Indigenous New Guinea males still display their penises, while Western men do so more subtly by wearing tight-fitting jeans, pocketsize swimsuits or by dangling a bunch of keys in their nether regions.

Studying pupils

University of Chicago bio-psychologist Eckhard Hess developed *pupillometrics* to assess the size of the eye's pupil as a means of gauging emotion or interest. Hess discovered that the pupil enlarges when people look at something that stimulates them. When someone looks at unpleasant or uninteresting things, the pupils contract. In one of Hess's studies, heterosexual men were shown retouched photographs of women. In half the photographs the women's pupils were made to look larger, in the other half the pupils were made to look smaller. With few exceptions, the men perceived the women with the larger pupils as being more attractive and friendlier than the same women whose pupils appeared smaller. When asked why they found one set of women more attractive than the other, the men were unable to give an answer. None of the men remarked on the difference in the size of the pupils.

Despite controversy regarding the negative effect of air-brushed photos on people's perceptions of themselves, retouching photographs of male and female models is still common practice in the advertising industry. The pupils are enlarged to make the models more attractive and alluring. Sales of manufactured goods, especially fashion, cosmetics and hair products, measurably increase when close-ups of the face are used to promote them.

If you want to kick-start a romance, arrange to meet your person of choice in a dimly lit place. Both your and your partner's pupils dilate because of the lack of light, creating the impression that you're interested in one another. The rest is up to you.

For more information on what messages you can send with a gaze alone, go to Chapter 5.

Progressing Through the Romance

As I describe in the earlier section 'Going courting: The five stages', the courtship procedure comprises a series of stages. Depending on how each person reacts to the other's signals, the courtship progresses or comes to a screeching halt. If you find yourself laughing, tickling and generally engaging in playful behaviour when you're with Cute Guy or Gorgeous Gal, you know that you're at least 'in like' if not yet 'in love' with one another. Goofing around and acting like puppies in a basket is harmless, unthreatening behaviour that allows you to show one another your nurturing and fun-loving sides.

Matching each other's behaviours

The closer two people are emotionally, the more similar their postures become. Certain postures and emotions are linked – especially those pertaining to sexual interest and anger – so when two people adopt the same physical position they may well be experiencing similar feelings. Observe a couple who are in tune with one another and you can see that their movements are co-ordinated and their postures match.

Take a look at photos or videos of the Duke and Duchess of Cambridge together and you may notice how their bodies move in sync with one another. An easy energy exists between them, and their bodies fit comfortably together. They walk in time with each other, with William often guiding his wife by placing a gentle hand on the small of her back. This intimate gesture reflects the sensuality they experience together.

Displaying that you belong together

People who establish a physical closeness give the impression that they're emotionally close as well. A man may put his arm around a woman's waist or shoulders, sending out the message that she's his woman. A woman may remove a piece of fluff from her man's jacket or straighten his tie, conveying the message to anyone who's watching that he belongs to her.

Other signs of togetherness are linking arms or holding hands while you're walking with your partner. People hold on to one another in these ways not to keep from falling over but to show that they're connected.

Angelina Jolie and Victoria Beckham are often photographed touching their husbands, Brad and David. Whether they're stroking his upper arm or resting a hand on his chest, both women are sending out clear signals that, while others may look at and fancy her man from afar, only she may touch him (see Figure 13-8).

When two people hold hands, either person's hand may be in front or behind. The position of the hands indicates who's in charge. The dominant person's hand is in front, with the palm facing towards the back. This position is more comfortable for taller people, both men and women, which is why you often see men taking the lead in this way. Short or tall, the person whose hand is leading with the back facing forwards is in charge. (For more about the meaning of hand movements and positions, go to Chapter 9.)

Figure 13-8:
Touching
your partner
demon-
strates that
he belongs
to you.

Chapter 14

Interviewing, Influencing and Playing Politics

....

In This Chapter

▶ Creating the right impression

▶ Conveying positivity and confidence

▶ Weighing up your best position

▶ Discovering effective negotiating behaviour

....

*H*ow you perceive and project yourself determines how people perceive and receive you. If you want to be seen as positive, powerful and influential at work, you have to act the part. Your gestures, actions and expressions need to celebrate and reflect your strengths and abilities. Based on what you reveal in the way you appear and move, people want to know more – or close the door on you.

From the moment you enter the work environment to your last day on the job, you're being watched. Make sure that the way you're moving, gesturing and behaving projects the image you desire. The higher up the hierarchy you go, the more focused your actions and the more contained your gestures need to be, in order to project the expected authority. You never see chief executives running down the hall or senior partners flapping their hands. You never see prime ministers and presidents sitting with their backs to the door.

Self-awareness is paramount if you're to work your way successfully through the office maze.

In this chapter, I look at how you can make a positive impact from the first impression through to the final exit. You discover that how you position your body impacts upon how people perceive you, and you gain skills to display confidence, commitment and credibility.

Making a Great First Impression: The Interview

I know, I know, you've heard it a hundred times or more, but here it is again: you never have a second chance to make a first impression. Make a good one and you're on to a winner. Make a poor one and you're going to struggle long and hard to be invited back.

Going for an interview involves being on show. People begin making evaluations from the moment they first see you. From top to toe, how you groom, dress and accessorise yourself sends out signals about who you are and the message you want to convey. Add to those ingredients your body language, manners and demeanour, and in less than seven seconds the impression you make is set. Although you may appeal to some, others may be less than impressed. This section describes how to push the odds in your favour.

Perfecting your interview behaviour

Getting yourself ready for a successful interview requires preparation and practice. In order to go in feeling good about yourself, and in control, follow the suggestions below:

✔ **Warming up:** Remind yourself of the purpose of the interview, what you want to achieve and how you want to be perceived. Think hard about the strengths and special qualities that make you unique and add value to all that you do. Before setting off for your interview, visualise yourself at your best. Only enter the interview room when you're looking, sounding and feeling like you do when you know you're on top-notch form.

Concentrate on breathing from your diaphragm, allowing the air to flow into your body with ease and strength. Visualise unzipping your torso and freeing the nervous butterflies in your stomach. See them fly out of you in a forward-facing, straight formation – light and free – guiding you to where you want to be. Notice how relaxed and energised you feel. Practise vocal warm-ups – humming and quietly repeating the phrases, 'The tip of the tongue, the lips and the teeth' and 'Red leather, yellow leather, red leather, black leather' or any of your favourite tongue twisters. Shake out your arms and legs, and again, breathe deeply. You may want to do these exercises in the privacy of a washroom if you're concerned about appearing a bit odd as you walk down the street and into the building. These exercises help to release any tension you may be harbouring in your body, connect with your voice and clarify your speech.

REMEMBER

Physical exercises, including raising and lowering your shoulders, letting your head roll from side to side and shaking your hands and fingers out before undergoing any tension-filled task, prepare you mentally, vocally and physically, enabling you to face your fears and get on with the task at hand.

✔ **Claiming your space:** Wherever you are, make the surrounding space yours and own it. (Check out the later section 'Claiming your space' for loads more tips.) Remind yourself that you wouldn't be there if you didn't have the right to be. You want to send out the message that you're ready and raring to go. Follow these tips:

- Relieve yourself of unnecessary clutter. Carry only what you need. Too much mess conveys a muddled mind (see Figure 14-1).

- Enter the reception area with a confident stride and greet the receptionist with a smile and a polite word. Give your name and that of the person you've come to see. Remove your coat and ask the receptionist to store it, if possible.

Figure 14-1:
People carrying fewer items look more in control than their colleagues.

Move away from the receptionist's area and, in spite of the invitation to 'take a seat', remain standing, unless the chairs are upright and easy to get in and out of. Some seating arrangements include soft, low chairs and couches that make you look small and can be awkward to navigate. Most reception areas have literature about the company, as well as newspapers and periodicals. If you haven't already read up on the company – and you really should have – flick through their annual report. If you prefer to stand, allow your hands to rest, one in the other in front of you at waist height, while taking in your surroundings. Known as the Power Position, standing like this makes you appear strong and in control and also calms your nervous energy.

✔ **Making your entrance:** How you move signals how you perceive yourself and expect to be treated. When you're invited to enter the interview room, do so with focus and energy. If you want to be perceived as someone with an upfront, upbeat and positive attitude, move confidently, smoothly and purposefully. And smile. Put down whatever you're carrying, shake the interviewer's hand if offered and only take a seat if you're invited to do so. You're demonstrating that you're comfortable and respectful entering another person's territory.

Move purposefully, avoiding any slight hesitation that may cause a small shuffle that makes you appear unsure of yourself. In order to project a commanding image, walk at a brisk pace, taking medium-length strides.

✔ **Showing that you're approachable:** Smiling at someone you're meeting for the first time makes you appear approachable, prompting the other person to open up and to engage with you. When you smile, you're indicating that you're willing to share yourself and connect at an emotional level. Smiling also lightens and relaxes a potentially tense atmosphere; it costs you nothing and yet enriches the lives of people who are at the receiving end. Although it may not last long, the memory of a genuine smile can last forever.

When you smile, make sure that you mean what you're doing. A fake smile is easy to spot and leaves the impression that you're not genuine.

✔ **Shaking hands:** Instead of shaking hands across the desk, which puts a barrier between you and the other person, move to the left of the desk to avoid receiving a palm down handshake and being put in a subservient position. Hold your palm straight and return the same amount of pressure that the other person gives. Let the interviewer decide when the handshake should end.

When you match the force of the interviewer's handshake, you're showing that you're sensitive and flexible and able to reflect that person's approach. If you crush the other person's fingers or offer a wet fish handshake in return for a firm one, you're showing that the two of you are mismatched and out of sync.

Include the person's name in your remarks twice within the first 30 seconds of having introduced yourself, including when you first meet. Speak for no longer than 20–30 seconds at one time.

✔ **Positioning yourself:** When you're invited to sit, make sure that your body is at a 45-degree angle from the other person. Move the chair to this angle, if you can. If you can't, shift your body. (The later section 'Creating a relaxed attitude with the 45-degree angle' contains lots more info on the importance of this position.) Facing your interviewer directly, especially if you're seated across the desk from one another and your chair is lower than his, makes you look like a child about to be reprimanded. If you're invited to sit away from the desk in a more informal area, silently rejoice. Few rejections are made from this position.

If the seat you're offered is soft and low, sit on the edge, leaning slightly forward to avoid sinking into the seat and lowering your status. If you don't, you'll look like a mini head perched on two sticks.

Respecting the other person's personal space is bound to win you points. When determining the appropriate space, keep these guidelines in mind:

- The greater the familiarity between you and the other person, the closer you sit; the less familiar, the farther away.

- Men tend to move closer to a woman they're speaking to, whereas women generally back away.

- If you're being interviewed by a person of a similar age, you sit closer than if you were being interviewed by someone significantly older or younger.

As the meeting progresses, and all being well, the parameters of this area close inwards, inviting you to come closer. If you move in too soon, the other person feels invaded and moves back and away from you.

✔ **Making your exit:** When the time comes to leave, move calmly and focus on what you're doing. Smile, shake hands with your interviewer, turn and head towards the door. No matter how fit you are, and even if your bottom puts Pippa Middleton's to shame, the final impression you want to leave your interviewer with is your face, not your buttocks. Of course, backing out of the room appears odd, and so to ensure that your face is the last thing your interviewer sees, when you reach the door, slowly turn, look your interviewer in the eye and smile again (see Figure 14-2). Finally, when you exit the room, leave the door in the same position as it was when you entered.

People who show that they're similar to the people they want to work with, sharing values, goals and beliefs, and demonstrating that they can benefit the business, are more likely to gain further interviews and land a job than the person who shows little interest or a lack of initiative.

Figure 14-2:
When leaving a room, turn to ensure that the last image the interviewer sees is your friendly face.

Using minimal gestures for maximum effect

You see fewer and more precise gestures displayed higher up the business hierarchy. Innocent, inexperienced and insecure people flap their hands, toss their heads and jiggle their feet, whereas people at the top keep their movements cool and contained; their gestures look precise, concise and devoid of extraneous activity.

During an interview, keep your gestures clear, simple and deliberate. When appropriate, mirror the other person's gestures and expressions. (I discuss mirroring in the later section 'Establishing rapport'.) Keep your hands away from your face and mouth and avoid any nervous-looking behaviour such as straightening your tie or fiddling with your hair. Leave alone any items you may nervously toy with, such as a pen or piece of jewellery. (Check out the later section 'Avoiding nervous gestures' for more details.)

Speaking more, moving less

Research shows that a direct link exists between people's vocabulary and their status, power and position. The higher up the corporate ladder someone rises, the greater that person's facility with words and phrases. Further research shows a connection between people's control of the spoken language and the number of gestures they use when communicating. People at the top don't need a lot of gestures to get their point across because they have their words. Lower down the pecking order, people rely more on gestures to convey their meaning, because they haven't acquired the skills or had the training or opportunities to develop their vocabulary.

Creating a Positive Environment

If you want to get ahead at work, you need to treat people with respect. Not everyone you work with is going to be the same as you – thankfully – or even like you (which you may find hard to believe, being the likeable person that you are). But each person brings a unique quality that can contribute to the success of an organisation when steered with sensitivity and compassion.

As well as treating people with respect, aim to establish rapport. When two or more people are reading from the same page and playing with the same goal in mind, miracles can happen. Or at least, deadlines can be met.

Demonstrating respect

Over and over again as I was researching material for this chapter, people told me that what they really wanted at work was to be treated with dignity and respect. When I broke down what they said, the following messages came through:

- ✔ **Treat people with courtesy and kindness.** Keep your body in an open position – where your weight is evenly distributed and your muscles are relaxed (see Figure 14-3) – to allow a free flow of information, inviting people to feel comfortable in your presence.

- ✔ **Encourage colleagues and staff to express their ideas and opinions.** Look them in the eye as they speak, and appear interested. Pay attention to people's facial expressions – are they frowning or smiling, are their lips taut or trembling? Refrain from multi-tasking when someone's speaking: fiddling with your phone and playing with paper, pens or pencils is rude and potentially distracting. If you don't agree with what you hear, keep your facial expressions and gestures neutral.

Figure 14-3:
An open
body invites
others to
enter the
space.

✔ **Listen to what others have to say before expressing your opinions.**
Never interrupt or butt in while someone else is speaking. If you struggle
not to interrupt, make a conscious effort to keep your mouth closed
while others speak. Refrain from clenching your teeth, however, as
doing so creates tension in your mouth, mind and body. Allow your lips
to lie lightly together and your tongue to float gently in your mouth.
Make sure that your eyes are open and not burrowed in a frown.

✔ **Encourage someone who offers an idea that may improve current conditions.** Lean forward, look them in the eye and smile as you speak if you
want to let them and others know that you think they're making sense.

✔ **Never insult, bully or disparage someone or their ideas.** Raising your
nostrils as if you're smelling something past its prime, pulling up your
upper lip, laughing with derision or physically prodding or pushing
another person is rude, unproductive and about as far away from demonstrating respect as a person can get.

✔ **Praise more often than you criticise.** Encourage a culture of praise and
recognition among employees as well as from management. When you
praise people, look at them face to face and smile. Doing so may feel
uncomfortable at first because many people shy away from giving and
receiving praise. To see the benefits, persevere.

✔ **Practise giving and receiving praise.** When you offer praise, be sure that you believe what you're saying or the person you're praising won't believe you. Like animals, people can pick up on physical vibrations including facial expressions and bodily tension. Nod as you speak in confirmation of what you're saying. Look the other person in the eye. Smile with pleasure as you give and receive the praise.

✔ **Treat others as they want to be treated.** Maintain an open mind and reflect your attitude in your open body language. Nobody wants to be spoken to in tense tones accompanied by tight gestures.

For more about body language in the office, refer to *Persuasion & Influence For Dummies* by Elizabeth Kuhnke (Wiley).

Establishing rapport

When you're in rapport, you feel a harmonious connection between yourself and others. All's right in the world and communication flows. You might even find yourself smiling and nodding in agreement as you converse.

The word *rapport* derives from the French word *rapporter*, which translates as 'to return or bring back'. English dictionaries define rapport as 'a sympathetic relationship or understanding'. The result is that people in rapport can create outstanding results.

When you have rapport with someone, taking on that person's style of behaviour – also called *mirroring* and *matching* – helps you become highly tuned to the way the other person thinks and experiences the world. Your whole body becomes involved in the observation process. *Mirroring* is a direct replication of the other person's movements while *matching* is more about moving in sync with them. Be attuned to the difference between moving in rhythm with someone and mimicking their actions, though, because people know when you're making fun of them or being insincere.

Mirroring

People who are in rapport tend to reflect one another's physical patterns. They move in time with each other and mirror behaviour that they observe.

Research on rapport indicates that, from an evolutionary perspective, mirroring body language facilitates interaction between people. When you mirror people – whether in the way they speak or move – you're unconsciously reproducing their state of mind within yourself (check out Figure 14-4). The more effectively you can do so, the more able you are to understand the other person's perspective.

Figure 14-4:
By mirroring
one
another's
body
language,
the man and
woman are
building
rapport.

When you're reflecting other people's behaviour back to them, avoid mimicry. If you recreate muscle movement for muscle movement and replicate exact gestures and expressions with precision, the other person feels mocked and disinclined to engage in a meaningful conversation with you.

Matching

Matching someone's behaviour indicates that you're in sync with one another, experiencing similar feelings and emotions. When you're matching someone's behaviour, you create a similar state to the other person that helps you understand their point of view.

Try to match the other person's:

- Body postures and gestures
- Breathing rates
- Rhythm of movement and energy levels
- Voice tonality, including pitch, pace and volume

Mirroring and matching effectively

People attempting to create rapport through mirroring and matching without also trying to understand and convey the state of the people around them come across like the worst of used-car salesmen. Those best at creating rapport match the *state* of the other person, feeling it within themselves much as the other person does. The goal in matching and mirroring behaviour is to adopt and replicate the state of the other person you're interacting with. Mirroring and matching the behaviour enhances communication only when the adopted physiology assists in replicating an emotional state. For more about creating rapport through mirroring and matching, see *Neuro-Linguistic Programming For Dummies* by Romilla Ready and Kate Burton (Wiley).

Standing tall and holding your ground

Having a superior position carries with it an implied authority. The same goes for tall people: they can command respect as a result of their height. Others have to look up to them and, because of their physiological make-up, they look down on others.

Some people don't feel comfortable being taller than others, so they stoop or slouch (see Figure 14-5). They diminish themselves in size and stature, giving away their authority. Shorter people have to create an image of height and stature. They do so by standing with their centre of gravity deep in their loins while lifting their upper torsos upwards and outwards. Rather than placing their energy in their upper chests – making themselves top heavy – they place their energy in their pelvic area, giving them a sense of firmness and control. Tom Cruise, Nicholas Sarkozy and Al Pacino, for example, are no taller than 5 feet 7 inches, and yet Cruise's bright smile, Sarkozy's purposeful stride and Pacino's brooding passion all manage to exude an aura of power.

To experience what being in control feels and looks like, try this short exercise, practising from both the seated and standing positions:

- ✔ Visualise another person who's challenging you, at an interview, in a meeting or at an assessment.

- ✔ Place your feet firmly underneath you, hip width apart.

- ✔ Maintain flexibility in your knees and ankles to avoid becoming stiff.

- ✔ Keep your head upright and maintain eye contact with the other person.

- ✔ Let your arms and hands be visible.

✔ Keep your chest open, feeling as if your shoulder blades are gently melting down your back.

✔ Keep your mouth closed while you're listening.

✔ Inhale from your diaphragm. Breathing deeply from your core grounds you and provides a firm foundation from which you can move, gesture and position yourself.

✔ Reflect on what you're going to say before speaking.

✔ Remind yourself of your strengths and how you want to be perceived.

✔ Respond.

Stooped shoulders, caved-in chest and hands in the fig-leaf position (covering your private bits) are protective signals and indicate that you're subconsciously feeling defensive.

Cecile stands at just over 6 feet tall. As an athlete, she was used to being with people of equal height, and felt comfortable with them. When her sports career ended, she obtained her law degree and joined a city firm. After several months, Cecile noticed that she was hunching her shoulders and sinking into her hips. Her chest caved inward, her head sunk into her neck and she was looking at people from under her eyes.

Figure 14-5
Someone who slouches fails to project authority.

As we explored the reasons for this new behaviour, we discovered several issues. Cecile was experiencing a lack of confidence and low self-esteem because she was still finding out about the job. Highly competitive, she was uncomfortable, fearing that she was being perceived as lacking in her work. In addition, the male partner she reported to was shorter than Cecile. She discovered that she was purposely making herself smaller to make him look bigger. With practice, Cecile regained her stature. We explored her mental attitude and made the necessary self-perception adjustments. Her new way of thinking and perceiving herself was reflected in the way she stood and gestured. Now, when Cecile sits and stands using her full stature she feels confident, looks credible and commands respect.

Moving with purpose

Whether you stride into a room with focus and direction, or wander in as though you've forgotten why you're there, you're going to create an impression. Unless you're purposely playing the role of someone from La-La Land, if you want to be noticed in a positive sense, put your muscles into your movement and propel yourself into the fray with focus, direction and positive energy. Other people then perceive you as vibrant, interesting and engaging.

Before projecting yourself into other people's territory, test the waters. Moderate your movements to mirror those of the people you're with (I discuss mirroring in the earlier section 'Establishing rapport'). If you come bounding into a room full of silent, contemplative folk, you may be perceived as a bit of a buffoon, if not an outright annoyance. Reflect back the energy you observe in the room and adapt your behaviour to match what you notice, still moving with focus and direction.

Matching mood and movements for results

I recently attended two training events led by two different trainers and the contrast was highly informative. At the first, the trainer bounded into the room like a puppy. Feeling overwhelmed by her exuberance – it was 6 p.m. and I was tired after a long day's work – I struggled to engage with her and left the session feeling disappointed that I hadn't gained anything from it.

The second training session took place early in the morning, and again I was tired – this time because I'd had a long journey to the venue. Here, the trainer established rapport by matching my mood and movements. Instead of imposing her energy on me, she allowed me to set the tone until I was ready to become more engaged and energised. By noticing my movements and purposely matching them to enhance our communication and build our relationship, I left the session singing the trainer's praises, having gained valuable knowledge while enjoying the process.

Positive energy draws people, whereas negative energy repels them. You don't have to bounce like Tigger to demonstrate focus and energy. Slow actions performed with a clear intention project authority and command attention.

An intentionally deliberate movement draws attention to the action and highlights the meaning behind the gesture.

Pointing Your Body in the Right Direction

How you position your body in relation to other people impacts upon their perception of you, which is particularly relevant in the work environment. If you stand directly in front of them, face to face, hands on hips and jaw jutted forward, you become a threatening force. Turn your shoulder to people, cross your arms and look down your nose at them, and you indicate that you think they aren't up to scratch. Turn your back completely on people and you better hope that they don't stick anything in it as a response to your dismissive attitude!

To create a more positive interaction, stand facing another person at a comfortable distance – with your arms open, your hands visible and a welcoming expression on your face – and see how constructive the mood becomes. Sit or stand side by side at a distance that feels right for your relationship, and sense the connection. Both consciously and subconsciously you're adjusting your body position in response to what's happening in your environment.

People who sit side by side tend to work in a collaborative way. People sitting across the table from one another are often at odds, relying on the furniture to act as a defensive barrier.

To make a positive impression, hold your head up, keeping your chin parallel to the ground. Think of something that makes you happy. Let your eyes engage and sparkle. Allow yourself to smile. Free your shoulders and permit your chest to open as if it were a plane about to take off (but don't puff it out, which over-eggs the pudding and reveals defensiveness, not strength). Breathe from your diaphragm. Ground yourself by connecting with your environment. Imagine roots coming out from the soles of your feet, providing you with a firm foundation. Pretend that you've a tap root driving deep from the centre of your sole, making you solid and strong. In addition, make believe that you've shallow roots coming out from the soles of your feet, providing you with flexibility.

If someone you're engaging with seems distracted, uninterested or even annoyed, aim to match that person's movements and energy as a means of creating rapport. When the person feels that the two of you are connected, you can more easily lead the conversation in the direction you desire.

Creating a relaxed attitude with the 45-degree angle

The angle at which you position yourself in relation to another person affects the outcome of your communication. If you want your interaction to be comfortable, co-operative and congenial, place yourself at a 45-degree angle to the other person. This position encourages openness and trust. By positioning yourself at this angle, you form a third point where you avoid being perceived as aggressive or flirtatious. Whereas face to face is confrontational, and side by side is intimate, placing yourself halfway between the two creates an atmosphere of confidence and equality. Neither confrontational nor intimate, the 45-degree angle allows people to see one another, gesture freely and maintain a comfortable space between themselves.

The 45-degree angle is a co-operative space that encourages discussion and the flow of ideas – it's perceived as neutral territory. The third angle allows another person to join you in the space, creating an equilateral triangle. If a fourth person enters the group they can form a square, and if one or two more people join, they can form a circle or divide themselves into two triangles.

Positioning yourself for co-operation

Say that you're the newly appointed head of a well-established and successful team. One by one, you invite your new colleagues into your office for a 'getting acquainted' session. They may feel a little wary of you and watch to see how you manage the meeting. By placing yourself in the neutral 45-degree zone, you encourage openness and honest discussion. No threatening aspect is associated with this position. Turn 10 degrees in either direction and the dynamics change. If you turn inwards, you indicate that intimacy is in the air. If you angle your body away, you shut out the other person.

Sitting with subordinates

When you want to create a relaxed, informal atmosphere when speaking to a subordinate in your office, open the session with both of you sitting in the 45-degree angle position, directing your bodies to a third point forming a triangle, suggesting agreement. From this position you can reflect the other person's gestures, creating a sense of ease and rapport.

If you want a direct answer to a question and you feel that you're not getting it in the 45-degree pose, shift your position to face directly towards the other person. This action says that you want a direct answer to your direct question.

Taking the pressure off

Positioning your body at a 45-degree angle relieves the potential stress of the meeting. When a sensitive issue needs addressing, go for this position. It takes the pressure off and encourages more open answers to your open questions. Unless, of course, you want to put the pressure on, in which case face the other person directly and look him in the eye.

Facing directly for serious answers

If someone asks you a direct question, look at the person directly – that is, if you want to be taken seriously. If you drop your head, avert your eyes and peer over your shoulder, you're conveying that you're unsure, doubtful and perhaps even scared; you've lost your power.

Serious questions require a serious attitude and so you need to reflect that attitude in your pose. When you're asked a direct question, follow these steps (seated or standing):

1. **Close your mouth.**
2. **Breathe deeply from your lower abdomen.**
3. **Hold your head vertically as if your chin is resting on a calm lake.**
4. **Align your hips and shoulders with your knees.**
5. **Place your knees directly over your ankles, with your feet planted firmly on the ground.**
6. **Open your chest.**
7. **Look the questioner in the eye.**
8. **Pause.**
9. **Answer.**

Emma works in the HR department of a telecoms company. She's ambitious and wants to progress in her career. During her annual appraisal she received disturbing feedback: her superiors weren't taking her seriously because her behaviour makes her appear unsure of herself.

When Emma came to me, she was alive with unfocused, nervous energy. She shifted her weight from leg to leg and slouched into her hips. Her shoulders stooped and her hands fidgeted. She tossed her head and frequently giggled.

She had difficulty establishing and maintaining eye contact. Her words said that she wanted to progress in her work, but her body language conveyed that she wasn't up to the job. When Emma saw herself on video she was shocked at the negative impression her gestures and behaviour were making. By adjusting her stance, she stood taller. By controlling her breathing, her actions calmed down. By opening her chest, she filled her space. Her fidgeting lessened and she began to project the image she wanted. Emma now comes across as confident, convincing and credible.

Picking the power seats

At work, stay away from seats that make you look small, awkward and insignificant (see Figure 14-6). Avoid seats that force you to look upward, lifting your chin and exposing your neck, one of the most vulnerable parts of your body. The person on the other chair is sitting upright and in control. Even if he's leaning back in his chair, he's still in a higher position than you. He can look down on you along the length of his nose. He can lower his glasses, looking over the top at you, sitting in a cramped and awkward position and thus feeling uncomfortable.

Figure 14-6:
Sitting in a low, soft chair diminishes your power.

Considering the back of the chair

The higher the back of the chair, the higher the status of the person it belongs to. The person with the support behind his back, the protective shield and frame that surrounds him holds a more powerful position than the person sitting on a stool at his feet. Kings and queens, popes and prime ministers, chief executives and oligarchs sit in chairs that reflect their power and status. The higher the back of the chair and the more luxurious the fabric, the higher the status of the person.

On the TV show *The Apprentice*, Sir Alan Sugar sits in a black leather chair with a high back. The back of the chair frames his face and gives him authority. The would-be apprentices sit in front of him. The backs of their chairs are lower. Before a word is spoken, the positioning makes clear who holds the authority in the room.

High-status people prefer to sit on high-backed chairs.

Rolling on casters

Chairs on casters have a power and mobility that fixed chairs lack. The person sitting in a chair that swivels has more freedom of movement and can cover more space in a shorter time than someone sitting in a fixed chair. The person who's sitting in the chair on wheels, with the arm rests and the high, reclining back, tends to be the person in charge.

Gaining height advantage

Height is associated with status and power: the higher you are, the more authority you hold. Savvy business types know that, by adjusting the seat height of their chairs, they gain a competitive advantage.

If someone invites you to sit in a chair that puts you at eye level with the other person's desk, politely decline and say that you prefer to stand.

Placing the chair

When you seat yourself directly across the desk or table from another person, face to face, the atmosphere is immediately confrontational. But place the chair at a 45-degree angle in front of the desk and you create a welcoming environment. If you want to reduce a visitor's status, arrange for him to be seated as far away from your desk as possible, into the public zone at least 8 feet away from where you're sitting.

Negotiating Styles

When crunch time arrives and you're at the final stage of a work or business negotiation, you want to win, right? The best negotiations result in everyone feeling like a winner. And to feel that you're a winner you have to look, sound and behave like one – you must act the part. If you want to know more about how to position yourself when negotiating, persuading and influencing, take a look at *Persuasion & Influence For Dummies* by Elizabeth Kuhnke (Wiley).

 Before you go into any meeting where you want to be seen performing well (interview, negotiation or assessment), find yourself a quiet spot in which you can gather your thoughts in peace. Five minutes is ample. Reflect on how you want to be perceived and visualise yourself behaving in that manner. See and hear yourself performing at your best and experience the feeling. By creating your desired image, you're able to act the part and convince others that you really are like that. Who knows, you may actually be that person.

Claiming your space

When you enter a negotiation, you need to claim your space right from the start. If you don't, the competition is going to have you for breakfast. *Claiming your space* means that you're taking responsibility for yourself and your actions, and that you act as though you've got the right to be where you are, doing what you're doing. When you walk into a space and make it your own, you're telling others that this territory is yours and woe betide anyone who tries to take it away from you. Dogs spend much of their time marking out their territory in order to let the rest of the pack know that they've been there, and the same applies to people (although in a less obvious manner!). Your intention is to let people know that you own this space and you're to be taken seriously.

Acting the part

The Russian director, Constantine Stanislavski, popularised a style of acting that became known as *method acting*, which requires actors to base their characterisations on the emotional memory process. The actors immerse themselves in their characters' lives, to experience that life as the characters would. Actors draw upon memories and incidents from their own lives and incorporate them into their roles, enriching and enhancing the portrayal. Devotees of method acting include Dustin Hoffman, Jane Fonda and Robert De Niro.

In a similar manner, by recalling how you felt and behaved when you negotiated a favourable outcome in the past, and by emulating the behaviours of negotiators you admire, you too can act yourself into the part.

When you claim your space successfully, you can act as if you belong there. Your gestures appear fluid, your posture is upright and you engage in eye contact with ease. You send out positive signals indicating that you're comfortable and in control.

Getting acquainted with the environment

One way of demonstrating that the space you're in belongs to you is to make contact with an item in the area. Say, for example, that you've been invited to speak at an event attended by many influential people, some of whom you know, others you don't. You want to appear confident and in charge of yourself and your material. To do that, follow these suggestions for getting comfortable in the space and making it your own:

✔ Walk into the room where the event is taking place as if you own the space. Move with purpose and authority.

✔ If you are expected to sit, pull your chair out and sit down without waiting to be invited. (Be advised, though, that if you do take this action at a first interview, you may be perceived as forward or rude.)

✔ Place your notes and pen in front of you with confidence and authority.

✔ Establish eye contact and open the discussion clearly and concisely.

Tricia is a highly qualified and respected lawyer. Practising for her partnership interview, Tricia felt nervous and awkward, as though she didn't belong. She fidgeted with her clothes, avoided eye contact and played with her jewellery. Her behaviour began shifting as she practised entering the room and taking her seat at the table in front of the imaginary panel. Before Tricia sat, she let her hands rest on the top of the chair's back as if staking her claim to that seat. By making contact with this object, she established a sense of ownership with the room. Her nerves steadied, and she gained an appearance of confidence and credibility.

Choosing a good seat

When attending meetings, arrive early so that you can pick your spot. Sitting facing the door gives you the upper hand. Research shows that people seated with their backs to the door experience stress, increased blood pressure and shallow, rapid breathing as the body prepares itself for a possible attack from behind. Save this weak and defensive position for your competition.

Filling your space

People who fill their space look more commanding and in control, which can be a challenge for small or slim people, who may appear to be devoured by space. The following tips can help people of smaller stature appear more in command of their territory:

✔ Hold your elbows slightly out from your sides when standing or sitting. (People who hold their arms close to their bodies look subservient, timid and fearful.)

✔ Lean forward when seated behind a table, letting your hands, elbows or lower arms rest on the table's surface.

✔ Never pull your arms in close by your sides at a meeting; you're reducing your stature and diminishing your influence.

Large people also need to consider the amount of space they fill, because lolling and ambling along or spreading across their space can be perceived as invasive. You don't need to draw your shoulders and arms in towards yourself. Just be aware that you take up more space than smaller people and that you may need to adjust your position to allow others in.

To avoid overwhelming others with your large presence, contain your gestures, making them concise and precise.

Displaying confidence

The way you stand and sit, your gestures and expressions, the actions you choose and the way you perform them, all reveal who you are and what you're about. Captains of industry, masters of the universe and doyennes of the theatre instinctively know, and are well trained in, how to project a confident countenance. With eyes clear and focused, posture erect and facial muscles engaged, they create a look of positive expectancy.

To be perceived as confident, you have to demonstrate confident behaviour, which requires that you know what confident behaviour looks, sounds and feels like. To clarify your concept, try the following exercise:

✔ Ask yourself, 'What's important to me about behaving confidently?'

✔ Reflect back on a time when you felt confident. Describe the feeling. What gestures and expressions did you incorporate into your behaviour?

✔ Think of someone who you believe demonstrates confident behaviour and describe how that person acts, including specific gestures, fluidity of movement, eye contact and facial expressions.

✔ Consider what you currently do that's similar to that person's behaviour.

✔ List the benefits of behaving with confidence.

✔ Practise the gestures, postures and expressions that denote confidence for you and avoid those that don't.

Avoiding nervous gestures

People who fidget and fiddle, pick at their fingernails and scratch their head, face, neck and/or chest during a negotiation are displaying nervous gestures and giving the game away. You don't need a microscope to see that such people are in a real state and are creating a nervous environment. Spend too much time with someone who's demonstrating nervous behaviour and you start feeling uncomfortable too.

You can't avoid gesturing nervously unless you're aware that you do it. Watch yourself on video, ask a trusted colleague for feedback and pay attention to yourself as though you're an outside observer. When you recognise the behaviour, you can do something about it.

Replace an anxious gesture with another action. If you're fiddling with a pen, put it down whenever you're not writing. Let your hands rest on the desk or table in front of you. If you don't have a surface that your hands can lie on, rest them in your lap. If you find yourself picking at your fingernails, swap that action for another, such as taking a quick note then folding your hands in your lap. You can also shift the way you're sitting or standing. Repositioning your body from a pose in which you're feeling uncomfortable also results in shifting your thoughts, feelings and intentions. After you shift your position, settle in. If you're bouncing from pillar to post, you're showing your nervousness.

Changing behaviours takes time, commitment and practice. In fact, research shows that habits can take anything from 18 to 254 days to form. For example, a relatively simple habit like drinking a cup of hot water and lemon every morning or going for a 10-minute walk every lunchtime, can take up to 66 days. Changing your habitual behaviours in stressful conditions may take longer.

In today's highly competitive business world, you need simple strategies to provide the extra *oomph* to get you where you want to be. Being good at what you do is no longer enough; you have to be *seen* to be good. Take stock and evaluate what you do well and where you see room for improvement. Consider your behaviour and the impact it has. When you're aware of these things, you can make the necessary adaptations.

Opening or closing your fingers

Short, sharp gestures hold more authority than open hands waving in the air (see Figure 14-7). By keeping your fingers closed and your hands below chin level when gesturing, you look confident and in control, and thus command attention.

Standing up for meetings

Research shows that, when people participate in meetings standing up, they speak for a shorter length of time. It encourages quick decision making, and cuts down on time spent socialising. The studies also demonstrate that people who conduct their meetings while standing are perceived as having higher status than the seated people.

Kate attended a marketing meeting at a company in Denmark. In the middle of the room was a tall stone table with no chairs. The table was at a comfortable height for people to stand at and lean on, and the room had enough space for them to walk around the table easily. The participants in the meeting were encouraged to mill around the room speaking with one another, and to come to the table when a point was being made and a decision required. Kate found the experience liberating, because the thinking in the room was more creative and energising than in meetings during which people remained seated.

Figure 14-7:
When you wave your hands above shoulder height you appear flustered.

If you want to appear caring, approachable or subservient, also keep your hands below chin level but gesture with open fingers.

Carrying only what's necessary

Keep your accessories slim and compact. A bulging briefcase indicates that you're the worker bee and not the queen making strategic decisions. They convey the impression that, although you may be buzzing away hard, you're not in control of your time.

Accessories are meant to enhance your image. Decide what image you want to project and choose your accessories accordingly. Also, to make a positive impression, invest in good quality accessories.

Watching your buttons

Tightly closed jackets indicate a tightly closed point of view. People who button up their jackets while making decisions indicate that they're closed to the idea put forward. When they fold their arms across their chests with their jackets buttoned, they're displaying real negativity. If you notice one or two people unbuttoning their jackets during a meeting, you can safely assume that they're changing their opinions and opening up to what's going on (see Figure 14-8).

Figure 14-8:
An unbuttoned jacket makes you seem relaxed and receptive.

Chapter 15

Crossing the Cultural Divide

*W*ith businesses spanning the globe, students travelling the world and the media bringing foreign lands into people's homes on a daily basis, no group can any longer believe in the infallibility of its own customs and culture. As the singer/songwriter Paul Simon says, 'One man's ceiling is another man's floor'. In spite of the 'shrinking' world, or perhaps because of it, people are holding on to their cultural customs and traditions with a mixture of pride, fear, and determination. Behaviours as simple as counting on your fingers, walking along the street and shaking hands vary widely across the globe.

When you know the rules that govern behaviour in cultures other than your own, you can avoid making major mistakes that, in addition to insulting your host, may lead to a diplomatic crisis – or at least an awkward situation. A huge number of countries, cultures and customs exist in the world and I don't intend to cover them all here. In this chapter I give you a taster: a few examples, tips and techniques to enable you to trek the globe with confidence.

I assume that you don't want to make a fool of yourself, offend your host or cause an international calamity because you don't know the difference between acceptable and unacceptable behaviour in a culture other than your own. When in doubt, ask. Natives are usually delighted to guide you in the ways of their country and are flattered that you want to behave in a respectful manner. One gesture that you're always safe using, no matter where your travels take you, is the smile. This gesture is the one expression that's understood by both the most sophisticated city person and the desert nomad.

Recognising the Different Strokes for Different Folks

As more cultures interact than ever before, knowing the acceptable non-verbal behaviours – and those that are verboten – can help you to make a friend and seal a deal. Although you may not need to become au fait with all the cultural intricacies around the world, discovering the basics – for example, meetings and greetings, handling business cards, managing personal space, and establishing and maintaining eye contact – sets you up for the next promotion or puts you in the driver's seat as regards building positive relationships with people from races, religions and creeds different from your own.

Some cultures – such as the Irish and the Italians – are known for their upfront exuberance, while others – including the Japanese and the Swedes – are acknowledged as the keepers of the keys when it comes to revealing emotions. Some encourage openness (such as the Spanish), whereas the English, Scots and Scandinavians prefer to protect their privacy. Even within the same country, behaviours differ. For example, Northern Germans tend to be contained in their expressions and movements whereas their Southern cousins demonstrate more freedom in their gestures and mannerisms.

By accepting differences and adapting your behaviour to meet what's expected in cultures dissimilar to yours, you can build respectful relationships and sail smoothly through challenging cross-cultural waters.

Pay attention to how the natives are behaving. Unless people's behaviour goes against your values, emulate their movements and expressions. Treat people's beliefs and customs with respect in order to communicate with honesty and openness as you engage with them.

The New Zealand haka

The Maori haka, an action chant with hand gestures and foot stamping, is traditionally performed by the New Zealand rugby team, the All Blacks, before an international test match. Originally acted out by warriors before battle, the haka proclaimed the soldiers' strength and prowess and served as a verbal challenge to the opposition. The most famous haka, 'Ka Mate', tells of the wily ruse that a Maori chief used to outwit his enemies and is interpreted as a celebration of the triumph of life over death.

On 28 August 2005, before a match against South Africa, the All Blacks unexpectedly introduced a new haka, 'Kapa o Pango'. The climax of this new haka is particularly aggressive as each player, staring at the opposing team, performs a throat-slitting action. In response to allegations that the gesture was offensive, the New Zealanders explained that in Maori culture and haka tradition the throat-slitting gesture signifies the drawing of vital energy into the heart and lungs. The All Blacks went on to win the match 31 to 27.

Positioning yourself and setting boundaries

One problematic convention that differs from country to country and culture to culture is the issue of personal space. In Latin America, it's natural and expected for people to stand close to each other whereas in Anglo-Saxon countries people give one another a wider berth. Watch the Spanish and Italians when in conversation. They stand close to one another when they're speaking and a casual touch on the arm or shoulder during conversation is the norm. Good friends typically greet one another with a hug or a kiss and seeing people of the same sex walking down the street arm in arm is normal. If you back away when an Italian or Argentine speaks to you, they may think that you're shy and move closer to fill the gap. In complete contrast, Australians require a lot of personal space – if you get closer than an arm's length an Aussie feels hemmed in.

People in Nordic countries are more restrained in their body movements. In contrast to their Southern European cousins, who embrace public physicality, Northerners back away from effusive gestures and consider hugging in public taboo.

If you want to avoid embarrassing your Nordic friend or acquaintance, particularly in public, refrain from behaving in an intimate manner. Save your hugs for home.

If you were a fly on the wall in an American manufacturing company, you'd see the plant manager walking around, casually dressed and chatting informally with the staff and factory workers. In France, expect to see the plant manager wearing a suit and beginning the day by greeting everyone in the office and factory with a handshake. These practices demonstrate the management structures within the two work environments: the French company is clearly more hierarchical.

In many Western cultures female friends greet each other by offering a kiss towards the sky rather than planting a proper kiss on one another's cheeks. Known as the 'air kiss', it avoids a messy exchange of lipstick. Like Southern Europeans, and unlike their Korean and Japanese neighbours, the Chinese demonstrate their regard for members of their own sex by publicly holding hands or making other forms of physical contact. Opposite sexes, however, don't engage in public displays of affection.

Getting up close and personal

Whether you kiss, bow or shake hands when you greet someone and say goodbye, how you do so indicates your culture's attitude toward bodily contact. In some countries – including France, Italy and Greece – the standard practice is to touch, whereas other cultures – such as those of New Zealand, Australia, Great Britain and the United States – view touching as intrusive, if not outright rude.

Islamic countries forbid public touching between the sexes and woe betide you if you get caught. Imprisonment and public hidings aren't out of the question. On the other hand, same sex couples walking down the street hand in hand or with their arms intertwined or draped over one another's shoulders is normal in Arab countries and implies nothing more than friendship or camaraderie. (Two men walking arm in arm in downtown Dallas may raise a few eyebrows whereas in Dubai no one would notice.)

If you've visited Latin countries, in South America to the Mediterranean, you know that the locals are comfortable with getting up close and personal. Embracing one another with big hugs and pats on the backs while planting kisses on your friends' and family members' cheeks is natural and expected behaviour. Even the workplace is filled with bear hugs and mutual kissing in place of a handshake.

No kissing please, we're German

The Knigge Society in Germany, an organisation that advises on etiquette and social behaviour, has called for a ban on kissing in the workplace. The society's chairman, Hans-Michael Klein, is purported to have received emails from workers expressing their concern about this overly familiar practice. His response is to stick to the traditional handshake. Although he admits that banning kissing outright may be impossible, he believes that society should protect people who don't want to be kissed. He suggests that if staff and employees don't mind being kissed

at work, they announce their feelings by placing a paper message on their desks. Mr Klein is reported as saying that kissing isn't typical German behaviour and that the habit is imported from countries such as Italy, France and South America. He indicates that kissing belongs in a specific cultural context and says that he's been told that Germans don't like to kiss while at work.

A survey shows that most German workers feel that kissing contains an erotic element and that the gesture is a way for men to get close to women. Other issues that the Knigge Society addresses include the appropriate way to end a relationship via text message and how to deal with a runny nose in public. Interestingly, the Russian custom of men exchanging kisses hasn't got in the way of Germany conducting commercial relations with the Big Bear.

In 2009, when Michelle and Barak Obama attended a G20 dinner, Silvio Berlusconi – Italy's then president – was desperate to embrace the bare-shouldered, tightly-toned, elegant woman. YouTube recordings of the three show Berlusconi pursing his lips, raising his shoulders and rubbing his fingers while extending his arms in a 'come-to-padre' pose. President Obama keeps a close and steely eye on Berlusconi, with taut lips and not a hint of a smile. His right arm, next to Berlusconi, is tense and tight. The First Lady smiles only with her lips while her eyes remain fixed on the Italian president. Her right arm juts forward like a steel rod and her fingers are tight, offering a handshake with no welcoming touch. The Obamas' message was, 'Don't even think about it!'

Gearing up your greetings

Greetings can be loaded affairs: to kiss or not to kiss; to shake hands or to refrain? The following are a few examples of the types of greetings you can expect in different areas around the world:

- ✔ **Brazil:** Upon greeting and departure, the custom is to shake hands with everyone present. After you establish a friendship with someone, expect to embrace.

    Brazilian women exchange kisses on alternating cheeks: twice if they're married, three times if they're single. The third kiss is to ensure 'good luck' in finding a spouse.

- ✔ **China:** A slight nod or bow from the shoulders is the proper form for greetings and departures. Wait for them to initiate the gesture and follow their lead. The Chinese are also, however, more comfortable greeting another person with a handshake than people from many other Far Eastern countries.

    The Chinese don't like being touched by people they don't know. This convention is especially true of older people and individuals in important positions. If in doubt, leave out the double-handed handshake.

- ✔ **France:** If you make friends with French people, expect them to kiss your cheeks three times when you say hello and goodbye.

✔ **The Middle East and the Gulf States:** Here, it's common for men to touch upon greeting. Wait for your counterpart to initiate the exchange because several styles of greeting are used.

When shaking hands, some people don't seem to want to let go, whereas a mere flutter of fingertips is more than adequate for others. The standard Asian handshake between men is more of a handclasp: it lasts between 10–12 seconds and is rather limp. This long hold contrasts with the North American handshake that lasts approximately 3–4 seconds and is firm. (For more about handshakes, flip to Chapter 9.)

Personal distance between male speakers is close in the Middle East and holding hands is quite common. Unless you want to insult the man, hold your ground and hold and hug him in return.

Elaborate greeting rituals are normal in Saudi Arabia. Although a Westernised Saudi man does shake hands with another man, the customary Saudi greeting between men is a more complicated affair. After saying the traditional 'salaam alaykum', you shake hands and say 'kaif halak'. Then you and your Saudi counterpart put your left hands on the other's right shoulders and kiss one another on each cheek. Finally, your new-found friend takes your hand in his. None of this applies if you're a woman, so don't be offended!

Traditionally, if a veiled Saudi woman is in the company of a Saudi man you don't introduce her. Although Westerners may wonder why women hide behind black veils, the ladies in burkas can watch how others behave while revealing little about themselves.

Acknowledging the no-touching rule

Although in many Far Eastern countries people greet one another by shaking hands, the Japanese in particular have an aversion to informal bodily contact. Japanese doing business in the West force themselves to shake hands although they are uncomfortable doing so. In their own country, the usual form of greeting is a long, low bow from the waist and a formal exchange of business cards.

Although young people are defying the norms of their parents, be aware that throughout the Middle and Far East male–female touching in public meets with disapproval.

Even if you feel awkward bowing to Far Eastern colleagues or customers, seeing it as a sign of subservience, do so anyway if you want to make a favourable impression. What you're saying is that you value their experience and wisdom and respect their culture and customs.

In the Far East, never put your hand or hands in your pockets when you're bowing, greeting someone or saying farewell or giving a speech. Doing so is considered rude, despite being accepted behaviour in the UK and America.

Japanese cities are very crowded and sometimes you need to push through the throng, as the locals do. To do so, hold your hand in front of your face, with a bent elbow (rather like a child pretending to be a shark or as if preparing a karate chop), while bowing and saying 'excuse me'.

When presenting your business card in the Far East, hold it in both your hands with your details facing towards the other person. When people from the Far East present you with their card, receive it with both hands and study it with respect before looking back, smiling at the person who presented it to you and accepting the card with a slight bow. Don't write on it!

Whether you're working in the Indian subcontinent, Central Asia or any country throughout the East, avoid slapping your colleagues on the back, playfully punching them on the arm or hugging the breath out of your new best friend. You'll be perceived as rude, disrespectful and invasive.

Waving farewell

The simple act of waving someone goodbye isn't so simple after all. What you may believe is a straightforward signal saying '*ciao bella*', '*à bientôt*', '*sayonara*' or 'see you later' can be interpreted as an offensive gesture or a sign to return. For example, if you give a business presentation in Argentina, and you wave goodbye to your audience, be prepared to present again. Your gesture of 'farewell' in fact signals to your audience that you want them to stay.

Most Europeans face their palms front and wag their fingers up and down with their arm stretched forward and held stationary. Americans hold their palms forward with their arms outstretched and wave their hand back and forth from side to side.

Throughout most of Europe, the American wave would be interpreted as 'no', except in Greece where the gesture is highly insulting and you can easily find yourself pleading innocence to the local authorities.

Observing the Conventions of Higher- and Lower-Status Behaviour

The concept of status refers to how important a role an individual plays in society. People with *high social status* are perceived as valuable and dominant and often fulfil leadership roles. *Low social status* people are regarded as dispensable in spite of their often playing important supporting roles in society. Across cultures and continents, people of lower status demonstrate deference to people holding higher status. Their body language is closed and they take up as little space as possible so as to appear non-threatening (see Figure 15-1). People with high status tend to fill the space they occupy. They're confident that they can handle whatever comes their way and aren't afraid of looking threatening. Their body language is both firm and relaxed, even in times of tension and panic.

Figure 15-1:
People in low status positions adopt submissive postures.

Your self-perception influences your behaviour. Whether you have a healthy sense of self-worth and confidence or feel like you're below pond life, your body language, no matter where you live, reflects your internal state. External factors cannot change your self-image. In contrast, external factors such as your job, financial standing and qualifications do affect the value and status others ascribe to you.

To determine a person's sense of herself, observe her non-verbal behaviour while she's interacting with others, particularly when under stress or pressure. Instinctive responses kick in at these times, revealing someone's true self-perception. The person who remains calm under pressure probably has a positive internal status; the person who shouts, screams and runs in panic at the first sign of stress is crying out for protection.

When the commanding officer enters a military barracks, enlisted soldiers stand up with shoulders back, stomachs in, eyes straight forward and not even a thought of smiling. When the soldiers are told to stand at ease, they widen their stance and clasp their hands behind their backs. At no time do they engage at a familiar level with their superior. Similarly, school pupils are taught to rise when an adult enters the classroom and staff members straighten up when the boss strides through the office. In Asian countries, subordinates don't look their superiors in the eye, whereas in Western cultures eye contact is the norm. (Check out the later section 'Playing by the local rules: Eye contact' for more on where to look depending on where you are in the world.)

Bowing, kneeling and curtseying

Bowing, kneeling, curtseying and lowering the head are low status behaviours. Within royal households, staff bow or curtsey when the monarch passes. By curling up the body and lowering it, you make yourself look small in relation to the other person. This behaviour can be traced to the animal kingdom, where creatures under attack cringe and crouch to protect themselves.

Bowing is of particular importance in Japan, where you can tell someone's status in relation to another's by how long and low the person bows. Someone holding a lower status bows lower and longer. If equals are bowing to one another, they match one another's bows. If one of the two people wants to show more respect, she adds an extra bow. The Japanese also add another bow for someone who's much older, as well as for a customer whose business they're hoping to obtain.

When you're bowing to someone who holds a higher rank than you, make sure that you out-bow the person and keep your eyes respectfully lowered. If you're unsure of who holds the higher status, bow slightly less low than the other person. Slide your hands down the front of your legs towards your knees or down the sides of your legs. Maintain stiffness in your back and neck and avert your eyes.

Standing to attention

Standing with a straight back, legs close together with your weight distributed evenly between them, arms by your sides and hands remaining still, is a sign of deference the world over. If you've experienced being called into the headteacher's office, standing up in court or serving in the military, you know the position. You look straight ahead and don't move a muscle until you're spoken to.

In some Western societies younger people stand up when an adult enters the room. They look people in the eye, shake hands firmly and say a polite 'hello, bonjour or guten Tag'. When dining out and someone stops by to say hello, men are expected to stand while women remain seated – confusing behaviour, isn't it, if we're supposed to have equal rights?

Getting Specific: Common Gestures, Multiple Interpretations

Just when you thought you knew the meaning of laughter, the 'thumbs up' sign and giving the 'okay' signal, you find yourself creating the most embarrassing faux pas. All you can plead is ignorance, which is hardly a viable excuse. This section fills you in to keep you out of trouble.

Giving the thumbs up . . . cautiously

The thumbs up sign means different things in different cultures. In North America and the UK, the sign means 'good'. The same gesture in the Arab world, Nigeria and parts of South America, however, has negative connotations, and in Germany holding up your thumb indicates the numeral one.

If you're travelling in Japan and want to indicate that everything's just great, stick your thumb up in the air with a clenched fist.

Ensuring that the okay sign really is okay

Traveller, beware. North Americans make a circle with their index finger and thumb – with the other fingers slightly raised – to indicate approval, but you're regarded as being vulgar if you make this sign in Brazil. To complicate the issue, when the Japanese make this sign they're signalling money, whereas, for the French, the gesture stands for zero.

Ask your host, or read ahead of time, what the okay sign means in a particular country. In America, it's a positive sign signalling success. In Arab countries, it's a rude sexual gesture, as is making the okay sign while shaking your fist in Japan. The okay sign can be a blessing or a curse. It may be safest to avoid using the sign at all!

Laughing your way into (and out of) trouble

When people laugh in the Western world, you're safe in assuming that they're happy. If you hear the same laughter – with a slightly different accent – in Asia, don't think that everything's fine. Individuals in the Asian world laugh as a means of controlling their displeasure and also to conceal embarrassment, confusion and shock. A young Japanese, Vietnamese or Korean woman may reveal her embarrassment by giggling behind her hands, which are held in an upright position, slightly away from her mouth, with the palm towards her face.

Cultures, like people, have personalities. Some are open, outgoing and extrovert. Others are closed, contained and restrained. Sitting in a restaurant in Rome you see people laughing, interrupting one another and touching a lot. Take yourself to Stockholm and experience the difference. People are quiet, more contained in their gestures and demonstrate less emotion. Both groups are equally friendly and caring; they simply express their feelings and goodwill quite differently.

Be careful when cracking jokes in different cultures. What tickles your fancy in the Arctic tundra may leave your colleague in the Congo cold. Although humour can translate across borders, you may struggle to grasp the subtleties. If you're in a culture different from your own and you're in doubt about what's funny and what's not, observe how the natives respond and follow their lead. You can also ask other people to relate their experiences of humour in different cultures.

Avoiding Problems and not Causing Offence

This section focuses in on an issue that in some ways runs through this whole chapter, which is to help you avoid embarrassing situations and steer clear of upsetting people in different countries and from different cultures.

A potpourri of local customs

Many conventions and common gestures can prove problematic when travelling. Here are a few to watch out for:

- ✔ When visiting Asian and Middle Eastern societies, use only your right hand for greeting and eating. The left hand is considered 'unclean' and using it in any greeting is highly insulting and eating with it is considered vulgar.

- ✔ Muslims consider pointing at anyone or anything rude.

- ✔ Asians and Arabs consider the feet to be unclean. When visiting Arab and Asian countries, be sure to sit with your feet flat on the floor; showing the soles of your shoes is highly insulting. Never prop your feet up on a piece of furniture, such as a desk or chair, or cross them over your knee.

- ✔ In Thailand, never step on a doorsill when entering someone's home. Thais believe that friendly spirits live below.

- ✔ Some Asian cultures, including Thailand and India, consider the head to be a sacred area where the soul resides. To touch the head of a Thai or an Indian, even a child or close friend, risks terminating the relationship.

Smoothing over difficult situations

Different cultures deal with difficult or embarrassing situations in different ways. Brazilians, for example, avoid giving bad news and saying no. They may change the subject, stretch the truth or put such a positive spin on the information that you don't notice the negative aspects. They're not trying to deceive or avoid losing face; they simply want to keep things positive and not disappoint.

On a cold winter's day, Carol, an American living in Tokyo, was travelling in the packed underground during rush hour. No seats were available and, in spite of her being pregnant, no one offered her theirs. She was forced to stand, pressed up against the safety glass of the door dividing her carriage from the next. Her train companions leant against one another for support rather than holding onto the straps.

With one lurch of the train, the passengers all swayed towards Carol and pressed against her. Her back went through the safety glass, leaving her covered in broken fragments. In spite of her condition, people ignored her. When the train arrived at the next station, however, one young man knocked out the rest of the glass to minimise the danger and another moved away to offer her a seat. These actions took place with no eye contact. Carol realised that she'd inadvertently created a scene and the Japanese, by not overtly paying attention to her, were 'saving her face'. Their lack of emotional reaction was their way of smoothing over an embarrassing situation for Carol, despite the incident having been an accident. This behaviour was their way of keeping the situation harmonious without offending her.

If you find yourself in a similar situation to Carol, follow your personal values and customs. If that means that you'd offer a pregnant woman your seat, do so without making a meal of the gesture. Establish eye contact with the person, smile, stand and indicate with your hand that your seat is for them. Make no contact with other people in the carriage, as doing so would cause them to feel uncomfortable and lose face.

Playing by the local rules: Eye contact

In North America and throughout much of Europe, eye contact is a necessary ingredient for demonstrating respect and signalling that you're a powerful business professional. The opposite is true, however, throughout much of Asia, Africa and Latin America, where making eye contact is viewed as rude, personally challenging or displaying a lack of respect. For example, in Africa, China and Japan you show respect to your superiors by avoiding eye contact.

As with so many of the issues I discuss in this chapter, though, things can be even more complicated. For instance, in the Middle East eye contact is considered a sign of trust or truthfulness, but Muslims consider eye contact between the sexes as inappropriate (eye contact with your own gender is acceptable).

Wherever you are in the world, as a general rule avoid staring or fixing your gaze on someone, because doing so can often be interpreted as confrontational.

When conversing with someone from the Far East, avoid making eye contact, except for an occasional glance to make sure that they're still present. Then, quickly avert your eyes again.

In some cultures eyes play an important role in communication. For that reason, always watch for even the smallest of eye gestures because they can highlight or undercut the spoken words.

Julia was working in Japan preparing a client presentation with a Japanese colleague. When she asked him if he was pleased with their work, he said that he was. Several days later, however, Julia heard through the grapevine that her colleague wanted to rework the presentation. When she asked him why he'd told her that it was fine when it wasn't, he replied, 'But I told you with sad eyes, Julia.' Julia left her colleague wondering how she could have spotted his sad eyes when he mostly averted his gaze.

Toasting the host and each other

Our Norwegian friend, Thomas, invited us to his home in Oslo for a long weekend. On Saturday night he hosted a formal dinner party for 16 people. Throughout the meal, toasts were frequently made. Every time our generous and gracious host raised his glass, he looked each guest directly in the eye as we raised our glasses in response. No one failed to engage in direct eye-to-eye contact with Thomas, as well as with the other guests at the table. Fortunately, we only toasted once during the serving of the hot food!

Although toasting details vary depending on which Nordic country you're visiting, direct and prolonged eye contact throughout the ritual is required.

In Nordic countries, Germany and Great Britain, eye contact is important for demonstrating sincerity and trust. If you're invited to a Scandinavian's home for dinner, be prepared for some serious eye contact (see the nearby sidebar 'Toasting the host and each other').

Many of the young Asian women I coach struggle to look their superiors in the eye. For them, doing so suggests arrogance and disrespect. Because they're working with British, American, Australian and Western European colleagues, establishing and maintaining eye contact is a must if they're to progress in their careers. In contrast, when coaching Westerners who are embarking on assignments in African, Asian and Arab countries, I get them to practise creating relationships with clients, superiors and colleagues while averting their eyes.

When you meet and deal with people from other cultures, pay attention and take every opportunity to discover more about how they behave in different situations. Doing so is bound to pay off as your personal relationships blossom and your career develops.

Adapting your style for clear communication

If someone asks me, 'Why do I have to adapt; why can't they?', I hear Aretha Franklin singing 'R-E-S-P-E-C-T/ Find out what it means to me!' Many people can't understand why they should adapt their behaviour to communicate successfully with people whose traditions and cultures are different. Take a moment to consider what that thinking leads to. Although business may be competitive, being deliberately disrespectful gets you nowhere; sooner or later you come unstuck. And on the way down, you have to face all the people you offended on the way up! For example, if you refuse to shake hands with a Western businesswoman when she extends hers in greeting, don't be surprised if she doesn't answer your phone calls or respond to your emails.

Remember that what seems strange to you is perfectly normal for someone else. For example, in North America and Europe men and women socialise individually and in groups; friendship between men and women isn't strange or unorthodox. This custom doesn't apply in Muslim countries, however. Men greet other male friends with a handshake, an embrace and by touching one cheek to the other and, when they're among their friends, Muslim women's behaviour is warm and affectionate. But never, however, shall the twain meet: the men stick with the boys and the women hang out with the girls.

You may be effusively affectionate, wanting to put your arms around your friends when you meet. This behaviour is great in Latin countries, and acceptable in China, too. However, unless you want to embarrass your Nordic buddy or German cohort, a polite hello suffices. You're not being unfriendly, simply respecting the norms of their culture and making your friend feel good. And isn't that what acting in a friendly manner is all about?

Being friendly means that you respect and conform to the traditions of the other person's culture, and are considerate of how your behaviour may be perceived in a land very different from yours. For more about communicating across cultures, pick up a copy of *Cross-Cultural Selling For Dummies* by Michael Soon Lee and Ralph R. Roberts (Wiley).

Chapter 16

Reading the Signs

In This Chapter

▶ Showing that you're interested

▶ Paying attention to all the signals

▶ Recognising different types of gesture

*I*n order to interpret body language accurately, you have to notice it first. If you think this sounds pretty obvious, you're right. And yet some people just don't pay enough attention to other people's behaviour – and are then surprised when they later express unhappiness, anger or even pack up and leave. 'But you never told me,' they say. 'If you'd paid attention, you'd have realised,' comes the reply.

Noticing how people behave is the first step towards understanding. After that, you can begin to interpret the meaning behind their actions. Be careful not to judge too quickly, however. The expert observer knows that it takes more than one gesture to convey a complete message.

Think of body language in the same way as you do the spoken word. If you want to communicate a thought you have to speak several words, or even a few sentences, to express what you mean. Body language works the same way. One gesture doesn't tell the whole story. It takes several actions, working together, to signal a person's feelings, thoughts and attitudes.

In this chapter you explore and interpret gesture clusters and identify where contradictions may exist between what someone says and how he says it.

Taking an Interest in Other People

When people are wrapped up in themselves they often don't notice how someone else is behaving. Big mistake. By failing to spot the signs, you lose valuable information. The way a person behaves can complement, supplement and even undermine what he's saying.

By observing people's body language you're on the inside track to knowing how they're feeling and how they may respond. Whether you're observing participants in a business meeting, a family negotiation or a couple in a restaurant, by being aware of how the people position and move their bodies, you may end up understanding more about their relationship than they do.

Here's a list of the telltale expressions for different emotions:

- ✔ **Happiness:** Lower eyelids are slightly raised, crinkling around the outer edges of the eyes and the eyes sometimes narrow; the corners of the lips move up and out and lips may part to expose upper teeth; cheeks are raised with an apple-like bulge; C-like wrinkles pull up from corners of raised lips to the sides of the nose. The body is open and forward moving.

- ✔ **Surprise:** The eyebrows zoom upwards in a curve; wrinkles spread across the forehead; eyes open wide showing their whites; the jaw drops; the mouth slackens. The head hunches into raised shoulders.

- ✔ **Sadness:** The inner ends of the eyebrows rise; eyes moisten; the mouth drops at the corners and the cheeks become limp; lips may quiver. The shoulders hunch forward; the body is slack.

- ✔ **Fear:** Similar to surprise but with subtle differences. Raised eyebrows are pulled together (not as much curve in the brow as in surprise). Forehead furrows in centre (when surprised, the furrow carries across the brow). Whites of the eyes show; lips are pulled back; the mouth is slightly open. Shoulders hunch forward, the chest arches inward and the body pulls backward.

- ✔ **Anger:** Eyebrows pulled down and inward; vertical crease between the brows; eyes narrow and stare with hardness. Lips close tightly, and turn down at the corners; nostrils may flare. Hands tighten and clench; the body is forward moving.

Be subtle when watching other people. If they feel they're being scrutinised, they may take offence and even become antagonistic.

James, a highly respected and acclaimed prize-winning scientist, is quite a bit older than his current wife. At a private dinner party held in his honour, he was invited to speak informally while coffee was being served. Earlier in the day, he had been the guest speaker at a luncheon meeting of colleagues and supporters. At that time, he spoke with reasonable authority and clarity. In public view, his wife looked at him adoringly, laughed at his jokes and led the applause. By the end of the evening, however, James was tired. His stories rambled, his words were mumbled and his jokes fell flat. As he spoke, his wife whispered and giggled with her young, handsome dinner partner, occasionally casting a glance towards her husband and pointing to her watch as if to tell him that it was time for him to wrap it up. When he finally sat down, his wife scowled at him across the table before turning again to the man on her right and resuming their intimate discussion. The difference in the way James's wife behaved on these two occasions demonstrated that their relationship was complex, complicated and compromised.

Drawing Conclusions from What You Observe

To read body language signals accurately, you have to consider the combination of gestures and whether they match what the person is saying and the context in which you're seeing them. For example, when someone scratches his nose, he's not necessarily indicating his guilt. He may just have an itchy nose. If, however, his eyes dart about, he's chewing his lip, his legs are crossed and one arm is tightly folded over his body, you're safe in betting that he's in a negative state of mind.

The following sections explain how to draw thoughtful conclusions.

Summing up the gestures

When observing body language, watch for all the behaviours a person is demonstrating. Making a judgement based on one gesture is unwise. If the sides of a person's lips are lifted up, don't assume he's happy. Look to see what his eyes are doing. If they're crinkling around the sides, he's feeling good; if they're dull and lifeless, he's faking his smile.

Continuing your search, if you notice a vertical line running between his brows, his head is tilted as he's leaning forward and his lips are lifted at the corners, he's showing interest, not anger. On the other hand, if his eyes are looking downward, the sides of his mouth are pulling down and he's holding his stomach, look out. He may be about to vomit. A smile isn't just a smile and a kiss isn't just a kiss, no matter what the song says. The sides of the mouth going up while the sides of the eyes pull down sends two contrasting signals. The mouth says happy and the eyes say sad. When in doubt, trust the eyes. (You can find out more about how eyes send messages in Chapter 5.)

If you want to be believed, make sure that your body language accurately reflects what you're saying. Get used to it. People always believe what they see more than what they hear.

Drumming fingers indicate different types of stress including boredom, anxiety, frustration and nervousness. Staring into space with dull eyes says he's bored, fed up or thinking about something else. Staring into space with engaged eyes tells you that he's listening. Crossed arms across his chest may indicate that he's feeling cold or is turned off by what you're saying. Always observe the gestures in context.

The following sections describe clues for recognising someone's mood.

Signalling stress

Observe someone's face and hands to see if he's stressed. If he's rubbing his eyes or the bridge of his nose, holding his head or stroking his neck, you can bet he's feeling the pressure. Like all self-touching gestures, holding and rubbing the head is comforting. Shutting your eyes at the same time helps to block out internal and external distractions (see Figure 16-1). Even if he says, 'I've just got a headache', he's still dealing with the pressure resulting from the pain.

Figure 16-1:
This man is comforting himself by rubbing his head.

Conveying boredom

If someone's eyes are dull and drooping and his head is resting in the palm of his hand, you can bet he's suffering a severe case of ennui. To keep himself awake, he may text, doodle or shift in his seat.

Wanda attended a conference to hear an expert in her field speak. Unfortunately, the expert was a better researcher and writer than speaker. Soon Wanda's attention began to wander. She noticed many of her fellow delegates shifting in their seats, looking at their watches and sitting with their arms folded across their bodies with their heads resting in their hands. Few of them were looking at the speaker and most seemed somnambulant.

Showing happiness

When someone is leaning towards you with outstretched arms and forward-facing palms, sporting a wide open grin and crinkling eyes, you're looking at a position of pleasure. If you want to show your happiness without going to such an extreme, a simple smile will do, as long as the laughter lines at the outer corners of your eyes are engaged. (Chapter 6 describes the difference between real and fake smiles.)

Spotting mismatches between words and actions

Words convey factual information and gestures convey feelings and attitudes. When a mismatch is evident between your words and the way you say them, people will believe what they observe rather than what they hear.

For example, if someone proclaims you that he loves you and he's sitting with his arms crossed over his chest, fists clenched, legs tightly crossed, head bent, mouth turned down at the corners and he has a big frown running across his forehead (see Figure 16-2), you might question his words. Should you suggest that he may be harbouring some unspoken feelings, such as resentment, anger or fear, and he scoffs at the suggestion and accuses you of putting too much emphasis on what you see, trust your instincts. You've got yourself a clear case of actions speaking louder than words.

Fernando approached his quarterly review with trepidation. Although his boss, Maggie, said that he was doing a fine job, her body language said something else. A lack of eye contact as she praised his work, fingers playing around her mouth and shifting body movements signalled all was not well. Although Maggie's words were supportive, her body language said that she wasn't happy with the job Fernando was doing. He left her office feeling confused and worried.

Figure 16-2:
The furrowed forehead, downward turn of the closed mouth, and crossed arms indicate a negative state.

Recall a conversation you had when you knew that something wasn't quite right. Describe the other person's gestures and facial expressions. What was he saying? How did you feel at the time? I'm willing to bet that a mismatch was evident between the words and the behaviours, leaving you feeling uncomfortable and confused. (For more about how gestures and feelings impact on communication, get yourself a copy of *Communication Skills For Dummies* by Elizabeth Kuhnke (Wiley).)

Over lunch with her friends, Jacqui was talking about her relationship with her husband, Michael. Although her mouth was formed in a smile and her words were positive, her eyes looked sad. She seemed distracted and kept twisting her wedding ring on and off her finger as she spoke. Several months later, Jacqui told her friends that she was leaving Michael. Remembering how she'd behaved at lunch that day, no one was surprised.

Considering the context

Just because someone sits bent forward with his head tucked into his shoulders, his arms crossed tightly over his chest, and his hands balled up in fists and tucked under his arms doesn't mean that he's angry. Look at the bigger picture. It may be cold where he's sitting and he's merely trying to keep warm. Or perhaps he ate something that he now wishes he hadn't.

If you want to read body language correctly, you have to take in all the signs.

Dr O'Connor is a tall, handsome and physically fit man. He gives the appearance of being strong and active. When I first saw him, I was pleased that my mother was in his care. However, when we shook hands I had my doubts. His hand felt limp in mine and I was aware that I was exerting more pressure than he was. Based on that handshake alone, I began to doubt his commitment. Thinking about him later, however, I recalled how gentle his touch was when taking my mother's blood pressure and listening to her heart, and how he lightly rested his hand on her shoulder as he encouraged her to take her medication. Because his hands are vital for his work, he must protect them and use them gently.

Honing Your Powers of Observation

Wanting to read body language accurately is your first step. Paying attention to the signs is your second. Practising, practising, practising is your third. Consciously observe other people's movements, gestures, facial expressions and body positions. Note the speed of their movements too. When you've got all the pieces of the puzzle in place, determine their inner state. Pick a place to practise where lots of people are busily getting on with their lives. Train stations, airports and restaurants afford the opportunity to observe people without being obvious. Practising at home and at the office is okay, too.

While you're picking up useful information, you may want to keep your observations to yourself!

Watch television with the sound turned off. Figure out what's going on by observing the body language of the people you're watching. After a few minutes, turn the sound on to confirm your interpretation.

Part V
The Part of Tens

Enjoy an additional Part of Tens chapter online at www.dummies.com/extras/bodylanguage

In this part . . .

- ✔ Find out more about the ten subtle giveaways that identify deceptive behavior.

- ✔ Learn about the ten ways that show you're interested in someone.

- ✔ Discover ten tips for reading other people's non-verbal behavior.

- ✔ Develop ten tactics for improving the silent messages you send out.

Chapter 17

Ten Ways to Spot Deception

'*O*, what a tangled web we weave, When first we practice to deceive!' The problem with trusting body language as the sole source of information is that human beings are complex creatures. One gesture cannot and does not reveal an entire story any more than a book's message can be contained in one word. Context is key and even forensic professionals can be stumped when it comes to spotting the giveaways. That said, by carefully watching for those uncontrolled gestures that appear when least expected, you may just be able to detect the deceiver.

Spotting deception is awfully difficult to do. If you know the person, the task can be easier, but not foolproof, because you can compare behaviours between how she acts when telling the truth and when you think she may be pulling the wool over your eyes. So, focus on a wide range of clues. If you think that just one single gesture is going to give the game away, you're just deceiving yourself.

Catching Fleeting Facial Expressions

If you've ever fibbed, fudged or fabricated – your secret's safe with me. Sometimes a little creativity with the truth is required. Not that I advocate lying as your default mechanism. And, when you've told a porky, you probably looked at your accuser in wide-eyed wonder as if saying, 'What? Who me? Never!', trying for all you're worth to appear to be telling the truth. What you can't control are those tiny, barely perceptible micro-expressions that flit across your face in a nano-second and die the moment after they've appeared. However, the well-trained observer and the highly intuitive bystander can spot this involuntary process that, like a traitor, betrays what you're feeling. The minor muscular twitches, dilation and contraction of the pupils, flushed cheeks and slight sweating that occur when you're under pressure can give the game away.

Watch someone's face carefully if you think she may be deceiving you. While the facade may look calm and composed, at some point the mask will fall, if only for a moment, revealing the truth behind the lie.

Imagine that you've recently taken up skiing. Someone asks you how you're getting on. You tell her you love it, that after your first week you tackled a black run and even though you wiped out and careened down most of the mountain flipping between your front and back sides, you're mad about the sport and can't wait to give it another go. While your words say 'Yes!' and you're smiling and laughing as you tell the story, for the briefest of moments a look of fear crosses your face, to be immediately replaced by your previous enthusiastic and excited expression. If spotted, that momentary look exposes your terror. It shows that, although you want to convey the impression of loving what you'd been doing, during that fall you feared for your life.

See Chapter 4 for more about facial expressions.

Suppressing Facial Expressions

A composed face, lacking expression, is hard to read and hard to hold. Known as a 'poker face', this expression is the best way to conceal what you'd rather not show. Narrowed eyes, a tense forehead and twitching lips are small, subtle signs that an emotion is being suppressed.

Say you're at the funeral of a dear friend. While your body is aching to cry, you feel uncomfortable exposing your emotions. You compose your face, holding your trembling lips in check by tightening your mouth or smiling slightly. The giveaway signs here are your moist eyes, creased forehead, and crooked smile or down-turned lips. Your words say you're fine while your body signals how sad you feel. You can find out more about masking emotions in Chapter 4.

Eyeing Someone Up

Some deceivers look you straight in the eye while telling a barefaced lie. Others look away. What you, as a lie detector, have to do is look for the intensity of the action and compare the behaviour to what you've noticed in the past. Possible signs of deception include:

- **Eye rubbing:** Deceivers often rub their eyes as they're speaking, as if their brain is erasing or blocking out the deception. Men rub their eyes vigorously whereas women use a small, gentle touching action just below the eye.

- **Inability to look you in the eye:** Both men and women tend to look away, avoiding your gaze. Their eyes dart back and forth from yours, or fail to connect with you at all.

If you think someone's telling you a tall story, interject a few simple, uncontroversial questions that you know will elicit honest answers. For example, ask her where she was born or what she had for breakfast. Check where she's looking. Follow this up with a trickier question and see where her eyes go then. If she has to make up an answer, her eyes go in search of it. If she's telling you the truth, her eyes follow the pattern established when answering the first set of questions.

Look for unusual patterns and over-compensation. If, for example, the deceiver doesn't usually look you in the eye when speaking to you and now can't connect with you enough, you can safely assume that something suspicious is going on.

Turn to Chapter 5 for more about how the eyes communicate.

Covering the Face

People frequently put their hands to their faces when lying. Hand-to-mouth gestures are typical of someone who's holding back information. This action stems from their childhood days when they covered their mouths while telling a fib. (Not that you ever did, of course!) With age, that gesture modifies, becoming less obvious.

If you're having a difficult conversation with someone and notice her resting her chin on her hand with her index finger covertly touching the corner of her mouth while she's speaking, she's signalling deceit. Several fingers playing across the mouth are another sign of containing information.

If someone puts her index finger over her mouth in the shh-ing gesture, she's telling herself to be quiet. She may even put her fingers in her mouth in an unconscious attempt to revert to the childhood security of her mother's breast.

Putting your finger in your mouth signals a need for reassurance.

Finally, when someone is holding back information, she quite often suppresses her words with a fake cough or a clearing of the throat.

In Chapter 6, you can discover more about mouth movements.

Touching the Nose

If the mouth cover is the easiest gesture to spot when you think someone may be deceiving you, the second-easiest is the nose touch. As the hand comes towards the mouth it is deflected to avoid being obvious. The nose, conveniently close by, serves as a suitable landing point.

When someone lies, it releases chemicals called catecholamines, causing the nasal tissues to swell. This is known as the Pinocchio Response because the nose becomes slightly enlarged with the increased blood pressure. A tingling sensation in the nose develops, resulting in an itch that screams to be scratched. The hand, already in position, vigorously squeezes, rubs or pulls at the nose to soothe the sensation.

During his Grand Jury testimony concerning the Monica Lewinsky affair, President Clinton touched his nose 26 times when answering probing, uncomfortable questions. When asked questions that were easy for him to answer, his hands were nowhere near his face.

The nose touch is an overworked action of deceit, so if you're ever in the position of having to be duplicitous, find yourself another gesture.

Faking a Smile

The smile is the easiest facial gesture to produce and is therefore the one most often used when someone is being deceptive. A smile is disarming. It makes other people feel positive, trusting, and unlikely to feel suspicious.

But there's something about a fake smile that causes warning signals to flash. Whereas a genuine smile involves many facial muscles, including the ones that crinkle the eyes as well as those that pull up the corners of the mouth, counterfeit smiles are different. First, they're confined to the lower half of the face. The teeth may show but the eyes remain unresponsive.

Second, the timing of a fake grin is an indicator. Someone assuming a phoney smile puts it on hastily and holds it longer than they would a genuine smile. While the artificial smile swiftly comes then disappears, an authentic smile evolves slowly and fades gradually.

Finally, a sincere smile is symmetrical with both sides of the mouth raising. A deceptive smile is asymmetrical, being more pronounced on one side than on the other.

If you're wondering whether someone's smile is fake or real, look to the eyes. If they're crinkled at the corners, the smile is genuine.

Refer to Chapter 6 for more details about spotting smiles and Chapter 5 for seeing the part the eyes play.

Minimising Hand Gestures

You can spot deception by observing people's hand movements. Most people are unaware of how they use their hands in conversation and tend to flap them about when they're excited. When someone's trying to deceive you, she controls her hand movements by tucking them into her armpits, shoving them into her pockets (where they can nervously jingle and jangle her keys and coins) or even sitting on them. She may tightly clasp one hand into the other or shrug her hands, facing her palms upwards, in a sign of helplessness. Whatever she does with her hands, be aware. A man who is being deceptive tends to keep his hands still, containing gestures he'd normally use to emphasise a statement, drive home a point or underscore an idea. Conversely, when a woman is being deceptive she tends to use her hands more than usual. She keeps them busy, as if deflecting attention from what's really happening.

You can find out more about hand gestures in Chapter 9.

Maximising Body Touches

In their unease, deceivers stroke their bodies in an effort to comfort and reassure themselves. They also touch themselves as a means of blocking out information or preventing it from escaping. Excessive chin stroking, lip licking and sucking, eyebrow scratching and hair grooming, when taken in context, are potential giveaway signs that something is amiss. In addition, the following gestures indicate deception when put into context:

- ✔ **The ear fiddle:** This person tugs at her earlobe, rubs the back of her ear and may even shove her index finger deep within the auricle as she seeks the comfort of bodily contact.

- ✔ **The collar tug or neck scratch:** When someone's with-holding information, she often tugs at her collar or scratches her neck. This action is in response to the tingling sensation and slight sweating caused by increased blood pressure in the delicate neck tissues. The neck scratch, in which the index finger may rub the neck up to five times, signals distrust and reservation.

- ✔ **The nose rub:** Several quick rubs below the nose or one quick nose touch also signals that someone's being deceitful. Like all possible signs of deception, however, you must be careful when interpreting the nose touch. The person may just need to give it a quick wipe for hygienic reasons.

- ✔ **Crossed arms and legs:** These are further signs of holding back an attitude or emotion. As always with body language, in order to obtain as clear a reading as possible, read the signs in context to avoid misinterpreting the message.

You can find out more about how your feet and legs give the game away in Chapter 10, and Chapter 8 looks in detail at arm movements.

Shifting Positions and Fidgeting Feet

Feet shuffle, toes twitch and legs cross and uncross when someone's being deceptive. She avoids bodily contact with others, preferring to keep her distance. While she may wriggle and squiggle, her actions appear stilted rather than animated.

Signs of deception are most prevalent in the lower part of the body. Legs and feet are farthest away from the brain so they're under the least amount of mental control. Therefore, they reveal vital signs that the deceiver may not even know that she's sending.

When a person is being deceitful, you may notice more frequent changes in her posture, as she struggles to find her comfort zone. If someone's jiggling her feet and shifting her posture you can bet she's feeling ill at ease. See Chapter 11 for more about how inner turmoil reveals itself in body language.

Changing Speech Patterns

People don't think of speech itself as body language, but the *way* you speak *is*. How you say something tells the observer more about your thoughts and feelings than the words you say. Your speech patterns, including your pace, rhythm and volume, reveal your attitude and emotions.

People who are purposely misleading you tend to say less, speak more slowly and make more speech errors. They're likely to take longer pauses before replying to a question, and hesitate more during their replies. They're inclined to quickly fill in any potentially awkward gaps in conversation.

A deceiver's tone of voice is likely to be higher than usual, lifting at the ends of sentences. (To learn more about how the voice reveals your inner state, have a look at *Voice and Speaking Skills For Dummies* by Judy Apps (Wiley).)

Chapter 18

Ten Ways to Reveal Your Attractiveness

In This Chapter

▶ Showing that you care

▶ Demonstrating openness

▶ Being yourself at your best

*B*eauty is in the eye of the beholder and attractiveness takes many forms. Some people like fair hair, others prefer brown. Although you may favour a lean, mean body, your best friend may fancy one that's soft and cuddly. Whatever your preference, the truth is that you don't have to look like Jennifer Aniston or Benedict Cumberbatch to be attractive. What most people find appealing is openness and someone who takes an interest in them.

'But why should I bother?' you ask yourself. Because people think that if you're attractive, you also have other positive attributes. Numerous studies show that people believe that attractive individuals are likely to be talented, warm and responsive, kind, sensitive, interesting, poised, sociable and outgoing. And if that's not enough to light your fire, attractive people are also seen as more intelligent and happier than the competition. Whether this is true or not doesn't matter. If that's how you're perceived, why would you want to argue the point?

Although appearance is a contributing factor in determining your attractiveness, people overlook a less-than-perfect face or physique if your body language is appealing.

Engaging With Your Eyes

Think about a time when someone gave you his full attention. Chances are that he looked you in the eye, kept his body still and offered you encouragement to express your thoughts and feelings. His attention was focused on you. Establishing and maintaining eye contact with other people shows that you're interested in them. And if you're attentive to other people, they'll be attracted to you.

When you look at someone, make sure that your eyes reflect your interest in who that person is. Establish and maintain eye contact and refrain from frowning or squinting. Scrunching up your face gives you lines and wrinkles long before they're due.

By paying attention and demonstrating care, you make the other person feel important. Anyone who makes another person feel significant and worthwhile is automatically perceived as attractive.

Refer to Chapter 5 for more info about the eyes.

Showing Liveliness in Your Face

Smile and the world smiles with you; cry and you cry alone. At least, that's what my grandfather told me. A natural, genuine smile, engaging the eyes and mouth, is appealing. People want to be with someone who makes them feel good. Frowning, pouting and a generally miserable face are definite turn-offs.

A face that shows liveliness, interest and enjoyment is like a magnet. It draws people to you and makes them want to be in your company. Through your positive expressions, including eye contact and smiling, you can get people to see you as an attractive person.

Don't walk around with an artificial grin plastered to your face – that's a definite turn off.

You can find out more about facial expressions and mouth movements in Chapters 4 and 6.

Offering Encouragement

By nodding, tilting and cocking your head while another person is speaking, you show that you're listening and are interested in what he's saying. And anyone who shows curiosity is consistently perceived as attractive.

Nodding encourages people to continue speaking and demonstrates care and curiosity. Tilting your head to one side also shows that you're involved and paying attention. When you display concern for, fascination with or involvement in someone's story, you seem connected and empathetic. And who doesn't find those characteristics attractive and appealing?

You can read more about head positions in Chapter 3.

Using Open Gestures

Open gestures welcome people into your territory. By showing that you are attentive, relaxed and comfortable, you come across as warm and approachable. And warm plus approachable equals attractive.

If your tendency is to cross your arms over your chest or to shove your hands into your pockets, resist the temptation and open your arms, showing the palms of your hands instead. Barrier signals keep people away and make you look cold, distant and uninviting. Open gestures encourage others to enter your environment and demonstrate your acceptance of and appreciation for who they are.

Turn to Chapters 8 and 9 for more about open gestures.

Showing Interest Through Your Posture

An upright, erect posture is infinitely more appealing than a slumped, unresponsive physique. That's not to say you have to be rigid and stiff. On the contrary, you want your body to be flexible and alert to draw people to you and make them feel at ease.

When you're seated in an informal situation, lean backwards and adopt an asymmetrical position. Have a go at resting one arm over the back of the chair. Try other positions. Open, relaxed postures are more inviting and attractive than having both arms squeezed tightly by your sides. They take less effort, too.

If you want to show interest, lean slightly forward using a symmetrical posture. This balanced position shows that you're focused on the other person. If you act as if you're curious about that person and care about him, he's going to be drawn to you.

In Chapter 7, you discover more about the power of posture.

Positioning Yourself

Attractive people respect others. They take into account their points of view and show consideration for their feelings. They strive to understand what makes someone feel good and what causes offence. They recognise when to move in and when to back off.

Respecting someone's personal space is an attractive quality. Whether at work or in a social context, by placing yourself next to another person you're indicating that you value him and are interested in what he has to say. Attractive people don't purposely embarrass someone else and never intentionally invade someone's territory.

If you want to reveal your attractiveness, respect the other person's space. All being well, when you sit or stand at an appropriate distance, he feels confident and comfortable in your company.

You can find out more about positioning yourself in various spaces in Chapter 12.

Touching to Connect

Attractive people aren't afraid to make physical contact and appreciate the power of an appropriate touch. Touching is an effective gesture for offering encouragement, expressing affection or compassion, and showing support.

Attractive people are respectful when touching others. Your attractiveness quota rises if you intentionally touch another person in these situations:

- ✔ When you're listening to someone's problems or concerns. Your touch indicates that you care and are offering support.

- ✔ When you're persuading someone to your point of view. Your touch is like a bridge, connecting the other person to your position.

- ✔ When you're giving information or advice. Your touch conveys encouragement and co-operation.

 Only touch another person if you have a relationship that permits deliberate physical contact. Touching implies that a bond exists between the people involved. Observe the kind of contact people feel comfortable with before initiating contact. If in doubt about how your touch is going to be received, keep your hands to yourself.

Lookin' good

Attractive people take pride in their appearance. They know which clothes look good on them and which items they should give to a charity shop. You don't have to spend vast amounts of money to make yourself attractive. Start by being clean and well-groomed. See that your hair is washed and styled to suit you. Are your fingernails clean and trimmed? Do you visit the dentist regularly? Are your clothes and shoes in good repair? What about their size, style and colour? Do they suit you? How you present yourself reflects how you feel about yourself. If you don't take the time and effort to show yourself at your best, don't expect to be seen as an attractive individual.

If in doubt about what colours and shapes work for you, treat yourself to a session with a personal stylist. The professionals can guide you in the right direction while your friends, family and your own personal taste may take you down the wrong path.

If you're physically out of shape, do something about it now. Life's short. Not only are you going to look better, you're going to feel better. You don't have to join an expensive gym or health club, although if that works for you, do it. You don't have to invest in lots of fancy kit to do stomach crunches, though a good pair of running shoes is vital if you're heading off for a jog. What you do need to do is find what works for you, commit to a plan and stick to it. Fat and flabby is neither healthy nor attractive.

Being on Time

The most attractive people demonstrate respect and care for others. Although you may not think that how you manage your time has anything to do with body language, time management is an integral aspect of non-verbal communication, which is why I include it here.

If you've ever been kept waiting, whether for an appointment, a date or even a response to an email, you know how annoying it is. Keeping to schedule and being punctual is more than a demonstration of good manners; doing so is a reflection of your core values. In some cultures, such as India and Saudi Arabia, being kept waiting isn't an issue; it's even expected. But in Western cultures, people are much more aware of time. (See Chapter 19 for more information about time in different cultures.)

If you're habitually late, consider the impact of your behaviour. Don't be surprised if people consider you to be a bit of a flake, if not rude and selfish. Although you may think that arriving at a dinner party 'fashionably late' is appealing, the host whose soufflé depends on precise timing won't be thrilled.

Synchronising Your Gestures

To enhance your face-to-face interactions, synchronise your movements and gestures with those of the speaker. Watch people in conversation and note how their bodies move in a rhythmic pattern, whether their heads are nodding or their hands are gesturing. Then observe yourself. Notice how your eyes are blinking and your head is nodding in time with the speaker's. These subtle reflective body movements show that you're engaged with the discussion.

When you're speaking and you want to prevent someone from interrupting you, keep your hand slightly raised as you end your sentences. When you're willing to let someone else speak you have several options for handing over the air space. You can pause, look steadily at the other person or conclude a hand movement that was accompanying your speech. By using these signals you're demonstrating the attractive quality of sharing conversation, rather than hogging the spotlight. For more about the power of synchronised behaviours turn to Chapter 14.

Enhancing Your Way of Speaking

Attractive people know how to adjust their voices to suit the environment. They tweak their volume, pitch, pace and tone according to the situation. They choose appropriate language and speak clearly, confidently and with commitment. In addition, attractive people give their full attention as others express themselves.

Because attractive people like to share their opinions and tend to talk more than their more introverted cousins, aim to encourage others to speak as you listen more and talk less. Good listeners are a valuable commodity. Behaving with confidence, moving with purpose and demonstrating that you are comfortable abiding by the rules of your environment are sure signs of your attractiveness. (You can read more about enhancing your way of speaking in *Persuasion & Influence For Dummies* by Elizabeth Kuhnke (Wiley).)

Chapter 19

Ten Ways to Find Out About Someone Without Asking

- -

In This Chapter

▶ Observing the signs

▶ Determining the meaning

- -

*S*o, you've seen someone who's caught your eye. Although she's interesting enough to investigate, you don't want to pump your friends for information at this stage. What do you do? Pay attention.

You have two eyes, two ears and one mouth. Use them in that order and you may discover what qualities this person possesses that float your boat or ring your bells, without you giving your game away.

Observing Eye Movements

Do they flash? Do they flicker? Are they dull and dreary? Turn to the eyes, the gateway to the soul, as your first point of reference.

No matter how much your mouth churns out information, your eyes reveal more. Eyes that turn downwards like Antonio Banderas's give the impression that the person is kind, trustworthy and caring. The Spaniard's combination of soulful eyes and strong physique is swoon-inducing. Daniel Craig's steely blue eyes and bronzed six-pack have a similar effect. Fans wiggle in their seats when Hollywood stars Bradley Cooper and Matthew McConaughey step onto the red carpet. Through their carefully orchestrated eye movements, this generation of heart throbs projects an image of hot and sexy men of steel. Like most mature members of the royalty, long-reigning Queen Elizabeth II seldom gives her emotions a public viewing, and quite rightly, too. Even though her eyes reflect a down-to-earth kindness, you may think that they're covered by a thin gauze curtain to keep her feelings concealed from her public. Long live the Queen!

The late Princess Diana, on the other hand, drew her public in with her soulful eyes, averted gaze and vulnerable appearance. She was naturally skilled at creating empathy and captured the world's compassion by lowering her head and gazing upwards from underneath her brows. Women of all ages continue to replicate this poignant pose designed to elicit care and compassion.

Politicians, celebrities, masters of industry and most people with a public persona to project establish direct eye contact with others, making them appear interested, confident and credible. When you act as if you're self-assured, people treat you as if you are. The more people treat you as if you are the image you project, the more you become what you want to be.

If the person in your sights returns your gaze with lowered eyelids, raised eyebrows and slightly parted lips, she's indicating that she's interested in you and is willing to take things further. How you decide to respond to that message is your choice.

For more on how to read eye messages, head to Chapter 5.

Looking at Facial Expressions

By looking at the position of the mouth, the movement in the lips and what the nose is doing – yes, really, your nose – you can spot another person's happiness or pain, anger or despair, or just plain boredom. The most successful people in the public eye manipulate their facial expressions in order to elicit desired responses. They know what to show and when to show it.

The saying goes that behind every successful man is a strong woman. Some women look at their partners with an unwavering passion, awe and adulation. By attaching themselves to another person in this way they raise their own stature in the eyes of others. Nancy Reagan, the wife of the late US president, Ronald Reagan, was an actress before becoming First Lady. She was expert at influencing public opinion via the looks she showered upon her husband. Resembling a love-struck teenager, she'd gaze upon him with Bambi-like devotion. Her public displays of affection sent the message that Ronnie was a terrific guy.

Chapter 4 has details on the range of emotions that faces display.

Watching for Head Movements

Observe someone nodding in agreement, understanding or with the desire to add her point of view to the discussion. Her eyes are engaged, her head is upright and her face is animated. Slow nods tell you that she's following the speaker, and fast nodding indicates a desire to jump into the conversation. A shake of the head tells you she's not buying what she's hearing.

Cocked, canted and tilted heads indicate that someone's

- ✔ Thinking about what they're observing
- ✔ Contemplating how to react
- ✔ Demonstrating deference
- ✔ Responding submissively

When you register head movements in combination with other gestures, such as lip and eye actions, you're well-equipped to determine a person's attitude and its underlying message.

Head to Chapter 3 for more on head movements.

Noticing Hand and Arm Gestures

The state of your hands conveys silent messages about your internal state. Are your fingernails filed and polished or chewed to the quick? Are your fingers tapping, fiddling, scratching, rubbing or picking at something indiscriminately? If so, stop. You're sending anxiety and stress signals. When you see a person flapping her hands like Prissy in *Gone With the Wind,* you can identify that she's, well, in a flap!

When someone's hand goes to her mouth, you're safe in betting that she's holding back some kind of feeling, emotion or attitude. And when her lips are firmly sealed, she's keeping her feelings to herself.

Anyone rubbing her hands and licking her lips at the same time is feeling happy and excited, as long as the speed's up tempo. If the hand and lip rub is slow and deliberate, be careful. This is the behaviour of someone concocting a scheme, devising a strategy or calculating a risk that's designed to benefit her and not you.

Arms crossed against the chest, hands tucked into the armpits or a lowered head and furrowed brow are not signs of a warm and welcoming person. Of course, she may just be reacting to a cold blast of air. Opened arms, a dropped-jaw smile and an eyebrow flash convey pleasure and excitement, whereas a pointed finger wagging in your face demonstrates aggression, dominance and a dictatorial attitude. You may want to stay out of the bully's way.

For more on hand and arm gestures, go to Chapters 8 and 9.

Observing Posture

Someone in a Superwoman pose – upright, wide stance and arms outstretched or with hands on hips – demonstrates strength, power and assertiveness. If her chest is thrust forward, and her jaw is clenched while her chin juts out, beware. This aggressive posture signals that she's ready to take you on. Slumped shoulders, hands protecting the privates and a downcast eye all indicate that the person is depressed, discouraged or despondent. Sit with your ankles crossed and your hands neatly folded in your lap and you're suggesting containment. Sit with your legs splayed, your arms stretched across the back of your chair and your chest puffed out, and you're showing your dominance. Careful how you splay your legs. You may be showing more than you intend.

You can read more about posture in Chapter 7.

Considering Proximity and Orientation

Does a person get up close and personal when she's not been invited to do so? Does she turn her back when you approach? You can tell a lot about a person's nature, attitude and culture by the amount of space she places between the two of you, as well as how she positions her body in relation to yours.

If someone is feeling co-operative, she sits next to you. If she's feeling competitive, she sits across from you. If she really doesn't get on with you, she turns away.

Notice where a single person places herself when there are other people sharing the space, be it a restaurant, airport lounge or the changing room at the gym. If she sits with her head down, averting eye contact, she's indicating that she doesn't want to engage with anyone, thank you very much. If she sits facing the room, her body angled in an open position, she's indicating that she's up for a chat.

Those with a sense of their own high status remain seated while lesser mortals stand. People with a low sense of status move tentatively, hanging behind their more dominant colleague when entering the boss's office. People of equal status naturally sit next to one another, unless they're adversaries, in which case they sit facing each other. Go to Chapter 10 for more information on the messages you send through the way you position yourself in relation to others.

Paying Attention to Touching

Being comfortable touching others puts you in a powerful position. People look up to those who are physically at ease and move freely, as long as their touches are appropriate and inoffensive. Granted, Anglo-Saxons have more difficulty embracing the gesture because their culture is more reserved than that of their Latin cousins. That small point aside, touching implies trust. People often touch when they are

- ✔ Offering information or advice
- ✔ Giving instructions
- ✔ Making a request
- ✔ Persuading
- ✔ Flirting
- ✔ Conveying enthusiasm
- ✔ Offering comfort or consolation
- ✔ In a dominant role

When another person touches you, she's implying that a bond of trust exists between you. Unless, of course, that person is a politician, in which case you can assume that she just wants your vote.

Go to Chapter 9 for more on messages conveyed through touch.

Responding to Appearance

Unless you're meeting a blind person who forms impressions of others through touch, sound and smell, people make judgements about others based on physical appearance. With few exceptions, your initial impression of someone is informed by the way she looks. You may start by noticing what she's wearing. The clothes you choose represent how you view yourself and influence how others view you. If you notice someone wearing clean, well-fitting clothes, who's had a recent haircut and has manicured fingernails, you're looking at someone with a sense of personal pride.

And what about fitness? Whatever your investment in clothing and accessories, without a fit body you struggle to convince others that you're in control of yourself. To find out more about the power of a positive self-image, take a look at *Confidence For Dummies* by Kate Burton and Brinley Platts (Wiley).

People who want to show themselves as being at the top of their game pay attention to their outward appearance. They know the impact their visual message has on people's opinion of them.

Go to Chapter 11 for more on personal appearance and perceptions.

Checking Timing and Synchronisation

A skillful communicator knows the impact that time has on relationships. In Western cultures, people place great importance on time management. They value pace, punctuality and a pre-determined schedule. Northern Europeans and North Americans don't like tardiness, slowness and unstructured time. If you want to keep your mother-in-law happy, show up on time with a plan in place.

In India, Saudi Arabia and other Eastern cultures, people have a more relaxed approach towards time. Here, keeping people waiting for appointments and allowing interruptions during meetings is common and not considered rude. Time is seen as flexible and schedules are simply loose guidelines by which to structure your life.

When you're interacting comfortably with another person and have established a good rapport, you may find that your body movements match one another's. Your gestures and actions harmonise while you both subconsciously copy or reflect one another's actions. Like two dancers, your movements are synchronised as you both move to the same rhythm. Imagine the ensuing chaos if your movements were waltz-like while the person you're interacting with was jitterbugging. You'd be bumping into and tripping over one another and your communication would be in a muddle.

If you pay attention to another person and match your body movements to hers, you enhance your communication. So, if you want to stay on your father-in-law's good side, get your body in sync with his. By nodding at his jokes, smiling at his stories and recognising by the cant of his head that the sun is over the yardarm and it's time for a cocktail, your body reflects and responds to the signals he's sending out, making him happy. Which is a good thing.

If you've been listening to a long-winded rant and have had no opportunity to share your views, move conspicuously when you get the chance by shifting in your seat or making a hand gesture. By changing your body language you're indicating that it's your time to speak.

Scrutinising Non-Verbal Aspects of Speech

Because we take meaning from the way a message is delivered as well as from the words themselves, pay attention to the non-verbal aspects of speech. The volume, pitch, pace and tone of a person's voice give you a pretty good idea of her mood and attitude. Add in accent, rate and emphasis and the picture becomes clearer, albeit more complex.

You can usually spot a person's inner state through her vocal patterns. If her voice is low in volume, sombre in tone, slow in speed and lacking in emphasis, you can assume that she's feeling sad or depressed. If her pitch is high, her pace quick and the words tumble out of her mouth, she's probably feeling excited.

When a person lifts the pitch at the ends of her sentences and is neither asking a question nor Australian, you're right in thinking she's feeling a bit insecure or uncertain. Nervousness and deception, characterised by stuttering, stammering or adding 'ums', 'ers' and 'ahs', indicate that someone's not clear about what she wants to say. Polished performers eliminate those space fillers and count on the pause to provide authority and indicate confidence.

Anyone who can make you laugh has got to be okay, right? Laughter is infectious. It makes you feel good. Laughter lifts the spirits and as long as you laugh with, rather than at, another person, the results are positive and beneficial.

Finally, the person who wants to demonstrate that she has higher status than another, aims to have the last word on a subject.

Chapter 20

Ten Ways to Improve Your Silent Communication

In This Chapter
▶ Creating impressions
▶ Being willing to adapt

*I*f you've ever been in awe of someone who's comfortable asking for what he wants, dresses in a way that suits him and leaves people feeling good about themselves, now's your chance to discover his secrets. Actually, they're not such big secrets. It's more a matter of attitude. If you're aware of your current behaviour and are willing to do what you have to do to get the results you want, you're well on your way to achieving them.

Taking an Interest

The best communicators take an interest in other people. They empathise with you and, just by observing you, know how you're feeling. Think about those people whose company you thoroughly enjoy. I'm willing to bet – and I'm not a betting woman – that you seek the companionship of people who make you feel good about yourself. At least, I hope you do.

If you think that you're a good communicator but for some odd reason no one else agrees, consider your behaviour. The problem could be that you're so busy focusing on yourself, your stories and your interests that you're failing to notice what's important to other people. If you want people to like you, take an interest in them.

ANECDOTE

I once described another person as 'boring'. The friend I was speaking to told me that, if I find someone 'boring', I should think about that person for five minutes, and continue to do so in five-minute chunks until I find something interesting about him. He also suggested that I may want to consider my own behaviour. Was I acting in a way that brought out the best in the other person? Was I demonstrating an interest in him or was I more interested in myself? This was a great lesson and I've never described anyone or anything as boring since. At least, not in public.

Knowing What You Want to Express

A clearly formulated thought, simply expressed and without apology, makes life so much easier for both speaker and listener. As the listener, you know where you stand. As the speaker, you clarify your position. Instead of umming, erring or ahhing, expert communicators speak clearly, concisely and with conviction. They leave the verbal space fillers to those who are anxious about stating their opinions and hesitate to express their feelings.

Before speaking, whether stating an opinion or asking a question, have your thoughts clearly formulated in your mind. If you're speaking at the same time as you're thinking about what you're saying, you may have to make several attempts before you get your words out coherently. By then, your listener may have left the building.

Before speaking, close your mouth, consider the one message you want your listener to remember and speak with conviction. (For more about speaking with conviction, pick up a copy of Judy Apps's book, *Voice and Speaking Skills For Dummies* (Wiley).)

Modelling Excellence

Every so often you meet someone who has a knack for communicating that fills you with awe, keeps you hanging onto his every word and makes you hunger to be in his company. That's the person whose behaviour you may want to model.

Modelling excellence requires that you take the time to observe and reflect on your own behaviour and that of others. By observing people you learn what works and what doesn't. If someone uses body language that's inclusive, encompassing, open and welcoming, you're going to feel comfortable in his company. If someone looks down his nose or jabs his finger at you, you'll wish you were somewhere else. If someone presents himself with conviction, belief and credibility, commanding your attention and eliciting your respect, you're onto a winner.

Claiming your space, moving with purpose and speaking like you mean it makes a positive and powerful impression.

Deciding what you consider to be excellent behaviour requires that you review and determine your own values in order to behave with personal integrity. Ask yourself the following questions:

1. What do I value – my standards, beliefs, morals and ethics?

2. What is important to me about those values?

3. How do I demonstrate my values in the way I use my body?

Evaluate your current behaviour and acknowledge where you may have some blind spots. Perhaps you act in a defensive way – frowning with your head down and your arms crossed, for example. Perhaps you dismiss feed-back with a flick of the wrist, turned down lips and a shrug of the shoulder. Perhaps you play the blame game by finger pointing at others. Concede that some of your behaviour may put people off. When you follow the examples of people you admire, and acknowledge what you do well and where you can improve, you've got yourself a foundation to build on. (You can find more exercises for modelling excellence in *Communication Skills For Dummies* by Elizabeth Kuhnke (Wiley).)

Mirroring Others

By mirroring – that is, reflecting the body language of another person – you can create a natural rapport that leads to successful communication. Mirroring someone's behaviour tells him that what he's doing is acceptable in the context of your interaction. Mirroring demonstrates that you're willing to echo what you're observing in order to create an environment where both you and he can communicate freely and comfortably.

Once you've matched the other person's behaviour, you can then take the lead yourself and get him to mirror yours. (You can find tips and techniques for effective mirroring in Chapter 14. I also recommend *Neuro-Linguistic Programming For Dummies* by Romilla Ready and Kate Burton (Wiley).)

Practising Gestures

Some people struggle to find appropriate gestures for expressing themselves. Smiling, opening their arms and expanding their chests just doesn't sit com-fortably with them. One client, who's a thoroughly pleasant fellow, habitually frowns, making him look angry and out of sorts. He wasn't aware that he had this habit until I pointed it out to him. His genuine interest in other people means that he really concentrates on what they do and say, causing his brow to furrow. He thought he was conveying interest but other people thought he was showing disapproval.

If you want to project a specific image or attitude, practise the appropriate gestures until they become a natural part of your behavioural repertoire. You may feel uncomfortable at first – this is natural when learning a new habit or skill. Stick with it. The more you practise, the more at ease you feel as the gestures become second nature. Actors apply this technique all the time, both on and off screen.

Developing Timing and Synchronisation

Timing is all. Don't believe me? Lean in for an unexpected kiss and don't be surprised if your lips miss your target. Bump into a stranger at rush hour and either make a friend or sour someone's day. Throw a ball at someone who's not watching and see him struggle to retrieve it. When you get your timing right, you can create magic. Get it wrong, and watch out.

Improve your timing by paying attention to your surroundings and anticipating what may happen based on what you observe. Scanning in anticipation is a particularly useful skill for anyone working with the public, such as waiters and airline personnel. A skilled interpreter of body language anticipates an individual's needs by identifying non-verbal signals, and responding to them before being asked.

If you want to show that you're paying attention to a person who's speaking, synchronise your body movements with his. When your gestures echo those of others, you produce a rhythmic pattern that enhances communication. (See Chapter 8 to see how kinaesthetics impact on communication.)

Dressing the Part

Glad rags, jeans or a pinstripe suit? What's it to be? Your choice depends on what message you want to convey. The way you dress is a sign of who you are. Think of your clothes as a costume, through which you create impressions. Feeling relaxed and casual? Loose trousers and an unstructured jacket may be just the ticket. Working in a formal environment? A tailored suit is more appropriate. If you want to fit in with the herd, note how your friends, clients and colleagues dress and adapt your style to match theirs. People feel comfortable when others dress in a similar manner to them. (For more about how people respond to similarities, pick up a copy of *Persuasion & Influence For Dummies* by Elizabeth Kuhnke (Wiley).) Sure, you want to be comfortable and dress in a way that reflects who you are. You also want to be appropriate. You really do. If your way of dressing is distracting and inhibits communication, you may want to reconsider your choices. Your clothes needn't be expensive. They do need to be clean, in good repair and suited to your shape and style.

If you work for a conservative organisation where a suit and tie for men and jackets and skirts or trousers for women are the norm, you're tempting fate to show up in tracksuit bottoms and a hoodie. To do so would make other people uncomfortable and they'd question your credibility.

Acting the Way You Want to Be Perceived

First, you dig deep within and uncover your values. You ask yourself, 'What really matters to me? What do I stand for? How do I reflect those values in my behaviour?' Then, you incorporate the appropriate body language to create the impression you want to project.

You may not give much thought to your non-verbal behaviour, rationalising that how you behave works fine for you and that's all that matters. Okay, whatever. Just remember, though, that the way you behave determines how you're perceived. If you want people to think that you're kind, caring and considerate, act as if you are. Reach out your hand, take time to listen, give them their space. If you want to come across as tough, move with force and deliberation, contain your gestures, and keep your facial expressions to a minimum. The trick is to demonstrate your thoughts, feelings and intentions through your movements, gestures and expressions.

Demonstrating Awareness

Some people just don't get it. They're blind to their own behaviour and the impact it has on others. When you're mindful of the actions and reactions of other people, you develop an awareness of what works well when and where. (To learn more about mindfulness, check out *Mindfulness For Dummies* by Shamash Alidina (Wiley).)

You may not care what other people think of you. Good for you. In certain circumstances, however, such as being interviewed for a job you very much want, speaking on behalf of a cause you care about or giving life-saving instructions, someone's opinion of you matters very much. Knowing how your listeners respond to specific behaviours, and adapting your actions to meet their needs, creates successful communication. As well as focusing on your own behaviour, observe how other people behave. When you pay attention to the actions of others, you can respond in a way that makes them feel noticed, valued and taken seriously. And if you make someone feel that he matters, you're going to matter very much to him. Of course, you could choose to denigrate or dismiss someone because of the way he acts, in which case don't count on building a long-term, respectful relationship.

Asking for Feedback

Asking how people perceive your behaviour doesn't hurt – at least, not very much. If their responses match your vision of yourself, all's well. If, however, they tell you one thing and you thought you were projecting something else, you may want to spend some time re-evaluating your views.

When you ask for feedback, be specific. Otherwise you leave the door open for all kinds of information to come flooding through, some of which may not be pertinent or helpful. By asking for and receiving specific and honest comments about your behaviour, you can continue what's working well and adjust what's not. Make sure that you're open and receptive to the feedback coming your way and listen attentively. If you don't, the person offering insights may become exasperated and walk away, leaving you none the wiser. If you don't understand, ask for clarification. Respect and acknowledge the other person's point of view. This doesn't mean that you have to agree with what he's saying, just that you value his input. Finally, thank him for his opinions. After all, you asked for them. (To learn more about giving and receiving feedback, pick up a copy of *Communication Skills For Dummies* by Elizabeth Kuhnke (Wiley).)

 If you're giving feedback, make sure that you're clear about what the other person wants feedback on. Comment on observable facts and avoid making assumptions about personality or motives.

Index

About the Author

Elizabeth Kuhnke is an Executive Coach, specialising in communication skills and personal impact.

A former stage, television and radio actor who holds advanced degrees in Speech and Communication and Theatre Arts, Elizabeth has written three books addressing communication skills in the *For Dummies* series (*Persuasion and Influence*, *Communication Skills*, and *Body Language*). She has designed university voice and movement programmes and teaches acting skills to students and professionals. She is an accredited Myers Briggs Type Indicator (MBTI) administrator and Neuro-linguistic Programming (NLP) practitioner.

Elizabeth combines her theatrical expertise and psychological understanding with a rock-solid business approach. She works at top level with Fortune 500 and FTSE 100 companies and leading professional firms providing training and coaching in key areas relating to interpersonal communication. Coming from diverse backgrounds including accountancy, law, manufacturing and telecommunications, Elizabeth's clients consistently achieve their goals and have fun getting there. Her keys to coaching are based on the principle of demonstrating respect, establishing rapport and producing results.

A highly entertaining speaker, Elizabeth is a popular choice on the conference circuit, and is often quoted in the media addressing issues concerning confidence, voice, body language and communication skills – all the ingredients that create a positive, powerful impact.

To learn more about how Elizabeth can support you, visit her website at www.kuhnkecommunication.com.

Author's Acknowledgements

They say you should be careful what you wish for, as it may come true. When I wrote the first edition of *Body Language For Dummies,* I harboured an unspoken dream that the book would be a runaway bestseller with translations across the globe. My fantasy did come true – and then some! Further editions, Apps, DVDs, enhanced e-books and international speaking engagements all followed.

I thank my beloved husband, Karl Hellmuth, for his continuous belief in my abilities and his never-ending support. And my children, Kristina and Max, who fill me with awe and pride. I thank my late mother and my father for teaching me the power of positive communication.   In addition, I want to thank Annie, Iona, Kate and the whole *For Dummies* crew who strove to make this book the best of its kind and who kept me on target. A special thanks to my mentor and role model, Annette Green, who believed in my abilities when others doubted. And finally, thank you, Kate, for introducing me to the wonderful world of Wiley, and for helping me to surpass my goals. You're all stars.

Most of what you read in these chapters I have learned from valued colleagues, clients, friends and family members. To list them all would take more pages than I am allowed, so those of you who know me, know you're in my heart as I write these words. Look for yourselves amongst the pages. Finally, to you, my readers. My wish for you is that you enjoy this book, further your knowledge and free your expressive bodies in the name of clear, congruent communication.

Publisher's Acknowledgements

We're proud of this book; please send us your comments at `http://dummies.custhelp.com`. For other comments, please contact our Customer Care Department within the U.S. at 877-762-2974, outside the U.S. at (001) 317-572-3993, or fax 317-572-4002.

Some of the people who helped bring this book to market include the following:

Acquisitions, Editorial and Vertical Websites

Project Editor: Iona Everson

Commissioning Editor: Annie Knight

Production Editor: Vinitha Vikraman

Proofreader: Kerry Laundon

Publisher: Miles Kendall

Photography: Stephen Walby (`www.stephenwalby.com`)

Take Dummies with you everywhere you go!

Whether you're excited about e-books, want more from the web, must have your mobile apps, or swept up in social media, Dummies makes everything easier.

 Visit Us

 Like Us

 Follow Us

Watch Us

 Join Us

 Pin Us

 Circle Us

 Shop Us

FOR DUMMIES®

A Wiley Brand

BUSINESS

978-1-118-73077-5

978-1-118-44349-1

978-1-119-97527-4

MUSIC

978-1-119-94276-4

978-0-470-97799-6

978-0-470-49644-2

DIGITAL PHOTOGRAPHY

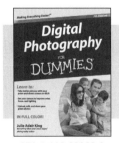

978-1-118-09203-3

978-0-470-76878-5

978-1-118-00472-2

Algebra I For Dummies
978-0-470-55964-2

Anatomy & Physiology For Dummies, 2nd Edition
978-0-470-92326-9

Asperger's Syndrome For Dummies
978-0-470-66087-4

Basic Maths For Dummies
978-1-119-97452-9

Body Language For Dummies, 2nd Edition
978-1-119-95351-7

Bookkeeping For Dummies, 3rd Edition
978-1-118-34689-1

British Sign Language For Dummies
978-0-470-69477-0

Cricket for Dummies, 2nd Edition
978-1-118-48032-8

Currency Trading For Dummies, 2nd Edition
978-1-118-01851-4

Cycling For Dummies
978-1-118-36435-2

Diabetes For Dummies, 3rd Edition
978-0-470-97711-8

eBay For Dummies, 3rd Edition
978-1-119-94122-4

Electronics For Dummies All-in-One For Dummies
978-1-118-58973-1

English Grammar For Dummies
978-0-470-05752-0

French For Dummies, 2nd Edition
978-1-118-00464-7

Guitar For Dummies, 3rd Edition
978-1-118-11554-1

IBS For Dummies
978-0-470-51737-6

Keeping Chickens For Dummies
978-1-119-99417-6

Knitting For Dummies, 3rd Edition
978-1-118-66151-2

Notes

Notes

Notes

Notes

Notes

Notes

Notes

Notes

Notes

Notes

Notes

Notes

Notes

Notes

Notes

Notes